Early Capitalism in Colonial Missions

Empire's Other Histories

Series Editors

Victoria Haskins (University of Newcastle, Australia), Emily Manktelow (Royal Holloway, University of London, UK), Jonathan Saha (University of Durham, UK) and Fae Dussart (University of Sussex, UK)

Editorial Board

Esme Cleall (University of Sheffield, UK), Swapna Banerjee (CUNY, USA), Lynette Russell (Monash, Australia), Tony Ballantyne (University of Otago, New Zealand), Samita Sen (Jadavpur University, India, and University of Cambridge, UK), Nurfadzilah Yahaya, (National University of Singapore, Singapore), Onni Gust (University of Nottingham, UK), Martina Nguyen (CUNY, USA), Meleisa Ono-George, (University of Oxford, UK)

Empire's Other Histories is an innovative series devoted to the shared and diverse experiences of the marginalised, dispossessed and disenfranchized in modern imperial and colonial histories. It responds to an ever-growing academic and popular interest in the histories of those erased, dismissed, or ignored in traditional historiographies of empire. It will elaborate on and analyse new questions of perspective, identity, agency, motilities, intersectionality and power relations.

Published:

Unhomely Empire: Whiteness and Belonging, c.1760-1830, Onni Gust

Extreme Violence and the 'British Way': Colonial Warfare in Perak, Sierra Leone and Sudan, Michelle Gordon

Unexpected Voices in Imperial Parliaments, edited by José María Portillo, Josep M. Fradera, Teresa Segura-Garcia

The Making and Remaking of 'Australasia': Southern Circulations, edited by Tony Ballantyne

Across Colonial Lines: Commodities, Networks and Empire Building, edited by Devyani Gupta and Purba Hossain

Imperial Gallows: Murder, Violence and the Death Penalty in British Colonial Africa, c.1915-60, Stacey Hynd

Arctic Circles and Imperial Knowledge: The Franklin Family, Indigenous Intermediaries, and the Politics of Truth, Annaliese Jacobs Claydon

Forthcoming:

Vagrant Lives in Colonial Australasia: Regulating Mobility and Movement 1840-1920, Catherine Coleborne

Early Capitalism in Colonial Missions

Moravian Household Economies in the Global Eighteenth Century

Christina Petterson

BLOOMSBURY ACADEMIC
LONDON • NEW YORK • OXFORD • NEW DELHI • SYDNEY

BLOOMSBURY ACADEMIC
Bloomsbury Publishing Plc
50 Bedford Square, London, WC1B 3DP, UK
1385 Broadway, New York, NY 10018, USA
29 Earlsfort Terrace, Dublin 2, Ireland

BLOOMSBURY, BLOOMSBURY ACADEMIC and the Diana logo are trademarks of Bloomsbury Publishing Plc

First published in Great Britain 2024

Copyright © Christina Petterson, 2024

Christina Petterson has asserted her right under the Copyright, Designs and Patents Act, 1988, to be identified as Author of this work.

For legal purposes the Acknowledgements on p. xii constitute an extension of this copyright page.

Series design by Tjaša Krivec.
Cover image: Coloured engraving conceptualized by Friedrich von Watteville (1700–77) and created by Philipp Jacob Ferber (1705–88). Genealogical chart in the shape of a vine showing places, people and events, and how they are connected to the crucified Jesus. The text is from John 15:5 "I am the vine, you are the branches". Moravian archives in Christiansfeld.

All rights reserved. No part of this publication may be reproduced or transmitted in any form or by any means, electronic or mechanical, including photocopying, recording, or any information storage or retrieval system, without prior permission in writing from the publishers.

Bloomsbury Publishing Plc does not have any control over, or responsibility for, any third-party websites referred to or in this book. All internet addresses given in this book were correct at the time of going to press. The author and publisher regret any inconvenience caused if addresses have changed or sites have ceased to exist, but can accept no responsibility for any such changes.

A catalogue record for this book is available from the British Library.

A catalog record for this book is available from the Library of Congress.

ISBN: HB: 978-1-3501-2208-6
ePDF: 978-1-3501-2209-3
eBook: 978-1-3501-2210-9

Series: Empire's Other Histories

Typeset by Deanta Global Publishing Services, Chennai, India

To find out more about our authors and books visit www.bloomsbury.com and sign up for our newsletters.

Til Carla. Liv og lys.

Contents

List of Figures	xi
Acknowledgements	xii

Introduction: What did early capitalism look like on the ground?	1
Historical context	4
Conceptual approach	6
Capitalism	6
Oeconomie as communal household	8
Methodology	12
Presentation style: A dialectic of archival narrative and	
theoretical reflection	13
Archival sources	14
Terminology	16
Chapter outline	18
1 The Moravian Brethren	21
Introduction	21
Individual	24
Community	26
Missionary ideals and missionary practice	29
History	34
Were the Moravians 'conservative'?	36
Conclusion	38

Bethlehem, Pennsylvania

2 Moravians and money	41
So, how *do* Moravians speak about economic issues?	41
Reprimand from Bethlehem	42
Bethlehem	45
Beginnings of the General Economy in Bethlehem	45
Transition towards waged labour	50

	Introducing a 'free economy'	51
	Projects and suggestions for the new organization	52
	Conclusion	57
3	Change in leadership and organization: The case of Bethlehem's General Economy	58
	Introduction	58
	Moravian leadership restructured	58
	Earlier attempts at organization	59
	The establishment of Central Council (*Ratsconferenz*) and Inner Council (*Enge Conferenz*)	61
	End of the General Economy: First steps	63
	July 1760: Communicating the impending change to Bethlehem	64
	November–December 1760: The appointed committee sets to work	66
	Plans	67
	January 1761: Results are presented to the Directorial Board	67
	February 1761: Blueprint for the restructure in place	68
	Spangenberg's letter (November 1760) with suggestions arrives from Bethlehem	70
	Execution	71
	March–April 1761: Decision sent to the leadership in Bethlehem	71
	Implications of the restructure: Market economy and mission work	73
	Market	74
	Mission	75
	Conclusion	77

New-Herrnhut in St Thomas, the Danish West Indies

4	Time of transition and change in mission: 1760–4 in the Moravian Unity	81
	Introduction	81
	The earlier missions: 1730s and 1740s	81
	Missions in 1760 and 1761: A period of transition	84
	The Mission Deputation: Establishment and tasks	87
	First General Synod in Marienborn, 1764	91
	Session one: Assessing specific missions	92
	Session two: Particular problems	93
	Session three: Reconstitution of the Mission Deputation	94
	Conclusion	96

5	'Plantation disposition': The 'outer' sphere and the accumulation of riches in the Danish West Indies	98
	Introduction	98
	Rude awakening in the Danish West Indies	101
	First years (1732–8)	101
	Purchase of a plantation	103
	Challenges to the ideal household	105
	Slaves and slave-owners in the mission	106
	'Inner' and 'outer'	109
	Expansion of the sugar industry	110
	Visitations to St Thomas	111
	Visitation of 1753: Early distinction between inner and outer duties	111
	Visitation of 1755: Addressing the question of Moravian-owned slaves	113
	Visitation of 1759: Clearer distinction between two types of Oeconomie	114
	Visitation of 1783–4: All eyes on the 'outer' Oeconomie	118
	Further divisions and distinctions	120
	Sale of the Bethel plantation	121
	Household after 1760	124
	Conclusion	128

New-Herrnhut in Greenland

6	Greenland and colonial authorities	131
	Introduction	131
	Relation to colonial authorities	133
	Danish colonial monopoly	133
	Nitschmann's letter to the Danish king, Christian VI	135
	The problem of passage	137
	The question of settlement	139
	Further restrictions	142
	Sustaining Moravian activities	144
7	Developing the 'inner sphere'	151
	Community organization: Developing the 'inner' sphere	154
	Choirs	154
	Households	158

Early organization	160
Implications and transformations in a colonial context	164
Days of celebration	167
Conclusion: The 'inner' sphere of the Greenland mission	170
Conclusion: Moravians and capitalism	171
Introduction	171
Religion and capitalism	171
Bürgergeist	176
Moravian particularities	180
Archival references	183
Bibliography	188
Index	203

Figures

1	Meeting minutes concerning admittance to communion	31
2	First page of Johann Arbo's notebook regarding the restructure of the Oeconomy of the Single Brothers' House	54
3	The first page of the constitution of the Mission Deputation in 1762	89
4	View of the plantation Bethel and the surroundings of New-Herrnhut on St Thomas, 1770	106
5	List of slaves and their children owned by the Moravians July 1755	108
6	New-Herrnhut in Greenland copper etching, 1770	132
7	Note from 1783 on items of payment and exchange, 16 June 1780	148
8	Floor plan of the mission station from 1750	152

Acknowledgements

This has been an incredibly challenging book to write, at an emotional as well as at an epistemological level. It began and was sponsored by the Gerda Henkel Stiftung (2016–18) – a tremendous opportunity for which I am still deeply grateful. This generous grant enabled me to identify, collect, process and transcribe the archival material which is the foundation of the present book.

Thank you to Maddie Smith and Megan Harris at Bloomsbury for their understanding and great patience with me as I hurled from crisis to crisis. Thank you to Victoria Haskins for suggesting my book for the series, *Empire's Other Histories*. Thank you to Emily Manktelow who encouraged me again and again to keep working, for telling me how important this book is. For their fortitude and perseverance, I have been enormously inspired by Katie Faull and Lyndall Ryan. And Roland would *not* let me give up, knowing full well that I would regret it immensely in the future. Thank you for seeing me through this. The reviewer of the manuscript gave me many excellent and constructive suggestions for improvement and clarification, and whoever you are, I thank you. Thea Olsthoorn helped me through the final hurdles.

During the initial stages of the Covid-19 pandemic (March–June 2020) I was in Herrnhut, unable to get back to Australia, I spent many hours working quietly in the company of Olaf Nippe and Katrin Wagner Fiebich, which gave me a daily routine. Thank you to Claudia Mai for being so supportive and understanding. My friends in Herrnhut were wonderful during this difficult time. I owe Olaf, Peter and Oscar, and Jill and Peter Vogt a huge debt of gratitude. And I would like to thank Christoph and Suse Beck for their hospitality. In their cozy flat so much work on this book has been carried out.

The archivists of the Moravian community are truly outstanding, not only in finding the most obscure documents and making all kinds of helpful suggestions but also just being friendly – up for a beer and a chat. Paul, Lorraine, Tom, Olaf, I am looking at you. Paul Peucker has read through many chapters in less than polished form and has contributed greatly to their final shape. I have also benefited much from talking through ideas and sources with Felicity Jensz, Josef Köstlbauer, Jessica Cronshagen, Frank Marquardt, John Balz, and Michael Leeman.

Friends, whose emotional support I could not have managed without: Anne Gudme, Jesper Tang Nielsen, Kirstin Mertlich, Pernille Østrem and Tine Reeh.

And then, of course, my family in both Denmark and Australia, who have given me so many happy moments – online and in person.

With all of you behind me, I did it!

Newcastle, NSW, 13 February 2023

Introduction
What did early capitalism look like on the ground?

The overall purpose of this book is to explore how an early global Protestant movement functioned economically and socially within different eighteenth-century colonial contexts and how their economic activities were conditioned by the various manifestations of an emerging global economy. It examines how a particular group of Protestants, the Moravian Church,[1] dealt with the relationship between missionary work and economic support in the mid-eighteenth century when the world in which they operated was changing and their own movement was undergoing significant transformation.

This purpose is achieved by examining and comparing the economic organization of Moravian mission households in three colonial territories in the mid-eighteenth century: the Danish colony of St Thomas in the West Indies, the Danish colony of Greenland and the British colony of Pennsylvania. By examining the considerations and practices of the Moravian Church, we gain a glimpse of the economic processes and developments of the global economic system we have come to know as capitalism. The best way of gaining insight into these developments is to look at households in the eighteenth century, because at this very small level, large changes took place. When Moravian missionaries in colonial territories found themselves in the midst of frontier economic development, they were faced with a number of issues and interactions with which they were not familiar from their rural European context and in which they had to adapt. How they did this in different colonial settings and at different stages of capitalist development is the focus of this book. Moravian household and community organization were not neatly aligned with capitalist development, and so the tensions with the global economy stand out more

---

[1] The proper term for this denomination is *Unitas Fratrum* ('United Brethren'), known in English as the Moravian Church and formerly Moravian Brethren. The German name is *Brüdergemeine*, which retains the gendered term. In the present book I use Unity and Moravians, and occasionally Moravian Church.

sharply at this analytic level as well as offer a glimpse into how these tensions were negotiated.

This study contributes towards the understanding of the relations between Protestantism and capitalism, and even Christianity and economy more generally, a field of questioning which has been dominated by Max Weber for more than a century. By focusing on the Moravian household, I demonstrate the messy and complicated interaction between one Protestant movement and early capitalism, and how these interactions generated complicated issues at the level of human life, religious understanding, and sociopolitical and socio-economic organization. We get a good look into a period where both economy and religion were being configured as distinct and ideological spheres of human life and action: economy as a pure sphere of exchange, value and profit, and religion as an internal and private matter.

On the one hand, the Moravian Church had a very practice-oriented religious organization which was an offence to the emerging structures of civil society – this is what makes it such a fascinating object of study. On the other hand, the Moravian Church was part of the Pietist awakening, which was highly influential in Germany and northern Europe in the wake of the Thirty Years' War (1618–48) and well into the eighteenth century. One of the central thrusts of Pietism, which dovetailed so neatly with the individualism of the developing liberal world view, was an increased emphasis on the awakened faith of the individual believer and his or her personal relationship with God.[2] In the Moravian variant of Pietism, it was the relation to the Saviour, the *Heiland* and his suffering, which entailed both direct encounter and continued relationship. This emphasis would prove to be very efficient in the Moravian missions, both within Europe and overseas in its colonies, and made them a useful supplement to imperialist expansion for the colonizing forces of Denmark-Norway, the Netherlands and Britain.[3]

Taking their small numbers into account, the fact that the Moravian missionary activity traversed all inhabited continents was astonishing. Along with their archival diligence, this means that most missions are substantially documented, not only in terms of diaries and correspondence but also in terms

---

[2] For an English introduction to Pietism in general, see Douglas H. Schantz, *An Introduction to German Pietism: Protestant Renewal at the Dawn of Modern Europe* (Baltimore: The Johns Hopkins University Press, 2013). For a recent German compilation, see Wolfgang Breul, *Pietismus Handbuch* (Tübingen: Mohr Siebeck, 2021).

[3] In her monograph on Protestant Empire, Carla Pestana notes that 'religion fueled expansion, justifying conquest and the authority that was established in the wake of those conquests'; however, the justification she provides is mainly in inner-religious terms, that is, an anti-Catholic agenda. Carla Gardina Pestana, *Protestant Empire: Religion and the Making of the British Atlantic World* (Philadelphia: University of Pennsylvania Press, 2009). See page 6 and chapters 2–3.

of meeting minutes, accounts and ledgers. Each mission thus provides more than enough material for a single study. The archival materials for the two mission stations of the present study, New-Herrnhut in Greenland and New-Herrnhut in St Thomas, are thus substantial, not only in and of themselves but also as part of their larger contexts. New-Herrnhut in Greenland was one of three eighteenth-century Moravian mission stations in Greenland,[4] and New-Herrnhut in St Thomas one of two Moravian mission sites in St Thomas alone and one of seven established by the Moravians in the Danish West Indies.[5] Clearly, neither of the two sites can be covered exhaustively. What this present study aims to examine, then, is how the missionaries supported and organized themselves in two very different contexts, which, while colonies of the same crown, were very different frontier zones. In Greenland the Moravians did not engage in commercial activity due to the nature of the surroundings and restrictions by the colonial powers, while St Thomas was a place of significant entrepreneurial development. Commercial activity included sugar plantations and workshops, which relied on and perpetuated slavery and human trafficking. Because the Moravian Church was a very centralized movement, however, it is also important to look at how the missions were organized and conceptualized from Europe, which is why I spend some time looking at the central management of missionary activity and how this changed after 1760 with the death of the founder, Count Nikolaus Ludwig von Zinzendorf. The most dramatic change with far-reaching consequences was the dissolution of the 'General Economy' or communal household of Bethlehem, Pennsylvania, which had since the mid-1740s upheld itself as a model of perfect mission organization. The transformation of this organization meant a fundamental change in the organization of the Moravian mission. For this reason, I devote several chapters to these years of transformation.

All of this is significant, since it gives us a look into the development of capitalism in practice, namely in relation to money, labour, organization and profit-management, and how people manoeuvred within its growing orbit. It shows us how the economic development also had a significant ideological dimension and how this affected the Moravians, at home and abroad, even as they tried to resist it. As such, we gain an on-the-ground insight into a profoundly and rapidly changing world.

---

[4] The other two being Lichtenfels, est. 1758, and Lichtenau, est. 1774. In the nineteenth century, three further Moravian mission stations were established, namely Friederichstal (1824), Umanak (1861) and Idlorpait (1864).
[5] Niesky in St Thomas (1750), Friedensthal (1751) and Friedensberg (1771) in St Croix, and Emmaus (1783) and Bethania (1749) in St John. In the nineteenth century Friedensfeld on St Croix was established in 1819.

Historical context

The period within which I am operating is one of transition in Europe. At a historical level, the analysis is situated within the period marked from the Peace of Westphalia in 1648 to the beginnings of the democratic revolutions in 1848. This period saw the breakdown and dissolution of the feudal socio-economic structure and the introduction of mercantilism, which in our period was overtaken by industrial capitalism. Apart from the increase in trade, especially the slave trade, the process included agricultural reforms, early manufacture, break-up of guilds and the increased demand for individual waged labour.[6] At a philosophical level, the period is characterized by contemplations on the social contract: Hugo Grotius in Holland, Hobbes and Locke in England, Pufendorf and Kant in the German principalities and Rousseau in Switzerland.[7] These were varying theoretical attempts at articulating individualism, recalibrating the relation between the individual and the community, and how this should be managed. Despite their variations, they all signalled the new social structure and its internal relations.[8]

All of these elements had an immense impact on communities and social organization. Changes took place in society, labour, households; people became gendered individuals and then citizens, divided into private and public personas; and the relation to the state had to be managed in a different way, as the state itself was being restructured and redefined.[9]

Connected to these profound changes were of course the imperial adventures of Europe as part of the emerging global economy. Missionaries

---

[6] Fernand Braudel, *Civilization and Capitalism, 15th-18th Century*, 1st U.S., 3 vols (New York: Harper & Row, 1982); Immanuel Maurice Wallerstein, *The Modern World-System 1-4* (Berkeley: University of California Press, 2011); Karl Marx and Friedrich Engels, *The German Ideology* (Moscow: Progress Publishers., 1964).

[7] C. B. Macpherson, *The Political Theory of Possessive Individualism: Hobbes to Locke* (Oxford: Clarendon Press, 1962); D. Baumgold, *Contract Theory in Historical Context: Essays on Grotius, Hobbes, and Locke* (Leiden: Brill, 2010); D. Boucher and P. Kelly, *The Social Contract from Hobbes to Rawls* (London: Taylor & Francis, 2003).

[8] M. Sonenscher, *Work and Wages: Natural Law, Politics and the Eighteenth-Century French Trades* (Cambridge: Cambridge University Press, 2012); Michael Sonenscher, *Jean-Jacques Rousseau: The Division of Labour, the Politics of the Imagination and the Concept of Federal Government* (Leiden: Brill, 2020).

[9] Isabel V. Hull, *Sexuality, State, and Civil Society in Germany, 1700-1815* (Ithaca: Cornell University Press, 1996); Jürgen Habermas, *Strukturwandel der Öffentlichkeit; Untersuchungen zu einer Kategorie der Bürgerlichen Gesellschaft* (Neuwied: H. Luchterhand, 1962); Michel Foucault, *Security, Territory, Population. Lectures at the Collège de France, 1977-78*, trans. Graham Burchell, Michel Foucault: Lectures at the Collège de France (London: Palgrave Macmillan, 2007); Thomas Ertman, *Birth of the Leviathan. Building States and Regimes in Medieval and Early Modern Europe* (Cambridge: Cambridge University Press, 1997); Philip S. Gorski, *The Disciplinary Revolution: Calvinism and the Rise of the State in Early Modern Europe* (Chicago: University of Chicago Press, 2003).

of all denominations played an important part in breaking down Indigenous traditions and communities and restructuring them according to the ongoing processes in Europe.[10] Indeed, the colonies were places where Europeans could experiment with different ways of making money, creating dependencies and instilling control.[11] Some colonies were granted the opportunity for explosive development through aggressive settlement policies, such as those in North America. Others were stripped and plundered for natural wealth and otherwise retained in a deliberately underdeveloped state, such as Greenland. And then some colonies, such as the West Indies, were treated as intensive production sites for wealth to be accumulated and consumed elsewhere.

Within this turbulent world the Moravians weaved deftly, due to their extraordinary ability to adapt to constantly changing circumstances. During the Unity's earlier years (before the late 1750s) the ad hoc organization secured this flexibility. After 1760, the increasingly centralized and bureaucratic leadership, I will argue, changed along similar lines as the economy, which ensured an ongoing suppleness in sync with 'external' changes.

The Pietist reform movement, of which the Moravians were a part, began in the second half of the seventeenth century across German principalities, the most well-known establishment being that of August Hermann Francke. Zinzendorf had himself attended Francke's school for aristocratic boys in Halle, because his grandmother Henrietta von Gersdorff (1648–1726) was a fervent Pietist and a great admirer of Philipp Jacob Spener and Francke.[12] When Zinzendorf and his fellow sojourners founded Herrnhut it was inspired by Halle; but after Francke's death, the already strained relations between Halle and Herrnhut deteriorated

---

[10] The best example is without a doubt Jean Comaroff and John L. Comaroff, *Of Revelation and Revolution I: Christianity, Colonialism, and Consciousness in South Africa* (Chicago: University of Chicago Press, 1991); Jean Comaroff and John L. Comaroff, *Of Revelation and Revolution II: The Dialectics of Modernity on a South African Frontier* (Chicago and London: University of Chicago Press, 1997). Their impressive analysis greatly inspired my analysis of Protestantism and colonialism in Greenland. Christina Petterson, *The Missionary, the Catechist and the Hunter: Foucault, Protestantism and Colonialism*, Studies in Critical Research on Religion 4 (Leiden: Brill, 2014).

[11] Focus on the disciplinary element was inspired greatly by Michel Foucault. See, for example, Søren Rud, 'Policing and Governance in Greenland: Rationalities of Police and Colonial Rule 1860–1953', in *Policing Empires: Social Control, Political Transition, Postcolonial Legacies*, ed. Emmanuel Blanchard, Marieke Bloembergen, and Amadine Lauro (Bruxelles: Peter Lang, 2017), 177–96; Søren Rud, *Colonialism in Greenland: Tradition, Governance and Legacy*, Cambridge Imperial and Postcolonial Studies (Cambridge: Palgrave Macmillan, 2017); Ann Laura Stoler, *Race and the Education of Desire: Foucault's History of Sexuality and the Colonial Order of Things* (Durham: Duke University Press, 1995).

[12] For a recent study into this period, see Otto Teigeler, *Zinzendorf als Schüler in Halle 1710-1716. Persönliches Ergehen und Präformation eines Axioms*, Hallesche Forschungen 45 (Wiesbaden: Harrassowitz Verlag, 2017).

and broke down completely in the late 1730s.[13] From then on, Herrnhut took its own very distinct path. On the surface the differences were a matter of religious taste as well as personal animosity, but the schism had deep roots and drew significant fault lines within the Danish and German ruling class.[14] Hallensian Pietism was a comparatively institutionalized and palatable form of Christianity, whereas the Moravian version was more excessive in all kinds of ways.[15] Hallensian Pietism had a wide range of patrons from the aristocracy, while the Moravians – operating with a different organizational structure – had many *members* from the German aristocracy, as well as sympathizers at the Danish court.[16]

Conceptual approach

In this book, there are several concepts which are central to the argument. These will be discussed here briefly but play an integral part in the following analysis.

Capitalism

Our current socio-economic system, capitalism, encompasses a global economy which until recently operated with a single uniform value system expressed in

---

[13] Hans Schneider, 'Die "zürnenden Mutterkinder". Der Konflikt zwischen Halle und Herrnhut', *Pietismus und Neuzeit* 29 (2004): 37–66.
[14] Thomas Grunewald, *Politik für das Reich Gottes? Der Reichsgraf Christian Ernst zu Stolberg-Wernigerode zwischen Pietismus, adligem Selbstverständnis und europäischer Politik*, Hallesche Forschungen 58 (Halle: Verlag der Franckeschen Stiftungen, 2020).
[15] See Paul Peucker, *A Time of Sifting: Mystical Marriage and the Crisis of Moravian Piety in the Eighteenth Century* (University Park: The Pennsylvania State University Press, 2015); Craig D. Atwood, 'Understanding Zinzendorf's Blood and Wounds Theology', *Journal of Moravian History* 1 (2006): 31–47; Craig D. Atwood, 'Sleeping in the Arms of Christ: Sanctifying Sexuality in the Eighteenth-Century Moravian Church', *Journal of the History of Sexuality* 8, no. 1 (1997): 25–51; Paul Peucker, '"Inspired by Flames of Love": Homosexuality, Mysticism, and Moravian Brothers around 1750', *Journal of the History of Sexuality* 15, no. 1 (2006): 30–64; Peter Vogt, '"Honor to the Side": The Adoration of the Side Wound of Jesus in Eighteenth-Century Moravian Piety', *Journal of Moravian History* 7 (2009): 83–106; Peter Vogt, 'Christologie und Gender bei Zinzendorf', in *Gender im Pietismus: Netzwerke und Geschlechterkonstruktionen*, ed. Pia Schmid (Halle: Verlag der Frankeschen Stiftung/Harrowitz Verlag, 2015), 63–92; Katherine M. Faull, 'Temporal Men and the Eternal Bridegroom: Moravian Masculinity in the Eighteenth Century', in *Masculinity, Senses, Spirit*, ed. Katherine M. Faull (Lewisburg: Bucknell University Press, 2011), 55–79.
[16] For a good overview of the problems between Hallensian and Moravian Pietism in Denmark and the social ramifications, see Juliane Engelhardt, 'Pietismus und Krise. Der hallesche und der radikale Pietismus im dänischen Gesamtstaat', *Historische Zeitschrift* 307, no. 2 (2018): 341–69. For an older study, see Jørgen Lundbye, *Herrnhutismen i Danmark: Det attende Hundredaars Indre Mission* (København: Karl Schønbergs Forlag, 1903).

money.[17] This monetary system had been underway since the twelfth century and with the increasing importance of bankers, credits and exchange[18] changed gear with the rise of Amsterdam in the late sixteenth century.[19] However, it did not become a global economic system until the nineteenth and twentieth centuries. One of the central features of capitalism is that money, from being one means of payment, became an end in itself and, as accumulated capital, the primary marker of wealth.[20] The transition between these two roles of money, from a minor element in one socio-economic system to the central element in another, took centuries, but it was the eighteenth century which saw the most dramatic shifts in the forms of wealth, as well as shifts in the owners of wealth. The Moravians initially relied on funds from their aristocratic members, however even this wealth had its limits, and eventually other paths had to be pursued.[21] As such, the Moravians are a good example of the mechanics within this transition to capitalism, in that it also underwent the movement from old wealth to new rules. In this chapter, I will analyse the ways in which economy is discussed in the Moravian community and the connection with household practice.

Capitalism is an enormous category, and it is not always clear, especially in historical research, what is being discussed.[22] While the constituent features of capitalism are the ones in which we in the Western world are currently embedded, this was not always the case. To this, the eighteenth century was certainly no exception.

Marx's own analysis in *Capital* is of the inner workings of capitalism and its constitutive and nebulous elements rather than a historical demonstration per se. He takes us through the development of exchange value as distinct from use value, the development of the commodity as an embodiment of exchange value and the main unit of a capitalist economy, the distinction between money and capital, surplus value and 'primitive accumulation' (the accumulation and

---

[17] Until the late 1960s this value was determined by the so-called gold standard, after which the US dollar became the default currency of the value system.
[18] See Fernand Braudel, *Civilization and Capitalism, 15th-18th Century Vol. 3: The Perspective of the World*, trans. Sian Reynolds, 1st U.S. (New York: Harper & Row, 1982), 89–174.
[19] Braudel, *Civilization and Capitalism* 3, 175–276.
[20] Karl Marx, *Capital*, MECW 35 (Moscow: Progress Publishers, 1996), chapter 3.
[21] Karl Müller, *200 Jahre Brüdermission I: Das erste Missionsjahrhundert* (Herrnhut: Verlag der Missionsbuchhandlung, 1931), 313–31.
[22] See the recent lecture: 'Capitalism: A Concept Too Big to Fail?: The Early Modern Period and the Formation of an Idea' by Craig Muldrew (https://www.youtube.com/watch?v=vObGIEC8kiA (accessed 15 May 2023)). See also Michael Sonenscher, *Capitalism: The Story behind the Word* (Princeton: Princeton University Press, 2022).

transfer of public land into private property and wealth) and so on.[23] What *Capital* demonstrates are the epistemological changes and social disruptions that were part of the birth-pangs of the global economy, and these are analysed in the service of defining this mode of production. What I will do in this book is to try and get a little bit closer to the economic experiments and their ideological effects. The Moravian Brethren are an excellent case study for a number of reasons, such as global presence and their entrepreneurial activity, and, last but not least, their archives, which inadvertently document all of these developments.

Oeconomie as communal household

The original meaning of the term 'economy' is derived from the classical Greek *oikonomos*, meaning householder.[24] In the eighteenth century, the term still retained this meaning, although new meanings were gaining traction.[25] Of the range of articles on *Oeconomie* in Zedler's *Universal-Lexicon* from 1731 to 1754, there is only a very brief entry on public economy (*Staats-Oeconomie*) as the science which teaches a prince how to manage fortune, both of the prince himself and the money and possessions of his subjects: 'Because the wealth of the princes relies on the purses of their subjects, it is impossible for a sovereign to advance his true happiness if he does not at the same time direct his attention to the country and the subjects.'[26] Even J. G. Krünitz's *Oekonomische Encyklopädie oder allgemeines System der Staats- Stadt- Haus- und Landwirthschaft* (1773–1858) uses the term Oeconomie in its Greek sense as household and uses the term *Wirtschaft*, meaning enterprise or economy, to designate the organization and

---

[23] Michael Perelman, *The Invention of Capitalism. Classical Political Economy and the Secret History of Primitive Accumulation* (Durham: Duke University Press, 2000). This is a fine study which historicizes the concept of 'primitive accumulation' in the context of classical economic theory.

[24] There has been a significant resurgence of scholarship on the household. For historical analyses, see Marion W. Gray, *Productive Men, Reproductive Women. The Agrarian Household and the Emergence of Separate Spheres during the German Enlightenment* (New York: Berghahn Books, 2000); Irmintraut Richarz, *Oikos, Haus Und Haushalt* (Göttingen: Vandenhoeck & Ruprecht, 1991); Lyndal Roper, *The Holy Household: Women and Morals, in Reformation Augsburg*, Oxford Studies in Social History (Oxford: Clarendon, 1989). For philosophical genealogies, see Giorgio Agamben, *The Kingdom and the Glory. For a Theological Genealogy of Economy and Government (Homo Sacer II, 2)*, trans. Lorenzo Chiesa with Matteo Mandarini (Stanford: Stanford University Press, 2011); Angela Mitropoulos, *Contract and Contagion: From Biopolitics to Oikonomia* (New York: Minor Compositions, 2012); Foucault, *Security, Territory, Population*.

[25] In Grimm's *Wörterbuch* (1854), the word has the meaning of order, generalizes the arrangement and purposeful organzsation of a whole. 'ÖKONOMIE', Deutsches Wörterbuch von Jacob Grimm und Wilhelm Grimm, digitalised edition im Wörterbuchnetz des Trier Center for Digital Humanities, Version 01/23, https://www.woerterbuchnetz.de/DWB?lemid=O01433 (accessed 4 January 2023).

[26] *Grosses vollständiges Universal-Lexicon aller Wissenshaften und Künste* (Leipzig: Zedler, 1732–50), vol. 39, p. 672. Then follows a cross reference to the article on *Cameral-Wesen*, since *Cameral-Wissenschaft* is another name for *Staats-Oeconomie*.

elements of industrial society.[27] In other words, while 'economy' was discussed and researched under the umbrella terms of *Wirtschaft* and *Kameralwissenschaft*, Oeconomie as a term has not yet come to designate this entity. Even then, *Wirtschaft* and other related terms, while including aspects of political economic organization and money, did not yet – in the eighteenth century – signify an abstract and distinct system of exchange and finance.

The Moravians used the term Oeconomie in several ways, such as distinguishing between the past and the present age.[28] There was even an understanding of 'outer Oeconomie', which indicates an outer sphere of circulation and exchange (see Chapter 6). In her brilliant study on Moravians and economy in Bethlehem, Pennsylvania, Katherine Carté Engel notes that the term implied a 'natural link between a practical earthly household and a larger spiritual order'.[29] To this I would add the notion of a self-contained unit of production and circulation within which everything had its place. Oeconomie, however, was above all used to designate the common household. As Paul Peucker has demonstrated, the communal household was a known structure within the Moravian community, in that a number of settlements practised communal house-holding.[30] The best known, however, is undoubtedly the communal household of Bethlehem, Pennsylvania, between 1744 and 1762, which was the most long-lasting and prosperous communal household in the Zinzendorf period.

The Bethlehem General Economy was a household organization, where an itinerant *Pilgergemeine* (i.e. pilgrim community) worked as missionaries among the Native Americans. As I will explain more fully in Chapters 2 and 3, this transient community was materially supported by a *Hausgemeine*, a house community, which worked solely for this purpose in Bethlehem. In the Danish West Indian mission, as we shall see in Chapter 5, this was also the case: In 1736–7 Friedrich Martin evangelized, while Matthäus Freundlich and Johann Bönicke worked to support the three of them. Because the mission/labour organization in St Thomas was born out of necessity rather than conscious planning, it also indicates a significant feature of the society in which such a division of labour makes sense, and this in turn influenced the Unity itself. In the missions in Greenland, however, this was not how the mission was organized,

---

[27] J. G. Krünitz's *Oekonomische Encyklopädie oder allgemeines System der Staats- Stadt- Haus- und Landwirthschaft*, Ökonomie. https://www.kruenitz1.uni-trier.de/ (accessed 4 January 2023).
[28] Peter Baumgart, *Zinzendorf als Wegbereiter historischen Denkens* (Lübeck/Hamburg: Matthiesen Verlag, 1960), 58–62.
[29] Katherine Carté Engel, *Religion and Profit: Moravians in Early America* (Philadelphia: University of Pennsylvania Press, 2009), 33.
[30] Paul Peucker, 'A Family of Love: Another Look at Bethlehem's General Economy', *Journal of Moravian History* 18, no. 2 (2018): 123–44, here 129.

and this is undoubtedly due to the fact that there were no means of income as such, and so all the missionaries shared in the various tasks of subsistence, to which the congregation also made a major contribution.

If we broadly think of these three household organizations and their distinct divisions of labour as three models, we have, first, the Greenlandic model, which is a subsistence economy community, based on a few trade skills but basically supported by annual food provisions from Europe and hunting and gathering in Greenland. Second, the Bethlehem model is one where the sole purpose of the house congregation is to support the missionaries and to make Bethlehem as a whole self-sufficient. Outside interaction was limited and only deployed when inner needs had been met. Furthermore, in Bethlehem, money was used only when dealing with the outside world. The model in Bethlehem was thus a self-contained economic circuit. Third, when the St Thomas mission began producing sugar in 1743, the Danish West Indian model became one of profit, where the profits generated were used to fund other missionary activities on the islands. In this sense, the Danish West Indian mission was an integral part of the plantation economy.

In 1760–4, a large restructure took place in the Moravian Unity, and one of the central events within this restructure was the dissolution of the Bethlehem model in 1760–2, and cracking open its closed circuit, so as to turn towards the Danish West Indian model, in which the surplus was centralized in Herrnhut and redistributed. This will become clearer in Chapters 2 and 3.

In comparison with the term 'family', which only really developed as a concept in the course of the eighteenth century, the term 'household' is less focused on the blood ties between the individuals within the household. Furthermore, there is emphasis on the dwelling in the very make-up of the word ('house'). So, household denotes the particular organization of people within a dwelling, insofar as these people constitute the basic unit of society and economy and contribute towards the reproduction of society and economy. As a *unit* of production within a larger social organization, a household is extremely vulnerable to change, which is why it also is a good place to monitor socio-economic transition. As we will see in the following, the Moravian household and its subdivisions, the choirs, was certainly a departure from the feudal household in Europe, and the introduction of this household structure in Greenland also meant a departure from the Kalaallit household, as we will see in Chapter 7.

Because capitalism did not erupt onto the world stage overnight, it is possible to trace the various stages of development in the Moravian Unity. This must be done by attention to a greater level of detail than what is possible through

Max Weber's ideal types. While Weber is usually assumed to be a significant contributor to our understanding of religion and economy in early modernity, he does not actually deal with the relation between economic development and religion; instead, his concern is with the affinities between the Protestant ethos and the essential spirit of capitalism. Within this particular framework, he dismisses Pietism. By arguing that Weber has misunderstood Pietism, or collapsed two dissimilar forms, or trying to disprove his thesis by demonstrating how Pietism did in fact contribute, we are operating and thus upholding his framework of separate spheres with or without affinity to each other. Once we shift to an understanding that does not from the outset presume a separation between theology and economy, we gain insight into crucial developments of the period.

Instead, I follow Werner Sombart, who is much more attentive to changes in the political outlook of the various agents of capitalism. This becomes evident in his distinction between the old-style bourgeois and the modern entrepreneur, a difference which he notes lasts until the end of the eighteenth century. Sombart defines the old-style bourgeois as one who in all his thinking and planning was still determined by the well-being of living humans. Until the end of the eighteenth century, Sombart holds, of all those who served capitalism – from the grand estate holder to the overseas merchant, the banker, the speculator, the manufacturer and the wool merchant – none of them ceased to adapt their business activity to the requirements of life: 'for all of them business remained only a means to the ends of life; for all of them their own life interests and those of the other people for whom they work decided the direction and extent of their activity'.[31] After a number of examples, Sombart concludes that in some cases the issues were of sustenance, in some cases of traditionalism and in some cases they were ethical concerns, 'but there is always something that inhibits the free development of the drive for acquisition, the spirit of enterprise and economic rationalism'.[32]

By contrast, Sombart identifies the concept of *Bürgergeist* as that which characterizes the spirit of capitalism, and its beginnings may be found in the Italian merchant cities of the fifteenth century. One of the characteristic features of new economic organization is the rationalization of management, which entails the creation of a sensible relationship between income and expenditure – in other words, a particular art of house-holding (*Haushaltungskunst*). The

---

[31] Sombart, Werner Sombart, *Der Bourgeois: zur Geistesgeschichte des modernen Wirtschaftsmenschen* (Berlin: Duncker und Humblot, 1987), 196.
[32] Sombart, *Der Bourgeois*, 211.

second characteristic of a good economy is the economization of business management, where saving becomes a virtue rather than being regarded as a necessity. Within this management, Sombart attributes substantial significance to double-entry bookkeeping, where profit is separated from 'all natural purposes of subsistence',[33] which enables not only the idea of acquisition and the organization of wealth but also the independent business. This independence is secured through the detachment of the enterprise from the entrepreneur and arranged according to purely objectified aspects, recognizable by a complete stranger. Such organization then enables the appreciation from the outside of the enterprise *as* an independent enterprise, without regard to a person or owner.

These points become very important when we turn to the restructurings of the Unity in 1760–4. One of the chief architects of the restructure of the Unity itself, and of the General Economy of Bethlehem mentioned earlier, was Johann Friedrich Koeber who, according to Hellmuth Erbe, was an embodiment of the *Bürgergeist* of the time (around 1760), and an indication that such an emerging *Geist* was also to be found in the Unity as a whole.[34] I discuss this in Chapters 2 and 3, and return to it in the concluding chapter.

Methodology

While the subject matter of the texts concern religion, my approach is a-religious: it endeavours to establish what Karl Marx called the truth of this world, which is only possible once the world beyond the truth has been dismantled.[35] This is, thus Marx, the task of *history* and is a task which should not only be left to the historians. History, along with the nomothetic disciplines of economics, sociology and political science, arose within the Enlightenment period and is thus framed within that particular ideological framework and its institutions.[36] In *Capital*, Marx observes:

---

[33] Sombart, *Der Bourgeois*, 119.
[34] Hellmuth Erbe, *Bethlehem, Pa. Eine Kommunistische herrnhuter Kolonie des 18 Jahrhunderts* (Stuttgart: Ausland und Heimat Verlags-Aktiengesellschaft, 1929), 133.
[35] Karl Marx, 'Contribution to the Critique of Hegel's Philosophy of Law: Introduction', in *Marx/Engels Collected Works 3* (Moscow: Progress Publishers, 1975), 175–87. I experimented with this approach in Christina Petterson, *The Moravian Brethren in a Time of Transition: A Socio-Economic Analysis of a Religious Community in Eighteenth Century Saxony*, Historical Materialism 231 (Leiden: Brill, 2021).
[36] See Wallerstein's genealogy of the emergence of history as well as the nomothetic discipline in Immanuel Wallerstein, *The Modern World-System 4. Centrist Liberalism Triumphant, 1789-1914* (Berkeley: University of California Press, 2011), 237–64. See also Hayden White, 'Interpretation in

Reflections on the forms of human life, and consequently, also, scientific analysis of those forms, take a course directly opposite to that of their actual development. It begins, *post festum* with the results of the process of development. The forms that stamp products as commodities, and thus presupposes the circulations of commodities, have already acquired the stability of natural forms of social life, before humans seek to give an account, not of their historical character, which are already considered immutable, but their content.[37]

This quote is also used by George Lukács to set Marx's 'critical philosophy' over against 'the rigid, unhistorical, natural appearances of social institutions' which Marx's critical philosophy aims to dissolve.[38] Following Marx, Lukács shows that by working within the parameters set by the self-same institutions which the 'bourgeois historians' examine, they leave the principles of society untouched, whereas a proper, critical historical analysis would analyse the history of these institutions *and* the parameters within which they take on this objective, seemingly immutable nature. The point of both Marx and Lukács is that forms and institutions are merely the *result* of a historical process, which is left unanalysed. Rather, the task of history is to analyse the actual historical developments leading up to the congealed and objectified forms.[39] As a scholar committed to anti-imperialism, and breaking with the institutions which produce inequality and exploitation, I find it imperative to identify and move beyond those parameters as best as I can.

Presentation style: A dialectic of archival narrative and theoretical reflection

My style of presentation moves between two focal points. First, I engage deeply with archival material (see below). This handwritten material is in the eighteenth-century *Kurrent* script. Not only are there different writing styles, but there are also many shorthand expressions. Needless to say, researching this material requires much patience, time and perseverance. Some of this material has been studied before but, with the exception of the material from St Thomas

---

History', in *Tropics of Discourse : Essays in Cultural Criticism* (Baltimore: John Hopkins University Press, 1978), 51–80, esp. 67–9.

[37] Karl Marx, *Das Kapital: Kritik Der Politischen Ökonomie*, MEW 23 (Berlin: Dietz Verlag, 1971), 89–90. I refer to the German edition, because I have heavily modified the translation. Compare with Marx, *Capital*, 86.

[38] Georg Lukács, *History and Class Consciousness: Studies in Marxist Dialectics*, Reprint (London: Merlin, 1990), 47.

[39] This was the purpose of my book on the developments of the choir structure in Herrnhut in the years 1740–60. See Petterson, *The Moravian Brethren in a Time of Transition*.

and Bethlehem, not extensively. In my presentation of the archival sources, I construct a type of archival narrative, which demonstrates how crucial events unfold through the material presented in the archival texts. These events often shed new light on understanding the period in question. Second, I also engage in what may be called a meta-theoretical analysis and questioning. Returning to the points made by Lukács, many of the social, economic and philosophical categories that are assumed to be settled and clear in our own day were not so in eighteenth-century Europe. These concepts and practices were in a rapid state of development, change and experimentation. The task of the meta-theoretical reflection is to grasp this process of change, transition and emergence. And it is precisely the archival material that enables us to do so.

Archival sources

The present book relies mainly on archival resources from three overall groups: (1) the material pertaining to organization (including Bethlehem) and missions from Herrnhut (Chapters 2–4); (2) the archival material on the Danish West Indies (Chapter 5) and (3) archival material on Greenland (Chapters 6–7). As we will see in the next three chapters, a number of significant changes took place in Herrnhut following the death of Zinzendorf, and the main documentation for these events I have ferreted out from a range of meeting minutes, both those from central governing boards, synods, and – after it was established – the Mission Deputation, later (after 1789) known as the Mission Department.[40]

The archival material from the central organization of the Moravian Unity is held in the central archive in Herrnhut, the Unity Archives in Herrnhut, Saxony (UAH). This material consists mainly of meeting minutes and synod reports. The material pertaining to the dissolution of the General Economy is held both in Herrnhut (meeting minutes and correspondence) and in the Moravian Archives in Bethlehem, Pennsylvania (MAB), where, in addition to the flurry of correspondence, and minutes of various meetings and discussions, we also find documents from the planning stage, such as drafts and plans for the new organization.

The material from the Greenlandic and Danish West Indian missions is held in the central archive in Herrnhut and smaller parts in the archives in Bethlehem. The material may roughly be divided into diaries, correspondence

---

[40] I would like to thank Olaf Nippe for not only impressing upon me the importance of these years in the overall Unity but also patiently helping me grasp the different strands of governance within the Unity as it developed and changed.

and minutes.[41] The diaries were kept by the missionaries at each settlement and document, as the genre indicates, the daily lives there. These diaries were sent back to Herrnhut annually, and some of the material would find its way into the *Gemeinnachrichten*, the handwritten compilation of diaries and news from all Moravian communities, which were distributed back to all Moravian communities. As Heinz Israel points out in his study of the mission to Greenland,[42] the diaries are a biased source, since in the process of writing the missionaries were conscious of the fact that their diaries would be read far and wide within the Moravian world.[43] Nevertheless, they provide a good overview of the daily activities and the communal practices of the mission: assemblies, commemorations, baptisms, visits to and from the colonial settlement (Greenland), and plantations (Danish West Indies).

The correspondence is, as Israel also indicates, much more revealing as to problematic issues. The missionaries would write to the Unity Elders' Conference (UAC) in Europe with grievances, requests and questions. Apart from general correspondence, one group within this overall genre is constituted by the annual reports from the head missionary to the UAC, and the response of the UAC to the missionaries based on scrutiny of these reports, as well as of their diaries. It is clear that the UAC read through the material with a fine-toothed comb in order to make informed decisions on future directions, such as change in organization, personal or the like. If matters in the mission in question seemed to be deteriorating, the UAC would send a senior member to the mission on a visitation, to assess the situation in person, implement reforms and report back to the UAC with suggestions for improvement.[44] The reports from these visits, which include instructions from the UAC prior to the visit (based on their reading of the incoming material), minutes of meetings held on site and the final report, constitute an important subgroup of archival material that I have used for my study.

---

[41] Gisela Mettele has an excellent chapter on the various forms of communication and how they fit within the Moravian global communication network. Gisela Mettele, *Weltbürgertum oder Gottesreich: Die Herrnhuter Brüdergemeine als globale Gemeinschaft 1727-1857*, Bürgertum Neue Folge, Bd 4 (Göttingen: Vandenhoeck & Ruprecht, 2009), 124–78.
[42] Heinz Israel, *Kulturwandel Grönländischer Eskimo im 18. Jahrhundert*, Abhandlungen und Berichte des Staatlichen Museums für Völkerkunde Dresden (Berlin: Academie Verlag, 1969).
[43] In the annual letter from the Inner Council to the missionaries in 1763, it is noted that they find the missionaries mentioning 'the sheep' too often in the diary and that this is unseemly. The missionaries 'can rather give news of this in your letters' (So wie wirs für unschicklich halten, daß dieselben so oft in Diario vorkommen–ihr könnet ja lieber in euren Briefen davon Nachricht geben–[. . .]). UA R.15.J.b.I.26a, 34: Inner Council to the missionaries in New-Herrnhut and Lichtenfels, 24 February 1763.
[44] See Mettele, *Weltbürgertum oder Gottesreich*, 139–45.

Finally, there are minutes from the internal meetings held on each mission. The more organized the missions became, the more specific did the meetings and their contents become. For example, in Greenland, after a visitation in 1770, the missionary group was instructed to organize specific meetings to discuss house and 'industry' matters – in other words, their economic affairs, how work was organized (e.g. turf and wood gathering), the pantry and provisions, and so on.[45] These meetings were to be attended by all European men and women. Another type of meeting, the Elders' meeting in both Greenland and St Thomas, was constituted by the missionaries in their capacity as missionaries, and here we find treatments of the organization of assemblies, the 'speakings' before communion, possible baptisms, communion, or exclusion of various members, and the process of deciding on these matters through use of the lot. These are very promising sources, since they were not intended for public use but rather for internal use. They also provide significant insight into the day-to-day practice of the missionaries and their management of the congregations.

All of these sources are used in various ways in the present book. The reader may think that there is already a significant amount of archival material mentioned, but I have only scratched the surface, and so this study cannot claim to be a comprehensive analysis of the mission to Greenland or the Danish West Indies. Given the enormous amount of source material that remains to be studied and analysed, this is a project for more than one lifetime. For this reason, I focus only on the first mission station in both places, both of which are named Neuherrnhut – New-Herrnhut – and mainly during the periods of 1740–60, when the mission is consolidated, and 1760–85, when many changes took place due to internal reorganization in the Moravian community.

Terminology

Before we move on to a chapter outline, I want to explain my choice of terminology. Eighteenth- and nineteenth-century material have ways of speaking about others which are unacceptable today. For the Indigenous population of Kalaallit Nunaat (Greenland), the Moravian missionaries mainly used the word *Grönländer* (*Greenlander*). *Grönländer* was also the more 'geographical' term, and when they referred to Inuit as a racialized group, they used *Eskimo* (but in the material I have used, this is very rare). For non-converted people

---

[45] UA R.15.J.b.I.7, 2: Minutes from the conference in New-Herrnhut, 29 June 1770.

they use *Heiden* ('heathens') or *Wilden* ('savages').[46] For the Black (slave or free) population of the Danish West Indies they use *Negern* ('Negros'), *Mohren* ('Moors') or *schwarzen* (Black),[47] while for the white population they use the local term *Blanken* (white).

When using source material, I have retained the wording therein – but, I translate *Neger* with Black to avoid repeating an offensive term. The original is retained in the footnotes. As for my own choice of words, I will use *Kalaaleq* (singular)/*Kalaallit* (plural) – man/woman/people – when dealing with Indigenous people of Greenland. These are the Greenlandic terms for the people of Greenland and is more specific than Inuit, which is a more abstract denominator and includes the Indigenous people of Labrador.[48]

The deliberation pertaining to the West Indies poses another level of complexity, given its particular history in which racial categories are sometimes necessary for comprehension. I will thus refer to white man/woman/people and Black man/woman/people where necessary. Furthermore, and perhaps more contentiously, I have opted to use the term 'slave' alongside that of 'enslaved person/people'. There are several reasons for this choice, one of which is perspective. Within the system of the emerging global economy, slaves were not considered humans. This dehumanizing economic system, in which we are still embedded, is what I want to emphasize by using the term 'slave'.

Furthermore, and this is connected to the first point, the concept of 'enslaved' suggests agency. My point in the entire book, however, is that liberalism rested on the systemic *exclusion* of non-white peoples, who thus are denied

---

[46] In her article on the early missions, Carola Wessel argues that the concept of *Heiden* (i.e. heathen) is a religious, and as such, a neutral term and not a geographical or ethnic term. Zinzendorf, she notes, did not see any difference between the disbelief and animosity against God in Europe and among 'heathens'. Carola Wessel, '"Es ist also des Heilands sein Predigtstuhl so weit und groß als die ganze Welt." Zinzendorfs Überlegungen zur Mission', in *Neue Aspekte der Zinzendorf-Forschung*, ed. Martin Brecht and Paul Peucker (Göttingen: Vandenhoeck & Ruprecht, 2006), 167. While she may have a point in the case of the early missions, I nevertheless use inverted commas for the category of 'heathens', except where it functions as a name.

[47] In his *History of the Caribbean Islands* completed in 1776, C. G. A. Oldendorp included a substantial section entitled 'Of the various nations of the Blacks, their fatherland Guinea, their religion there and other customs, as well as their languages' which was based on a range of travel stories, but also conversations with slaves conducted during his time in the Danish West Indies. C. G. A. Oldendorp, *Historie der caribischen Inseln Sanct Thomas, Sanct Crux und Sanct Jan: Insbesondere der dasigen Neger und der Mission der Evangelischen Brüder unter denselben*, 2 vols, Abhandlungen und Berichte des Staatlichen Museums für Völkerkunde Dresden: Forschungsstelle, Bd 51 (Berlin: VWB, Verlag für Wissenschaft und Bildung, 2000), 1, 365–465.

[48] Åmund Norum Resløkken, 'The Soul of the Arctic: David Cranz's Account of the Religion or Superstitions of the Greenlanders and Its Impact on Nineteenth-Century Descriptions of Religion in Greenland', in *Legacies of David Cranz's 'Historie von Grönland' (1765)*, ed. Felicity Jensz and Christina Petterson (London: Palgrave Macmillan, 2021), 185–205, here 202, n. 20.

individuality, reason and agency, the effects of which are fully visible today.[49] In retaining the word 'slave', I am thus trying to demonstrate the systemic inhumanity and reification present at the birth of the modern age. I see this as an obligation to history. That said, I use the term 'enslaved Moravians' to indicate the slaves who became part of the Moravian community in St Thomas.[50] This is in acknowledgement of the principle of the common humanity of all believers, which I see as fundamental in Moravian thought and practice, and a principle at odds with the political and economic ideology of the time. I discuss this in more detail in Chapter 1.

Chapter outline

The argument will be presented as follows. In the first chapter, I present some of the more idiosyncratic features of the Moravian Brethren, in that there are important differences in practice and outlook that need to be articulated, so as to better understand their way of operating. This is focused on their understanding of individual, community and history, which I will argue are in conflict with the emerging liberal ideology of the time. The following chapters are divided into three larger sections: Bethlehem, Pennsylvania (2–3), New-Herrnhut, St Thomas (4–5), and New-Herrnhut, Greenland (6–7). These chapters are all different pieces of the puzzle that is Moravian mission organization in the eighteenth century. Chapter 2 looks at the Moravian terminology of 'inner and outer' so as to distinguish between spiritual and organizational matters, and how this is practised in Bethlehem, Pennsylvania. This leads into the analysis in Chapter 3, which looks at the leadership changes that took place in Herrnhut in the years following Zinzendorf's death in 1760 and the immediate restructuring of Bethlehem in Pennsylvania. This restructure, I argue, is intrinsically connected with changes to the individual missions and the way they were organized in terms of economy, household and mission work. This is, in other words, where

---

[49] As analysed from different perspectives in Charles W. Mills, *The Racial Contract* (Ithaca: Cornell University Press, 1997); Roberta James, 'Rousseau's Knot: The Entanglement of Liberal Democracy and Racism', in *Race Matters: Indigenous Australians and 'Our' Society*, ed. Gillian Cowlishaw and Barry Morris (Canberra: Aboriginal Studies Press, 1997), 53–75; David Theo Goldberg, *The Racial State* (London: Blackwell, 2002); Domenico Losurdo, *Liberalism: A Counter-History*, trans. Gregory Elliott (London: Verso, 2011).
    The publication which opened my eyes to this fundamental inequality and its implications for the present is Gerald M. Sider, *Lumbee Indian Histories: Race, Ethnicity, and Indian Identity in the Southern United States* (Cambridge: Cambridge University Press, 1994).

[50] Persuaded by Heike Raphael-Hernandez, 'Black Caribbean Empowerment and Early Eighteenth-Century Moravian Missions Documents', *Slavery & Abolition* 36, no. 2 (2015): 319–34.

the separation of 'inner' and 'outer' takes place, with the 'outer' taking on an independent function and role. Chapter 4, while not preoccupied with St Thomas as such, provides a crucial insight into changes that enabled the developments of mission and economy in St Thomas, which is analysed in Chapter 5. In Chapter 4, I focus on the change in leadership structure and how the missions become integrated into a larger organization, the Mission Deputation, instead of being separate and opportunistic initiatives. These changes took place in the years between Zinzendorf's death and the first General Synod in Marianborn in 1764. Examining the changes in a single missionary organization makes it possible to examine the effects of the global economic system on missionary practice. The reason for doing so is that the changes in practice took place during some of the most formative centuries of Europe and its colonies.

Chapter 5 analyses the Moravian mission in St Thomas, the Danish West Indies, one of the present-day US Virgin Islands in the Caribbean. Here, I am interested in the development of an economic sensibility which came to rival the missionary purpose in its zeal and scope. To finance an impoverished mission within a frontier economy, the missionaries turned to sugar production and slave-holding as a way of financing the mission on the three islands of the Danish West Indies. This emphasis on economic development created significant unrest and discord between the mission in the Danish West Indies and the supervising mission in Bethlehem. After the early 1760s and the central transformation, as well as the significant restructure of Bethlehem, this tension was resolved.

Chapters 6 and 7 take us to Greenland, a mission which was established in 1733, during the period of the Danish absolute monarchy. This was before any civil government, before any systematized interaction with the Indigenous population was in place and before trade was central to the economy of the colonial powers. Further, the Moravians were engaged in intense competition with the Lutheran state-sponsored mission, which was connected to and sponsored by private trade. As the systematization of colonial administration set in over the nineteenth century, the Moravians were outside any sphere of influence and left Greenland in 1900. In this mission, they attempted to replicate the structure of the European communities and implemented the so-called choir structure in their missionary settlements from the mid-eighteenth century. This meant dividing their congregations into groups (choirs) according to gender, age and marital status, which became a feature of several early missions. Within this structure, all the believers were designated as either Brother or Sister, which also became the practice in the early Indigenous congregations. Chapter 6 deals with relation to the colonial authorities, while Chapter 7 deals with the Moravian settlement and its organization.

In the conclusion I pull it all together in order to address the elephant in the room, namely Max Weber and the vexed question of the relationship between Protestantism and capitalism. I draw on the analyses throughout the book to discuss the assumptions and implications of Weber's analysis and offer some reflections on how the developments within a small seemingly insignificant Protestant community have significance for our understanding of the developments of the industrial world of capitalism, the way in which our lives are organized and compartmentalized, and how some of the categories we take for granted came into being. I do not mean that the Moravian Brethren generated all of these things, but that the development within the Moravian Brethren makes it possible to show how these various elements of capitalism were consolidated across the Atlantic world.

1

The Moravian Brethren

Introduction

In this chapter, I present an introduction to the Moravian Brethren and some of the key points in their world view, their missionary practice and the promotional nature of their missionary histories. Because the Moravians are somewhat idiosyncratic, this brief explanation is to ensure that they are not understood on different terms than on those in which they operate. This is all the more necessary, because their published accounts and histories tend to downplay their most distinctive and eccentric qualities in order to place them in line with other, more socially conformist missions. This becomes a problem when the accounts are used as source material for analyses of missions. But it is precisely the distinctive features which will help us understand the organization of the economy and household practice to be analysed in the following chapters.

To the history of the (re)establishment of the Moravian Brethren in Herrnhut in 1722[1] belongs the story of Count Zinzendorf. Having been raised and schooled in a Pietist environment, he had been seeking to establish a Christian community that transgressed confessional divides, and to this end he had purchased an estate in Berthelsdorf in the Oberlausitz region of Saxony. Here the Moravian community grew quickly, after the settlement of the first thirty refugees from Moravia. The first years were highly unstable, but eventually Zinzendorf, who had been employed at the court in Dresden, returned and took charge in 1727.[2]

---

[1] The Moravian Church regards itself as a re-establishment of the Czech Reformation which began with Jan Hus, the Bohemian reformer denounced as a heretic by the Roman Catholic Church and burned at the stake in 1415. In the Moravian and Bohemian lands, the movement did not dissipate but continued. See Craig D. Atwood, *The Theology of the Czech Brethren from Hus to Comenius* (University Park: Penn State University Press, 2009).
[2] For a recent excellent study of the first decade of the Moravian community, Zinzendorf's Philadelphian ambitions, and the settlement of Herrnhut, see Paul Peucker, *Herrnhut, 1722-1732: The Early Years of the Moravian Community*, Pietist, Moravian, and Anabaptist Studies (University Park: Penn State University Press, 2021). For older studies, see Otto Uttendörfer, *Alt-Herrnhut. Wirtschaftsgeschichte und Religionssoziologie Herrnhuts während seiner ersten zwanzig Jahre (1722-1742)*

Zinzendorf was a *Reichsgraf* (imperial count) and was related to the Danish crown princess, Sophie Magdalene von Brandenburg-Kulmbach. This meant that he was invited to the celebrations when her husband was anointed as King Christian VI in June 1731 at a very exclusive ceremony at Frederiksborg castle, north of Copenhagen. Here, Zinzendorf met two Kalaallit and a young Black footman, Anton, the property of Privy councillor and director of the Danish West India Company, F. A. Danneskiold-Laurvig. This encounter, so the story goes,[3] reignited Zinzendorf's missionary zeal, which had been dormant for many years. According to the count himself, his missionary desire was first awakened when as a student in Halle he had met missionaries from the Danish-Halle mission to Tranquebar in India. Now he felt that the time had come. He made an agreement with the new Danish king, and borrowed Anton, who came with him to Herrnhut to appeal to the congregation. The following year, in 1732, Leonhard Dober and David Nitschmann left for St Thomas in the Danish West Indies to begin their mission to the slaves. Then followed a mission to Greenland in 1733, Suriname in 1735 and Georgia in North America, also in 1735.

The 'messengers', as they were called in Moravian parlance, were not trained theologians but tradesmen who had to work to sustain themselves while seeking out and speaking to the prospective believers. This emphasis on self-sufficiency meant that the missionaries were required to have at least one trade. Ordination became an issue only when the question of baptism arose. In St Thomas, Friedrich Martin was ordained by letter in 1738, and the Greenland missionary Matthäus Stach was ordained in Marienborn in 1741. Before then, baptisms had been carried out either by a visiting ordained Moravian[4] or by the Lutheran missionary at the colonial settlement in Greenland.[5]

(Herrnhut: Verlag Missionsbuchhandlung, 1925); Hanns-Joachim Wollstadt, *Geordnetes Dienen in der christlichen Gemeinde*, Arbeiten zur Pastoraltheologie 4 (Göttingen: Vandenhoeck & Ruprecht, 1966).

[3] James E. Hutton, *A History of Moravian Missions* (London: Moravian Publication Office, 1922); Hartmut Beck, *Brüder in Vielen Völkern: 250 Jahre Mission der Brüdergemeine*, Erlanger Taschenbücher, Bd 58 (Erlangen: Verlag der Ev.-Luth. Mission, 1981), 29–34; Müller, *200 Jahre Brüdermission I*, 3–9.

[4] For example, during August Gottlieb Spangenberg's visitation on St Thomas in 1736, where the first three converts, Immanuel, Clas and Jost, were baptized and received the names Andreas, Petrus and Nathanael. Oldendorp, *Historie der Caribischen Inseln*, 2/1, 179–81.

[5] However, the first Kalaallit to be baptized in 1739 were baptized by Matthäus Stach, who was not ordained until 1742. Henrik Wilhjelm argues that this is the reason David Cranz does not dare mention who baptized Qajarnaq in his *History of Greenland*. Henrik Wilhjelm, 'How a Man Accused of Being Wizard and Murderer Determined the Development of the Moravian Mission in Greenland', in *Edice Moravian 13 (The Moravians in Polar Areas – Conference Proceedings from the VI. Moravian Conference)* 13 (2015): 35–41, here 37. Indeed, in Cranz's *History*, the narration of the baptism is kept in passive (they were baptized) without any mention of the agent. See David Cranz, *The History of Greenland: Containing a Description of the Country, and Its Inhabitants and Particularly, a Relation of the Mission, Carried on for above These Thirty Years by the Unitas Fratrum*,

While the organization and growth of the Moravian Brethren had changed several times in the course of Zinzendorf's lifetime, it was not until after his death in 1760 that the organization of the Moravian Brethren changed significantly. Zinzendorf had been the undisputed leader of the community, although his influence in monetary matters and industrial development had been significantly curtailed from 1755. Filling the gap and determining the future of the Moravian Brethren became a significant and all-encompassing task in the years after 1760.[6] However, the death of Zinzendorf was not only the death of a leader; it was also the death of a feudal lord, a high-ranking aristocrat with a fundamentally conservative view on social organization, which he saw as an organic whole. Already during his lifetime, there were opposing forces to his view of social cohesion and interdependence, which came from members attracted to emerging liberal principles, including individualism and unfettered economic development. His death, then, opened up possibilities for economic development and significant social reorganization.

These economic and social transformations will be the concerns of the following chapters, and it is the central argument of the present book that the Moravian missionary organization changed as well, a change which influenced their whole approach and local organizations, and ultimately, the relations to the 'heathen' populations. Importantly, however, these changes should not be seen only as internal to the Moravian community or limited to matters of religious encounters. They also reflected larger structural changes at a socio-economic level. In her groundbreaking study on the Moravian Brethren as a global community,[7] Gisela Mettele notes that the converted members in the missions were not fully recognized members of the global Moravian community. One of the tasks of the present book is to understand how this 'externalization' took place. How did the Indigenous and converted members come to be on the outside of the global community? Following Mettele, this externalization was a feature of the global nature of the Moravians, but I will also argue that this particular understanding of 'global nature' really materialized only after the 1760s.

I would like to introduce some specifics of Moravian ideology and practice, which are important for understanding their work in the mission fields. These

---

at *New Herrnhuth and Lichtenfels, in That Country*, trans. John Gambold, 2 vols, vol. 1 (London: Printed for the Brethren's Society for the Furtherance of the Gospel among the Heathen and sold by J. Dodsley etc., 1767), 400–1.

[6] See Peucker, *A Time of Sifting*, 147–64, for a good overview of the areas under transition after 1760. This is one of the very few substantial discussions of the first years after Zinzendorf's death.

[7] Mettele, *Weltbürgertum oder Gottesreich*. All translations of Mettele's book into English are my own.

specifics are at this point in the form of an overview, to be followed up in the coming chapters.

Eighteenth-century Moravian ideology contained what may be named a non-liberal strain, summarized in three overall points: an emphasis on the common humanity of members, an emphasis on community and an emphasis on history. These features are heuristic and distilled from a broad range of Moravian material. Because the Moravians are a religious group, these categories are theologically grounded in that they testify to the creation of humans in the image of God, a self-understanding as constituting the chosen people guided by the Saviour to do his will, and that this interaction between community and the divine is manifest in the history of the community. However, as mentioned in the introduction, my focus is a more profane one, and my interest lies in the relationship between these aspects of Moravian ideology and how they clash or merge with secular developments.

Individual

As studies in many different areas have demonstrated, the idea of selfhood was a foundational feature of the emerging Enlightenment West. This selfhood was found in areas such as economy, philosophy, religion and eventually in literature, although an early example may be found in Daniel Defoe's *Robinson Crusoe* (1719).[8]

Despite the insistence on the individual as the beginning point, disciplines and thinkers differed in how they envisioned the level of connectedness individuals have with their surroundings.[9] The most radical individualism arose in the field of economics. Whereas the former form of socio-economic organization was primarily collective in nature, namely agriculture and crafts organized in guilds, the new economic basis was that of manufacture and trade, and the individual wage-worker or entrepreneur. There was a slow but steady shift away from subsistence life, where one produced what one needed to survive supplemented by the exchange or purchase of some items, to waged labour, a life where one

---

[8] Daniel Defoe, *The Life and Strange Surprizing Adventures of Robinson Crusoe: Of York, Mariner: Who Lived Eight and Twenty Years, All Alone in an Un-inhabited Island on the Coast of America, Near the Mouth of the Great River of Oroonoque; Written by Himself*. Oxford Text Archive. http://hdl.handle.net/20.500.12024/K061280.000.

[9] I would like to thank the participants in the seminar series at Oldenburg University (Jessica Cronshagen, Dagmar Friest, Gabrielle Robilliard and Frank Marquardt) for pushing me on this point.

worked for a living and bought the majority of what one needed, supplemented by a few home-grown items. For such a new socio-economic order to develop, a new understanding of self was required, one which saw the self as a distinct entity, an owner of property,[10] responsible for one's self, and one's own survival, rather than as an indistinguishable part of a community. Whatever communities arose were based on individualism and thus constituted communities of individuals rather than an 'organic' community.[11] For example, the communities proposed by Adam Smith in *Wealth of Nations* are conceptualized as communities of individuals, who relate to one another as distinct individuals.[12]

While the self in philosophy demonstrated a larger range of positions, the individual itself was not challenged. Kant's transcendental subject and Rousseau's citizen clearly differ in many respects,[13] especially in their interconnectedness to others. The key was to define how an individual functioned in a collective context – through various 'social contract' theories – while still retaining individual rights.[14] Kant is closer to the liberal economic individual, and Rousseau's individual is closer to that envisioned by Marxists in the conception of class.[15] But the individual is firmly in place.

While the Moravians were part of the revival movement of Pietism, and as such were wedded to the intensified idea of the individual believer that came to the fore with the Reformation, the Moravian individual is different in two respects.

First, the Moravian individual was never fully individual but always connected through their choirs to a community of relative equals. The individual's relationship to their Saviour was the basic relationship, no doubt, but since the Moravian choir structure grew out of identifying with the Saviour in one's particular developmental stages, one's choir community was also part of one's

---

[10] In his study of individualism in seventeenth-century British political philosophy, C. B. MacPherson termed this 'possessive individualism'. Macpherson, *The Political Theory of Possessive Individualism*.
[11] By organic community, I mean communities that think as communities and not in terms of individuals. This would have been the case with most subsistence-survival communities, ranging from peasants in Europe to Indigenous tribes in the rest of the world.
[12] Adam Smith, *An Inquiry into the Nature and Causes of the Wealth of Nations*, 2 vols (London: Printed for W. Strahan; and T. Cadell, in the Strand, 1776). See, for example, book 1, chapter 10, book 2, chapter 1, book 4, chapter 1.
[13] Etienne Balibar, 'Citizen Subject', in *Who Comes after the Subject?* ed. Eduardo Cadava, Peter Connor and Jean-Luc Nancy (London: Routledge, 1991), 33–57.
[14] Sonenscher, *Jean-Jacques Rousseau: The Division of Labour, the Politics of the Imagination and the Concept of Federal Government*, 69–73.
[15] See Marx's use of Rousseau in Karl Marx, 'On the Jewish Question', in *Volume 3: Marx and Engels 1843-1844*, Karl Marx, Friedrich Engels: Collected Works (Moscow: Progress Publishers, 1975), 146–74.

relationship to the Saviour, meaning that it was never conceptualized as a fully developed individuality.[16]

Second, this individuality, this believing and elected subject status, was extended to all believers.[17] This was in contrast to liberal political thought which excluded certain people – non-whites, women, slaves and children – from the category of the subject. As Domenico Losurdo, Roberta James, Charles Mills and David Theo Goldberg have demonstrated in different contexts,[18] liberalism is *based* on the exclusion of non-white people from the category of the individual and personhood. This is especially evident in the epistemologies of John Locke and Immanuel Kant, but even in Jean-Jacques Rousseau, who is regularly regarded as more progressive. On the one hand, the Moravians in the eighteenth and nineteenth centuries were both slaveholders and estate-owners and thus part of exploitative systems of inequality.[19] However, they also subscribed to an understanding of (relative) equality *within* their church community, a community which included Indigenous peoples, as well as enslaved men and women. Indeed, the mission to the slaves in St Thomas was the first Moravian mission – and scandalous in its time – until Christianity's potential for creating subservient slaves was realized by the plantocracy.[20] Early Moravian missions thus saw converted Kalaallit, Native Americans and enslaved Africans as brothers and sisters.

Community

The order of the estates of feudal society in Europe was not in line with liberal ideology and its individualism, and the upheavals caused by the transition affected all estates in society – albeit in different ways and with very different

---

[16] I have dealt with this extensively in Petterson, *The Moravian Brethren in a Time of Transition*, chapter 4.
[17] In the conclusion to his study of the Moravian mission to Greenland from 1969, Heinz Israel states that 'it certainly did not go unnoticed by the Greenlanders that during the long period of their activity, the Moravians endeavoured to treat them as human beings in the spirit of their Brother/Sister idea'. Israel, *Kulturwandel*, 103. My translation.
[18] see chapter 1, note 49.
[19] Josef Köstlbauer, '"I Have No Shortage of Moors": Mission, Representation, and the Elusive Semantics of Slavery in Eighteenth-Century Moravian Sources', in *Beyond Exceptionalism: Traces of the Slave Trade and Slavery in Early Modern Germany, 1650-1850*, ed. Rebekka von Mallinckrodt, Josef Köstlbauer and Sarah Lentz (Berlin: de Gruyter, 2021), 109–36.
[20] Svend Erik Green-Pedersen, 'Negro Slavery and Christianity: On Erik Pontoppidan's Preface to L. F. Roemer Tilforladelig Efterretning Om Kysten Guinea (a True Account of the Coast of Guinea), 1760', *Transactions of the Historical Society of Ghana* 15, no. 1 (1974): 86.

outcomes.[21] The communal forms that were broken up in the transition to capitalism were those based on agriculture,[22] the guilds[23] and older forms of household, where cohabitation with apprentices, farmworkers and servants was the norm.[24] This process took centuries, as we know in hindsight. Two of the ways in which collectives were reshaped after older forms of community had been dismantled were in terms of gender and class.[25] Within this process, the Moravians did play a role since the Moravian emphasis on community *is* the 'new' understanding of community, and as such they took part in the process of dismantling older forms of society and fashioning a new one. However, their social organization and its individual/community dialectic meant that the individual was never fully individual but could be understood only as part of the community; conversely, the community was never fully a community but could be understood only in light of the individuals.

This is most clearly expressed in the choir system of the eighteenth and the first half of the nineteenth centuries, which was a dominant feature of Moravian settlements in Europe.[26] This was an organizational feature that subdivided the community into groups according to gender and marital status (adults) and the children according to gender and age/maturity. While the word 'choir' turns up here and there in early archival material in Herrnhut, it is not until the early 1740s that it became the defining feature of Moravian settlements, with most settlements sporting so-called choir houses for the unmarried members and some for the widowed members as well.

---

[21] See especially Marx and Engels, *The German Ideology*. But also Werner Conze, 'Stand, Klasse VII: Zwischen Reformation und Revolution (16-18 Jahrhundert)', in *Geschichtliche Grundbegriffe: Historisches Lexicon zur Politisch-Sozialen Sprache in Deutschland (Studienausgabe)*, ed. Otto Brunner, Werner Conze, and Reinhart Kosselleck, vol. 6 (Stuttgart: Klett-Cotta, 2005), 200–17.
[22] See Silvia Federici, *Caliban and the Witch: Women, the Body and Primitive Accumulation* (New York: Autonomedia, 2004), especially chapter 3.
[23] Sheilagh Ogilvie notes that political support of the guilds waned from the beginning of the seventeenth century, although the actual abolishment sometimes did not occur until the mid-nineteenth century in some countries. Sheilagh Ogilvie, *The European Guilds: An Economic Analysis* (Princeton: Princeton University Press, 2019), 531–6. See the overview in Sheilagh Ogilvie, 'The Economics of Guilds', *The Journal of Economic Perspectives* 28, no. 4 (2014): 169–92, which also demonstrates why, from a liberal perspective, the guilds were an impediment to economic development.
[24] Although his focus is on the development of separate gender roles in the Enlightenment, Marion Gray's depiction of the pre-modern household provides insight into the population of a seventeenth-century household. Gray, *Productive Men, Reproductive Women*, 59–74.
[25] E. P. Thompson, *The Making of the English Working Class* (New York: Vintage Books, 1966) is the best demonstration of the process of breaking up earlier forms of community and the emergence of a working-class consciousness. I also discuss class as well as gender as early modern communities in Petterson, *The Moravian Brethren in a Time of Transition*, especially chapter 6.
[26] Petterson, *The Moravian Brethren in a Time of Transition*, 22–3.

The choirs were a mix of many things. They were kinship groups and liturgical fellowships, but they were also pastoral groups and economic entities.[27] A significant purpose of the choirs was to cultivate a sense of community across the different backgrounds of the members, mainly class and local backgrounds, by privileging gender as the fundamental organizing principle, together with age and marital status. In Herrnhut, Herrnhaag and Niesky – the earliest Moravian settlements – choir houses were both dwellings and workshops for the choirs of the single sisters and brothers. However, not all Moravians lived in settlements. In cities such as Copenhagen, Amsterdam, Stockholm, the members did not live together but attended meetings and gatherings according to their choirs.

The community was thus a very tight-knit collective and is one of the most central aspects of Moravian ideology.[28] Indeed, if one looks for 'Moravian theology' as an abstracted set of dogmas and doctrinal statements, one looks in vain, because Moravian theology is found in its worldly actions and engagements, its community structure and its relationships. The primary relationship was that of the believer with the Saviour (the *Heiland*, the Lamb), which was confirmed, witnessed and discussed in the fellowship of believers. So, while the Moravians, as a Pietist fraction, saw the individual encounter with the Saviour as the turning point, this was also the turn to becoming part of a larger fellowship of believers. When one became a member, or a limb on the collective body, this meant entering a set of concentric circles, where the progression towards the centre is one of many steps: in Europe, where people were already baptized, acceptance into the community and one's corresponding choir was followed by admission to communion.[29] In the colonies, matters were somewhat more complicated (more detail later). Here, baptism did not mean acceptance into the Moravian community but to a more general Christian community, and in some cases even communion was not indicative of having been accepted into the *Moravian* community. Nevertheless, an Indigenous congregation, say in Greenland, was under the administration and management of the Moravian missionaries and as such constituted a community. This strong communal emphasis of Moravian

---

[27] Petterson, *The Moravian Brethren in a Time of Transition*, 36.
[28] Gisela Mettele's splendid study into the Moravian Brethren as a global community demonstrates how this sense of community was forged and practised. Mettele, *Weltbürgertum oder Gottesreich*. In his study on imagined community, Benedict Anderson shows how one of the ways in which a shared consciousness arose was the newspaper and its way of connecting disparate individuals: Benedict Anderson, *Imagined Communities: Reflections on the Origin and Spread of Nationalism* (London: Verso, 2006). The Moravians mastered this even earlier, in the connections forged between far-flung missionaries through the extensive communication network, as Mettele demonstrates.
[29] The memoirs, *Lebensläufe*, of the European Moravian's spiritual path follow the line of awakening—application for acceptance—permission to settle or join—acceptance into the community—acceptance into a choir—communion.

ideology was perhaps part of the attraction for the multitudes in the mission fields. For the missionaries, however, the colonial contexts posed challenges to their communal understanding, in that they were regarded as belonging to a different community than that of their congregants, namely that of the Europeans in Greenland and whites in the Danish West Indies.

Missionary ideals and missionary practice

In order to gain an insight into Moravian missionary ideals and practice, I would like to begin with a particular example. It comes from the records of the house-meetings from New-Herrnhut in Greenland. The earliest minutes begin in October 1749 and state as follows:

> We had a meeting. First the main matter of the teaching was talked about, namely the side hole as the birthplace of all souls, especially among his small hearts, and the Saviour and all his wounds, how mildly he bled to death on the cross for our destitution['s sake], to paint in front of the eyes of all people.[30]

This is typical Moravian eighteenth-century affective language, with singular emphasis on 'the Saviour', that is, Jesus, and his wounds. Special prominence is given to the side-hole, namely the wound in the side afflicted by a Roman officer, when Jesus was on the cross according to John's Gospel.[31] For eighteenth-century Moravians, the side-wound was regarded as a place of refuge, but also, as the quote states, spiritual birth.[32] The 'painting in front of the eyes of all people' is, as argued by many, the approach of the Moravians, not only in Greenland and other colonial contexts but also in Europe.[33] Zinzendorf was himself an

---

[30] UA R.15.J.b.I.7, 1, Anno 1749, d. 14 October: 'Hatten wir Converenz. Erstlich wurde gereth von den Haubt matterien der Lehre, nehmlich das Seiten-hölgen als die Geburtsstatt aller Seelen, besonders unter seinen Hertzeln, und den Heilland mit allen seinen Wunden, wie er am Creütz so milde sich vor unsere Noth zu Tod geblutet allen Menschen vor die Augen zu mallen'.

[31] John's Gospel, chapter 19, verse 34. The entire passage (19, 31-34) is: Since it was the day of Preparation, the Jews did not want the bodies left on the cross during the sabbath, especially because that sabbath was a day of great solemnity. So they asked Pilate to have the legs of the crucified men broken and the bodies removed. Then the soldiers came and broke the legs of the first and of the other who had been crucified with him. But when they came to Jesus and saw that he was already dead, they did not break his legs. Instead, one of the soldiers pierced his side with a spear, and at once blood and water came out. New Revised Standard Version (Anglicized).

[32] Vogt, 'Honor to the Side'; Atwood, 'Blood and Wounds'.

[33] On the missionary context, see Hermann Wellenreuther and Carola Wessel, *The Moravian Mission Diaries of David Zeisberger, 1772-1781* (University Park: The Pennsylvania State University Press, 2005), 55-8. On the European context, see Katherine M. Faull, 'Faith and Imagination: Nikolaus Ludwig von Zinzendorf's Anti-Enlightenment Philosophy of Self', in *Anthropology and the German Enlightenment: Perspectives on Humanity*, ed. Katherine M. Faull (Lewisburg: Bucknell University Press, 1995), 23-56, here, 38, 50. Also Burkhard Dohm, *Poetische Alchimie: Öffnung zur Sinnlichkeit in der Hohelied- und Bibeldichtung von der protestantischen Barockmystik bis zum Pietismus* (Berlin:

avid user of this technique, making use of simple and graphic affective language to paint the Saviour before the eyes of his listeners, and believed that through such simple and non-allegorical language, it was possible to summon an unmediated presence of the divine.[34] This mention of 'the main matters of the teaching' is not a regular occurrence in the minutes from the house-meetings. More regular is use of the lot to determine whether or not a person should be admitted to the congregation, whether or not a certain congregant should be baptized or admitted to communion and so on. Thus, we find page after page names of Kalaallit with a lot sign '*' followed by a 'Yes' or a 'No'. The lot-practice was regarded as consulting the will of the Saviour on a range of issues from the names of places to marriage partners and, as mentioned here, admission to congregation, baptism and communion (Figure 1).[35]

The scope of the Moravian mission was not to convert entire nations, but rather to seek out the souls prepared in advance by the Saviour.[36] Hence, the process entailed one-to-one conversation, rather than delivering public sermons, as was the practice with other missionaries.[37] The messengers from the Moravian community were not trained missionaries but ordinary men and women who worked to sustain themselves in the mission field. This meant living among the people, working with them and sharing their daily lives. Living in such close proximity meant that the occasions for conversation were common and that social hierarchy was, as Hermann Wellenreuter and Carola Wessel put it, 'notably absent'.[38] Wellenreuter and Wessel's comment relates to the mission among the Native Americans in the Muskingum Valley in the Ohio region. However, their description of the everyday life of the Moravian missionaries is very close to what we see in the Moravian mission in Greenland, where the Indigenous Kalaallit and the missionaries lived side by side. While the Moravian missionaries were the ultimate religious authorities, they began from the mid-1740s to make use of 'national helpers', that is, leaders from

---

De Gruyter, 2000). The rhetorical terms are *ekphrasis* (Preston 2007), descriptive speech that brings the thing vividly before the eyes, or *enargia*, the rhetorical term for the ability to create a vivid presence through language. Heinrich F. Plett, *Enargeia in Classical Antiquity and the Early Modern Age: The Aesthetics of Evidence* (Leiden: Brill, 2012), 12 and 26.

[34] See further discussion in Petterson, *The Moravian Brethren in a Time of Transition*, chapter 4 on language.

[35] Elisabeth Sommer, 'Gambling with God: The Use of the Lot by the Moravian Brethren in the Eighteenth Century', *Journal of the History of Ideas* 59, no. 2 (1998): 267–86.

[36] Wessel, 'Zinzendorfs Überlegungen zur Mission', 168.

[37] In his diary from Greenland, Paul Egede (the son of Lutheran missionary Hans Egede) remembers how the Kalaallit asked his father to stop talking, when they felt his sermon had gone on for too long. Poul Egede, *Efterretninger om Grønland uddragne af en journal holden fra 1721 til 1788*, Det Grønlandske Selskabs Skrifter, XXIX (Copenhagen: Det Grønlandske Selskab, 1988), 33.

[38] Wellenreuther and Wessel, *The Moravian Mission Diaries of David Zeisberger, 1772-1781*, 67.

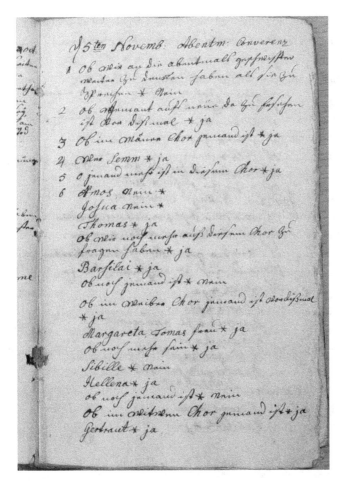

Figure 1 A page from UA R.15.J.b.I.7, 1 showing a meeting for admittance to communion, with the lot sign next to the name of the catechumen. Reproduced with permission from the Unity Archives, Herrnhut.

the Indigenous congregation as 'apostles for their nations'.[39] This deployment of Indigenous leadership marked a shift in the purpose of the mission. As mentioned earlier, the initial purpose was not to convert nations but to draw out those prepared in advance by the Saviour.[40] However, with the explosive growth of converts and new congregations, the necessity for producing home-grown helpers became a more urgent matter.[41] In the Danish West Indies,

---

[39] See Müller, *200 Jahre Brüdermission I*, 311.
[40] See A. G. Spangenberg, *Von der Arbeit der Evangelischen Brüder unter den Heiden* (Barby: Christian Friedrich Laur, 1782), 76.
[41] Müller, *200 Jahre Brüdermission I*, 311.

this practice of using enslaved helpers as 'apostles' was necessary due to the missionaries' irregular access to the plantations and thus a way to maintain order among the enslaved Moravians.

Another change in practice, although one which is less discernible, is the shift away from the original desire to avoid all church schisms: initially, the aim was to convert people to Christ and not to a specific brand of Christianity and the Moravian missionaries were to downplay differences to other Christian denominations and churches, and instead promote the unity of the community of Christ.[42] As Paul Peucker and Hans Schneider have been arguing for some time, early Moravian thought was characterized by the radical idea of Philadelphianism,[43] the belief that the true church was not present in one of the schismatic established churches but was an invisible community of Christians gathered from across denominational boundaries.[44] Thus, the Moravians were not setting out to build national churches but to contribute to a common missionary endeavour. At some point, however, this must have changed, because they began to accept converted people into the larger Moravian community. In the diary from New-Herrnhut in Greenland, from 19 January 1783, there is an entry concerning the celebration of the first fifty years since the departure of the first three missionaries, or messengers, from Copenhagen.[45] As part of the celebrations, a series of noteworthy events from the previous fifty years is listed. It is noted that in New-Herrnhut, the first mission post in Greenland, 1,254 had been baptized, which included 569 newborn children and 685 adults,

---

[42] 'Einfältiger Aufsatz der Evangelish-Mährischen Kirche wegen ihre bisherigen und künftigen Arbeit unter den Wilden, Sclaven und andern Heyden' (1740), pkt 2.h. in Otto Uttendörfer, *Die wichtigsten Missionsinstruktionen Zinzendorfs* (Herrnhut: Verlag der Missionsbuchhandlung, 1913). 30. Quoted in full in Wessel 'Zinzendorfs Überlegungen zur Mission', 170. See also Spangenberg, *Von der Arbeit der Evangelischen Brüder unter den Heiden*, 61.

[43] Hans Schneider, '"Philadelphische Brüder mit einem Lutherischen Maul und Mährischen Rock." Zu Zinzendorfs Kirchenverständnis', in *Neue Aspekte der Zinzendorf-Forschung*, ed. Martin Brecht and Paul Peucker (Göttingen: Vandenhoeck & Ruprecht, 2006), 11–36; Peucker, *Herrnhut, 1722-1732*; Peucker, 'A Family of Love'.

[44] Wolfgang Breul has argued that this is one of the three distinctive features of the Moravian missions and that they were instructed to downplay denominational differences rather than advocating them. Wolfgang Breul, 'Theological Tenets and Motives of Mission: August Hermann Francke, Nikolaus Ludwig von Zinzendorf', in *Migration and Religion Christian Transatlantic Missions, Islamic Migration to Germany*, ed. Barbara Becker-Cantarino (Leiden: Brill, 2012), 41–60, here 56. Philadelphians named themselves after the church of Philadelphia ('brotherly love') in the Book of Revelation as the church that will be saved because they had kept the word of God (Rev. 3:7-10). And, although she does not mention the concept of Philadeliphianism, Carola Wessel also emphasizes this non-sectarian aspect of early Moravian missions. Wessel, 'Zinzendorfs Überlegungen zur Mission', 170. Wessel also draws attention to the idea that certain people had been prepared in advance by the Holy Spirit and were in this way open to the message, such as the Ethiopian official in Acts of the Apostles 8 and Cornelius in Acts 10. These were the people to be targeted, rather than whole populations of so-called heathens.

[45] UA R.15.J.b.I.3.a: Diary, New-Herrnhut, Greenland, 19 January 1783.

who had 'arrived from among the wild [people]'. There is further mention of thirty-three from the Danish mission who were baptized. The first baptism of a Kalaaleq was that of Samuel (Qajarnaq) with his family on 30 March 1739. His daughter Aennel was still alive in 1783 and served as a national helper. In 1747, on 28 October, the record states, the first Kalaallit received communion, and since then the number had risen to 516. In 1772, on 18 October, the first Kalaallit were accepted into the community and by 1783 the number had risen to 100 people, covering both people born into the community and accepted into it. The account continues with a range of other statistics concerning marriages, deaths, European members and so on. Of interest here is the small number of people who are members of the community over against the larger number of people who are baptized. Being baptized and admitted to communion, then, was not the same as being members of the community (also noted by Mettele). Particularly notable is the late date of the first admissions of members, namely 1772. By comparison, the minutes of the so-called Helpers' Conference in St Thomas, in the Danish West Indies, show that actual membership was mentioned in 1763. Further, the Moravian historian Christian Georg Oldendorp mentions that an enslaved man, Matthias, was admitted to the St Thomas congregation as early as 1744 – almost thirty years earlier than in Greenland.[46] Clearly, the practice of accepting non-European members was not consistent across missions.

This is an important matter, because it goes straight to the heart of questions of community and belonging. In her work *Weltbürgertum und Gottesreich*, Mettele points out that baptized converts in the mission fields were not full members of the Moravian community but that they were baptized into Christianity rather than Moravianism. This is substantiated by the claim that while life on the mission stations was to follow the pattern of life and the liturgical forms of Herrnhut, 'there is no indication, however, that a monthly community day was held in the mission stations, as was customary in worldwide communities, to keep each other abreast of the developments in the other parts of the Unity'.[47] Hence, according to Mettele, the converts were not incorporated into the global structures of communication and were thus seen as of inferior rank. However, there were regular *Gemeintage* in both Greenland and St Thomas. Furthermore, the incorporation of converted slaves into the global Moravian community is

---

[46] Because the church records from St Thomas (UA R.15.B.a.16.b) are practically disintegrated, it is impossible to verify this and also impossible to check whether it says anything about membership.
[47] Mettele, *Weltbürgertum oder Gottesreich*, 107.

mentioned by Johann Loretz during his 1784 visitation in St Thomas.[48] Loretz noted that the Unity Elders Conference (UAC) based in Barby wished

> that the Black congregations from time to time receive and are read noteworthy pieces from the *Gemeinnachrichten*, to remind them of our community which we have in Christ Jesus, and to encourage them to partake in a brotherly way in the whole work of God in the Moravian Unity and each other, as members on one body.[49]

History

Along with the individual, the liberal understanding of history is another product of the Enlightenment's political project and consolidated itself in the course of the nineteenth century. As observed by Louis Dupré, the new orientation of the modern world view 'was supported by a philosophy that viewed the person as the source of meaning and value'.[50] This emphasis would only be strengthened through Leopold von Ranke's dictum, that the task of history is to show events as they actually happened, which thus elevated the individual historian to the rank of the supreme observer and source of all historical knowledge. This was formulated explicitly against G. F. W. Hegel, whose philosophical approach to history, in Ranke's view, did not take the individual into account.[51] However much Ranke's objectivism and positivism are refuted, the individual as the master of historical knowledge remains. This also means that the individual is regarded as being outside history and thus not accountable for its events.[52] The

---

[48] Visitations were trips made by leaders in the Moravian community to various mission posts, to inspect the congregations and the missionaries, and to implement changes. We return to this in the following chapters.

[49] ,daß den Negergemeinen von Zeit zu Zeit einige merckwürdige Stücke aus dem Gemeinnachrichten communiciert und vorgelesen, dieselben dadurch an unsere Gemeinschaft, die wir in Christo Jesu haben, erinnert und zu brüderlicher Theilnehmung an dem ganzen Wercke Gottes in der Brüder Unität und an einander, als Glieder eines Leibes ermuntert würden.' Vistiation report of Johann Loretz, St Thomas and St Croix, 1 May 1784, MDF.1920. A similar sentiment is repeated during Verbeek's visitation, 2 May 1797.

[50] See Louis Dupré, *The Enlightenment and the Intellectual Foundations of Modern Culture* (New Haven: Yale University Press, 2004), 229.

[51] See the excellent chapter on history 'Trials and Tribulations of Cleo', in Frederick C. Beiser, *After Hegel. German Philosophy 1840-1900* (Princeton: Princeton University Press, 2014). See also Werner Sombart's charge against history without theory in Werner Sombart, 'Economic Theory and Economic History', *The Economic History Review* 2, no. 1 (1929): 1–19.

[52] Hayden White has repeatedly drawn attention to this position of the historian in his publications. Hayden White, *Tropics of Discourse: Essays in Cultural Criticism* (Baltimore: John Hopkins University Press, 1978); Hayden White, *Metahistory: The Historical Imagination in Nineteenth-Century Europe* (Baltimore: The Johns Hopkins University Press, 1983); Hayden White, *The Content of the Form: Narrative Discourse and Historical Representation* (Baltimore: The Johns Hopkins University Press,

most extreme version of this may be found in Francis Fukuyama's essay from the last year of the Cold War,[53] where he argues – paradoxically – that Hegel was the one who had envisaged the end of history.[54] Hegel's understanding of history as the process of the dialectic influenced Marx and Engels and their conceptualization of history as a history of class struggle. Neither Hegel nor Marx and Engels would subscribe to the notion of the individual apart from the collective movement of history: Hegel, because the fullness of history was precisely when individual consciousness became sublated into the absolute, where the individual over against the absolute was but a step on the way; and Marx and Engels because of their emphasis on class as the true subject and driving force of history.[55]

Of these three ideologies of history (liberal, Hegelian and Marxist), the Hegelian comes closest to the view of history in the Moravian community, mainly because of its emphasis on a totality as that which consumes and determines the individual.[56] The strong sense of community in Moravian self-understanding means that there is a connection to a totality outside of the individual member, made up of the greater fellowship of Moravian believers, but also the shared history, the lived history, the sense of generations past, the lives sacrificed to the cause, the global connectedness and the fact that the Moravians are here today as a result of what happened in the past. This is demonstrated, above all, in a rich archival tradition that has produced the treasure trove that is the Moravian archives.[57] But it is also a collective and sedimented history, manifested in each individual. In an article based on fieldwork in the Danish Moravian community of Christiansfeld in the southern Jutland of Denmark, Rasmus Rask Poulsen shows how Moravian memory and identity are understood as 'a somewhat coherent religious and social unit that transcends time'. Poulsen quotes an

---

1987); Hayden White, *The Fiction of Narrative : Essays on History, Literature, and Theory 1957-2007* (Baltimore: Johns Hopkins University Press, 2010).

[53] Francis Fukuyama, 'The End of History?', *The National Interest* 16, Summer (1989): 3–18.

[54] Fukuyama's Hegel, however, is Hegel as mediated through Alexander Kojeve. A. Kojève, *Introduction to the Reading of Hegel*, ed. R. Queneau (London: Cornell University Press, 1980). For a more balanced reading of Hegel, see Domenico Losurdo, *Hegel and the Freedom of Moderns* (Durham: Duke University Press, 2004). For those who see Hegel as exhibiting a repelling Eurocentric mindset, however, the connection between Fukuyama and Hegel is less surprising. See George Ciccariello-Maher, *Decolonizing Dialectics* (Durham: Duke University Press, 2017), 1.

[55] Best expressed in Karl Marx and Friedrich Engels, *The Manifesto of the Communist Party*, Marx and Engels Collected Works 6 (Moscow: Progress Publishers, 1976).

[56] However, Schleiermacher, who was one of Hegel's great adversaries, had spent his childhood in the Moravian community, and his Christology was influenced by his Moravian past. His history, nonetheless, was anti-Hegelian and thus very liberal.

[57] The continuity with the past is set in stone on the gable of the Moravian Archives in Herrnhut, where we find the biblical reference Deuteronomy 32,7 (Remember the days of old, consider the years long past; ask your father, and he will inform you, your elders and they will tell you).

informant, Simon, as reflecting on the renovation of the stairs in the Sisters' House:

> When I walk up the stairs of the Sisters' House, I miss my old dented steps.... You think, 'These stairs are bumpy because someone has walked on them throughout two hundred years,' and that means something to me, because those people [who] walked there did so for a reason and that was the church life.

Poulsen notes that this expression of a notion of fellowship with those who went before is an example of how Moravians relate to other Moravians in the past.[58] I have also attempted to pinpoint this notion of a shared history: while coherent from the inside, it appears to outsiders as 'fragments of an inaccessible entity, which contains both the inner and outer history of the Moravian community'.[59] It is a deeper, more multidimensional view of history than one ordinarily finds in Protestantism and one that has more in common with Jewish or even Roman-Catholic understandings of and obligations to tradition.

Were the Moravians 'conservative'?

Clearly, liberal ideology was not a fully developed package, which the Moravians could assess and subsequently discard or modify but a world view in the making, with a number of categories changing shape and meaning. At the time when liberalism was emerging, there was a reaction from what we today would call conservatism:

> Conservative ideology was thus 'reactionary' in the simple sense that it was a reaction to the coming of what we think of as modernity, and set itself the objective of either reversing the situation entirely (the hard version) or of limiting the damage and holding back as long as possible the changes that were coming (the more sophisticated version).[60]

Now, clearly, this struggle within conservatism was not a once-and-for-all showdown but an ongoing struggle with shifting positions. For example, in the mid-1750s, the Lutheran pastor in Rennersdorf (near Herrnhut in Saxony),

---

[58] Rasmus Rask Poulsen, 'Living with World Heritage: Authority and Knowledge in Contemporary Moravian Christiansfeld', in *Crossroads of Heritage and Religion: Legacy and Sustainability of World Heritage Site Moravian Christiansfeld*, ed. Tine Damsholt, Marie Riegels Melchoir, Christina Petterson and Tine Reeh (New York: Berghahn Books, 2022), 125–44, here 134–5.

[59] Christina Petterson, 'The Community Archive in Christiansfeld between Local and Global', in *Crossroads of Heritage and Religion: Legacy and Sustainability of World Heritage Site Moravian Christiansfeld*, ed. Tine Damsholt, Marie Riegels Melchoir, Christina Petterson and Tine Reeh (New York: Berghahn Books, 2022), 194–210 here 205.

[60] Wallerstein, *The Modern World-System 4. Centrist Liberalism Triumphant*, 3.

Johann Gottlob Seidel published a furious attack on Zinzendorf and his 'gang', accusing them of undermining social norms and being a plague on church and state.[61] Seidel believed that if Zinzendorf could only be stopped, then everything could go back to normal – what Wallerstein refers to as the 'hard version'. One might object that the Moravians were radical Pietists and point to the Blood and Wounds theology and the mystical marriage that caused such an outrage in the first half of eighteenth-century Europe as very non-conservative and highly radical.[62] My own position on this is that these aspects were symptomatic of the changing world and as such testify to the flux of the times. However, if we look underneath, we can see that there is a concern with maintaining order, holding on to community, protecting and even reinforcing the institution of marriage. Furthermore, Zinzendorf's economic policies, if he can be said to have had any,[63] were certainly not liberal. An ongoing discussion in Herrnhut in the early 1750s demonstrates that Zinzendorf was against constructing 'factories' for several reasons, one of them being that '300 people could live off one factory today, and when the factory is stopped tomorrow, then all the people are without work, and have no bread'.[64] Another reason, given the following year, was that he was afraid that their 'neighbours would suffer under this'.[65]

I do not mean to imply that the Moravian position was officially and conclusively conservative, since this was hardly a defined political ideology at the time, but if we think of a spectrum from fully embracing the changes of modernity to wholesale resistance and the desire to revert to the former state, then the three elements above indicate that the Moravians are to be found on the 'holding back' position.

This distinct Moravian world view did not dissipate through encounters with the secular world, although they would be significantly challenged in encounters with Indigenous people, as well as slaves in the Americas. What interests me is how these central tenets fared in a number of different colonial contexts and

---

[61] Christina Petterson, "'A Plague of the State and the Church": A Local Response to the Moravian Enterprise', *Journal of Moravian History* 16, no. 1 (2016): 45–60.
[62] Peucker, *A Time of Sifting*; Peucker, '"Inspired by Flames of Love"'; Faull, 'Temporal Men and the Eternal Bridegroom'; Atwood, 'Sleeping in the Arms of Christ: Sanctifying Sexuality in the Eighteenth-Century Moravian Church'; Atwood, 'Blood and Wounds'; Vogt, 'Honor to the Side'.
[63] Zinzendorf's first wife, Erdmuthe Dorothea von Zinzendorf, was the one with business acumen and in charge of the household, including Herrnhut. Barbara Becker-Cantarino, 'Zur Bedeutung der *Oeconomia* im Engagement adliger Frauen im Pietismus: Erdmuthe Dorothea von Zinzendorf', in *Pietismus und Adel: Genderhistorische Analysen*, ed. Ruth Albrecht et al. (Halle: Verlag der Franckesche Stiftungen, 2018), 155–77.
[64] UA.R.2.A.33, B2, p. 204. Quoted in Otto Uttendörfer, Otto Uttendörfer, *Wirtschaftsgeist und Wirtschaftsorganisation Herrnhuts und der Brüdergemeine von 1743 bis zum Ende des Jahrhunderts*. (Herrnhut: Verlag der Missionsbuchhandlung Herrnhut, 1926), 40.
[65] UA R.2.A.No.35.b, p. 336. Quoted in Uttendörfer, *Wirtschaftsgeist Herrnhuts*, 45.

laissez-faire economic principles. What did increased alignment with the world mean? Did the acceptance of capitalist economic principles and the gradual integration into a global economy have any effect on the understanding of common humanity, community and history of the Moravian Brethren?

Conclusion

To sum up, this chapter has sought to provide some background for the analyses to follow. I have also sought to demonstrate that the Moravians had some distinct ideas that were not aligned with the emerging liberal ideology. I grouped these ideas together as common humanity, community and shared history. These ideas informed their missionary practice, which entailed seeking out the children of God from among the 'heathens' of the world, building communities and inscribing these endeavours into their collective history. Drawing attention to these differences is important, because by obfuscating what was different, indeed radically different about the Moravian missions, as the published Moravian missionary accounts tend to do,[66] the normalizing discourse upholds itself as, well, normalized.

What follows is the first of three large sections dealing with different missionary contexts and how this is negotiated by the leadership in Europe. The first is Bethlehem, Pennsylvania, where I will examine how eighteenth-century Moravians spoke about economic issues and how this related to the purpose of the missions. The significance of this for the larger argument is that the very understanding of the household implied a balance between mission and economy, which changed around the mid-eighteenth century, which is the topic of Chapter 3, and which would have an impact on how the Moravians organized the missions henceforth (Chapter 4).

---

[66] Cranz, *The History of Greenland*; C. G. A. Oldendorp, *Geschichte der Mission der Evangelischen Brüder auf den caraibischen Inseln S. Thomas, S Croix und S. Jan*. Hrsg. durch J. J. Bossart, 2 vols (1777). Spangenberg, *Von der Arbeit der Evangelischen Brüder unter den Heiden*; George Henry Loskiel, *Geschichte der Mission der Evangelischen Brüder unter den Indianern in Nordamerika* (Barby, Leipzig: P.G. Kummer, 1789).

Bethlehem, Pennsylvania

2

Moravians and money

So, how *do* Moravians speak about economic issues?

To Moravian parlance of the eighteenth century belonged the distinction between inner and outer things, *innerlich* and *äußerlich*. The inner things are connected with community organization, spiritual matters, congregational practice, liturgy, mission (soul work), while the outer things relate to business and enterprise. In his *Historie der Caribischen Inseln*,[1] C. G. A. Oldendorp includes an appendix to the year 1768 entitled 'Of the Outer and Inner State of the Brethren's Mission'. The appendix describes at length the possessions, industries and economic circumstances of the brothers in the Danish West Indies in 1768 (the outer), as well as the spiritual state of the congregations (the inner). This distinction, while in operation before Zinzendorf's death,[2] would become a central organizational feature of Moravian administration after 1760.[3]

---

[1] Oldendorp, *Historie der Caribischen Inseln*, 2/3: 1913–2059.
[2] Zinzendorf himself uses the distinction in relation to individuals and their inner (core) and outer (changing) circumstances. This is especially the case in Zinzendorf's many speeches to the various choirs in Herrnhut, which I have analysed in Petterson, *The Moravian Brethren in a Time of Transition*. Zinzendorf emphasizes that once the proper relationship is in place, that is, once the inner connection to Lamb is established, then proper submission to outer circumstances will follow naturally, and the individual will let the Lamb have his way with the choir and the members of the choir, be it death, missionary, marriage or a profession in Herrnhut or the West Indies. Commercial undertaking, evangelization and marriage are all cogs in the machine of the one divine plan, within which the Saviour distributes people to carry out this or that task. It is just as important to be married in Neuwied as it is to be building an oil-mill in Bethlehem or sent out as a missionary to Paramaribo. The significant thing is the inner relation to the Saviour.
[3] For example, in the collection of reports on the 'inner and outer course of the community in Neuwied 1750-59', which was organized in the decades after Zinzendorf's death. The documents themselves, from 1750 to 1759, do not operate with the distinction, but the archivist Erich von Ranzau in charge from 1769 to 1796 (with a four-year hiatus from 1775 to 1779) has given this title to the collection. Thank you to Olaf Nippe for identifying Rantzau's handwriting to me.
    In his memoir, clothmaker Gottlieb Oertel (1714–67) complained about being put to use in external business (*äußerliche Dinge*), that is, the establishment of three Moravian factories, instead of being used for something more meaningful or innerly (*innerlich*). UA R..22.109.9. The memoir is amended and printed in *Nachrichten aus der Brüder-Gemeine* (Gnadau: C.E. Genft, 1825), 771–80.

While the leadership of the choirs already in the 1740s were divided into two offices, the *Pfleger* (helper) in charge of the spiritual affairs and the *Vorsteher* (warden) in charge of outer, administrative tasks,[4] inner and outer were not regarded as separate spheres. They were understood to be connected, and regarded as complementary, with the outer enterprise always in service of and subordinated to the inner. This was all very well in a European context where economic developments were going at a moderate pace. In the rapid economic development of the colonies, such as the Danish West Indies and Bethlehem, the introduction of these distinct spheres had much more substantial consequences. The decisive point was the transformation of Bethlehem's 'common household' into a European-style organization with outer and inner spheres. As part of a general reorganization of the Unity, these steps were taken only weeks after Zinzendorf's death in 1760.[5] From this time, *äußer* increasingly serves to denote an external sphere of economic action which supports the spiritual sphere but is, in effect, separated from it. This is a crucial step in Moravian economic organization and administration, and we may see this process as a displacement of feudal organicism into the compartments of early capitalism. While the clear demarcation of an outer sphere had a significant effect on decision-making processes (see further Chapters 3 and 4), my concern in this chapter is a deep tension: the organic connection between inner and outer as it was understood in Bethlehem, Pennsylvania, and a demarcation of the outer economic sphere as it was practised in the Danish West Indies. For the Moravians in Bethlehem, the developments in the Danish West Indies were deeply disturbing.

Reprimand from Bethlehem

On 14 July 1747, the young bishop in Bethlehem, Friedrich Cammerhof wrote a letter of rebuke to the Moravian missionaries in St Thomas in the Danish West Indies. This rebuke demonstrates the difference in understandings of the ideal Moravian household, its spheres of concern and its management. One of his

---

[4] Uttendörfer, *Wirtschaftsgeist Herrnhuts*, 209; Heidrun Homburg, 'Glaube – Arbeit – Geschlecht: Frauen in der Ökonomie der Herrnhuter Ortsgemeine von den 1720er Jahren bis zur Jahrhundertwende. Ein Werkstattbericht', in *Gender im Pietismus. Netzwerke und Geschlechterkonstruktionen*, ed. Pia Schmid (Franckeschen Stiftungen Halle: Harrassowitz Verlag, 2015), 56–7.
[5] Erbe, *Bethlehem, Pa*. See also Katherine Carté Engel, 'The Evolution of the Bethlehem Pilgergemeine', in *Pietism in Germany and North America 1680–1820*, ed. Hartmut Lehmann and James Van Horn Melton (London: Routledge, 2009), 163–81. For an excellent analysis of the end of the General Economy and the particular missionary system it supported, see Engel, *Religion and Profit*.

points of admonition relates to the relationship between economy and mission. Cammerhof insists that the mission is the primary purpose of being present in, say, the Danish West Indies and that *'the outer profit should not be drawn into consideration at all',*[6] when determining the plans for a missionary's duties, rest, skills and so on.[7] Thus, whatever skills a certain brother may bring to a given mission station should not be the primary parameter according to which his usefulness is assessed, since 'the pilgrim plan', that is, the mission, must always take precedence over profit, and the primary purpose must always be to carry out the will of the Saviour and to be of service to his objectives. Cammerhof states that this is how matters are managed in 'our dear Bethlehem', where any changes indicated by the Saviour, however inconvenient to their industry, were happily complied with.[8] He insists that it is necessary to maintain 'pure apostolic thinking' and to *subordinate economic matters*, however good arguments to the contrary may be made. So, ideally, the brothers should not let themselves become fixed on outer (economic) matters, except to the extent that the outer matters serve the most basic needs; instead, they should be in charge of a blessed, apostolic economy in accordance with the cross:

> In addition, our common household helps us, and that is one of the inexpressible blessings that are contained therein. Because if everything is arranged according to the heart of the Lamb with a simple and pure eye on him, all the opportunities are cut off that can occur a thousand times in private housekeeping, whereby someone of witness and disciple disposition can be brought into an economic and plantation disposition and be displaced.[9]

---

[6] Friedrich Cammerhof, Bethlehem, to George Weber and Abraham Meinung, St Thomas, 14 July 1747: 'So erfordern es doch die ersten Grundt principia unsers Pilger plans und zeugen Berufs, daß ohngeachtet alle Vortheile die wir sonst von einem solchen Bruder haben, und des Nuzzens den er schaffen könnte, dennoch der anderwärtige Beruff vorgehe, und der äußerliche Profit dabey gar nicht in Consideration gezogen werde, denn sonst würden wir uns um die Crone unsers Berufs bringen, und von unsern Rufen in Christo etwas vergeben, den wir doch durch seine Gnade gerne behalten wollen.' MAB MissWI 129, 3. MAB refers to Moravian Archives, Bethlehem.

[7] The direct occasion for this pointed remark is, as noted in Cammerhof's letter, that there had been an agreement or plan to send brother and sister Böhner along with brother Segner to Bethlehem for a rest, as requested by the missionaries on St Thomas, and approved by the leadership in Bethlehem. Subsequently, this had suddenly been delayed, and they were not sent off as agreed.

[8] This refers to the practice of sending out members as missionaries according to decisions of the lot, which sometimes could be economically extremely counter-productive, if, say, a master carpenter who had finally brought the workshop into a good working order was called away as a missionary. See Engel, *Religion and Profit*, 52.

[9] Cammerhof to Weber and Meinung, 'dazu hilfft uns nun besonders auch unser gemeinschafftliche Haußhaltung mit, und das ist eins von den unaussprechlichen Seegen mit die drinnen liegen, denn dadurch werden, wenns alles nach den Herzen des Lämmleins eingerichtet wird mit einen einfältigen und lautern Auge auf Ihn, alle die Gelegenheiten abgeschnitten die bey der privat Haußhaltung tausendfältig vorkommen können, dadurch einer von den Zeugen und Jünger Sinn auf einen oeconomischen und plantagen Sinn gebracht und verrücket werden kan.' MAB MissWI 129, 3.

Cammerhof states that in the common household of Bethlehem all the intricacies and complications of private household organization are avoided, intricacies and complications that would throw a true faithful disposition into 'an economic and plantation disposition' and thus drive out matters of faith. By not concerning themselves with issues of economy and profit ('plantation disposition') the pure heart of a missionary (witness) and a disciple can be maintained. This is possible, says Cammerhof, within the structure of the communal household of Bethlehem.

Cammerhof's concerns were taken up at a synod in Bethlehem in September of the same year (1747), where discussions of the situation in St Thomas, Cammerhof's letter and the Moravian 'Pilgrim- and Disciple-calling' in the world took place.[10] The sessions devoted to this issue led to the recommendation stated in the results of the synod as follows:

> We heartily wish that the Saviour take care that our brothers and sisters in St. Thomas will not become too deeply entangled in the household and plantation matter, so that nothing is neglected in their main calling, which is to win the souls of the Blacks to the Saviour.[11]

This is followed by a more general recommendation on the relation and proper balance between the inner and outer matters.

At one level, Cammerhof's letter and the synod debates relate to the sugar production on the Moravian plantation, New-Herrnhut. At a deeper level, however, it relates to the organization of the missionary household and its priorities. In a proper Moravian household, industry and money-making should never be ends in themselves; instead, they should serve the mission. From the viewpoint of Bethlehem, the St Thomas missionaries have given in to a 'plantation disposition' and are following the order and priorities of the world instead of those of 'the Lamb'. We now turn to take a closer look at Bethlehem and the dismantling of this communal household also known as the General Economy.

---

[10] The minutes include correspondence between St Thomas and Bethlehem from 1746 to 1747, some discussions of the process on St Thomas and a statement in the resolution of the synod. Thomas McCullough, assistant archivist in Bethlehem, found these references in the minutes, digitized them and sent them to me, for which I am incredibly grateful.

[11] 'Wir wünschen von Herzen, daß der Heiland verhüten möge, daß unsere Geschwister in St. Thomas nicht zu sehr in die Haußhaltungs- und Plantagen-Sachen verwickelt worden, damit nicht darüber etwas in ihren Hauptberuf, die Seelen der Neger vor dem Heiland zu gewinnen, versäumet werde.' Results of the synod held in Bethlehem between 3/14 September and 8/19 September 1747 (AmSyn), MAB.

Bethlehem

Bethlehem, Pennsylvania, was settled in 1741 as a missionary base from where to convert Native Americans. After Zinzendorf's faithful attendant August Gottlieb Spangenberg's intensive legwork in Georgia and Pennsylvania, the Moravians settled Bethlehem at the Monocacy Creek, a tributary of the Lehigh River.[12]

Bethlehem was constructed on the model of what was called 'the General Economy'. The men and women lived in choir houses, which contained both dormitories and workshops. Living and working in these houses, the brothers and sisters did not work for wages but for room and board, and the surplus went to support the hundreds of brothers and sisters working in the mission fields. As Katherine Carté Engel put it, 'the town's raison d'être was its pilgrims'. Further, 'all economic decisions flowed from that fact'.[13] We have seen this approach expressed in Cammerhof's letter (see previous discussion). Already in the second half of the 1750s, this communal system began to come under internal pressure due to increased involvement in the fur-trade and other opportunistic ventures.[14] It also came under some pressure from the central board in Europe, but Zinzendorf insisted that it remain in place, primarily due to his high regard for the missionary work. On 9 May 1760, Zinzendorf died. The Central Council (*Ratskonferenz*) that met for the first time on 30 May 1760 took it upon themselves to continue the business of the Moravian community.[15] Amid a flurry of decisions and in-depth reorganizations, the decision was made to dissolve the General Economy in Bethlehem. This decision itself and the part it played in the general restructure is the focus of the following chapter. Here, we will look at the nature of the change and how it is discussed in economic terms.

Beginnings of the General Economy in Bethlehem

The architect of the General Economy in Bethlehem is Spangenberg, who drew up the plan of the community on his trip from Europe to Bethlehem in 1744.

---

[12] The beginnings of Moravian activity in Savannah and Pennsylvania is of course much more intricate. See Joseph Mortimer Levering, *A History of Bethlehem, Pennsylvania, 1741-1892, with Some Account of Its Founders and Their Early Activity in America* (Bethlehem: Times Publishing Company, 1903), 31–58; Engel *Religion and Profit*, 21–9.
[13] Engel, *Religion and Profit*, 38.
[14] Thank you to Katherine Faull for pushing this point.
[15] This is the so-called *Ratskonferenz*, Central Council meeting. The minutes of these meetings are found in UA R.3.B.4.c.1.

It consists of sixteen points,[16] the core feature of which was the communal household. Before he joined the Moravians, Spangenberg was a radical Pietist and had been a follower of Gichtel, who advocated against marriage.[17] Spangenberg also lived for three years on Christoph Wiegner's farm near Skippack, the dwelling place of the Associated Brethren of Skippack, which practised communal living.[18] Thus, Spangenberg's role in planning the General Economy of Bethlehem is no surprise given his earlier radical proclivities and his ability to think outside the norms of his time.[19] When conceiving the plan, Spangenberg was travelling back to Bethlehem from Europe, where he had taken part in a range of community formations in the Moravian communities between the years 1739–44.[20] He had spent time in the Wetterau (Herrnhaag and Marienborn), where he and his wife were in charge of the household, the so-called *Pilgergemeine*.[21] He also had tried to get the communal economy of Heerendijk back on its feet in 1740,[22] a plan which was rejected by the lot, and he spent 1741–3 establishing the Moravian communities in England.[23] He possessed, in other words, an exceptional organizational talent and had experience from a number of different political contexts (Dutch Republic, England and the principality of Hesse). To be added are his previous experiences from North America, namely establishing the settlement in Georgia and the aforementioned sojourn in Skippack.

Spangenberg's plan consists of sixteen points, but here we focus on the ones that pertain immediately to the question of household organization.[24]

1) In America there should be a pilgrim community (*Pilger-Gemeine*) and a settled community (*Orts-Gemeine*).

---

[16] 'Spangenberg's Plan', that is, the plan sketched en route from Europe to America in 1744: General-Plane mit welchen ich an 1744 von Europa nach America abgereiset. Held in MAB Spangenberg Papers, Box II, 1a, Moravian Archives, Bethlehem. Thank you to Tom McCullough for digging them out for me.
[17] Vosa, Aira, 'Von der Tugend der Ehelosigkeit. Johann Georg Gichtels Einfluss auf August Gottlieb Spangenberg', *Unitas Fratrum* 61/62 (2009): 9–21.
[18] Peucker, 'A Family of Love', 128, 137–8. See also Spangenberg's description of the communalism in Skippack explained in a 1737 letter to Zinzendorf, quoted in Erbe, *Bethlehem, Pa*, 13–14.
[19] This is ironic given his reputation for being a conservative, due to his role in mainstreaming the Moravian Church after Zinzendorf's death.
[20] For an overview of these years, see Jeremias Risler, *Leben August Gottlieb Spangenbergs, Bischofs der Evangelischen Brüderkirche* (Barby and Leipzig, 1794), 159–211.
[21] Risler, *Leben August Gottlieb Spangenbergs*, 163–4.
[22] Peucker, 'A Family of Love', 131.
[23] Geoffrey Stead, *The Moravian Settlement at Fulneck 1742-1790*, vol. 9, 2 (Leeds: The Thoresby Society, 1999), 7–8, 57–9.
[24] Joseph Levering has an outline of all sixteen points in Levering, *A History of Bethlehem*, 178–9.

2) The pilgrim community has its meeting place (*Rendezvous*) in Bethlehem, but moves around as a cloud of grace, to where the wind of the Lord drives it, and makes everything fruitful.
3) However, there should also be a house-community in Bethlehem, to look after the Oeconomie in the service of the pilgrim community, and their intentions, and to stay in place, when this moves around (*locomovirt*) for a while.

On the one hand, there was the so-called *Pilgergemeine*, a transient pilgrims' community, which refers to the missionaries working among the Native Americans, 'a cloud of grace' wandering around wherever the wind of the Lord would take them, making everything fruitful.[25] This cloud of grace was materially supported by a *Hausgemeine*, a house community.[26] As far as possible these communities should be self-sufficient. The division of the community into a *Pilgergemeine* and a *Hausgemeine* was not as such instituted by Spangenberg but had already been decided upon and organized in 1742 during Zinzendorf's presence in Bethlehem.[27]

Until 1754, the groups were not fixed, in that the lot decided who was to be sent out on missionary work. So, Engel notes that of the adult men in Bethlehem in 1752, 32 percent had worked as missionaries at some point in their lives.[28] As we saw in Cammerhof's letter, the mission was the primary object, and the economic benefits were subordinated to the missionary work. It is a wonder it could work at all, as Cammerhof ponders in another letter.[29] According to Erbe, Spangenberg instituted a number of changes in 1754, which introduced a separation between spiritual and economic 'calls' – but it is far from clear to what this refers.[30]

---

[25] 'Spangenberg's Plan', point two. The term 'cloud of grace' is a biblical imagery and likely refers to the narratives in Exodus, Leviticus and Numbers, where the cloud indicates the presence of the divine, and the tabernacle and people follow this cloud around in the desert.

[26] 1. Die Pilgergemeine hat ordinarie ihr Rendevouz in Bethlehem: zieht aber als eine Gnadenwolke herum, nach dem sie der Wind des Herrn treibt, und macht alles fruchtbar.
2. Doch soll auch in Bethlehem eine Hausgemeine seyn, die dortige Oeconomie zum Dienst der Pilgergemeine
und ihrer Absichten, wahrzunehmen, und in loco zu bleiben, wenn diese auf eine Zeitlang locomovirt.

[27] See *The Bethlehem Diary Volume I: 1742-1744*, trans. Kenneth G. Hamilton (Bethlehem: Moravian Archives, Bethlehem, 2001), 17–20.

[28] Engel, *Religion and Profit*, 50. As Engel also notes, this statistic does not include the women, who also served as missionaries with their husbands, thus removing two people from the productive arena of Bethlehem.

[29] Cited in Engel, *Religion and Profit*, 52.

[30] Erbe, *Bethlehem, Pa*, 110 and 127.

Construction began in 1743, with initial dwellings, the grist mill on the creek and the tannery. By 1745 Bethlehem sported a blacksmith, sawmill, pottery shop and an oil mill.[31] By 1752, forty trades were in operation,[32] which had increased to almost fifty in 1754, as witnessed by the British colonial administrator Thomas Pownall.[33] This work was all part of building a town and producing what was necessary to meet their own needs. Apart from the artisanal work, the community also relied on agriculture, mainly for their own sustenance. This was produced in Nazareth, Gnadenthal, Friedensthal and Christiansbrunn, and apart from wheat, oats and barley, it included buckwheat, maize and flax, as well as orchards and vineyards, and substantial livestock.[34] All of these crafts, skills and produce were primarily to serve the community in this big household. But they also did work for outsiders, and the surplus from this was redirected into the pilgrim community (the mission).[35] In 1752, the store was opened, which served as the contact point between Bethlehem and the outside world.[36]

Importantly, this was a closed circuit of production and had a singular purpose: to support the missions in North America and the Caribbean – so much so that when a request was made to contribute to a debt recovery fund (*Mitleidenheit*), Spangenberg replied that Bethlehem was unable to contribute, since all their surplus was tied up with the mission work. This response created enormous resentment in Herrnhut, especially since parts of the Unity debt came from expenses for Pennsylvania.[37]

The debt recovery fund was set up in 1757 to collect annual funds to collectively contribute to bringing down the debts of the church, which had risen rapidly after the collapse of a banker holding church deposits and the added complications of the Seven Years' War (1756–63).[38] The amount each community had to pay was determined centrally, based on the various means of income.

---

[31] Engel, *Religion and Profit*, 36. See also Carter Litchfield et al., *The Bethlehem Oil Mill 1745-1934: German Technology in Early Pennsylvania* (Kemblesville: Olearius Editions, 1984).
[32] Among which are tanner, dyer, cloth-maker, saddle-maker, shoemaker, tailor, weaver, stocking-maker, lace-workers, soap-boilers, mason, butcher, carpenters, millwrights, hat-makers, brick-makers, potters, clockmakers, waggoners, blacksmith, nail-maker, baker, brewer, bookbinder, cabinetmaker, cooper and locksmith. See full list in Erbe, *Bethlehem, Pa*, 65. taken from UAH R.14, A.19.12.
[33] See list in Engel, *Religion and Profit*, 52.
[34] Erbe, *Bethlehem, Pa*, 58–68.
[35] Engel, *Religion and Profit*, 53.
[36] Levering, *A History of Bethlehem*, 257. Engel, *Religion and Profit*, 114–21.
[37] Engel, *Religion and Profit*, 155–6.
[38] Engel, *Religion and Profit*, 155.

The reluctance to contribute to the debt recovery fund angered the leaders in Herrnhut. The role this played in prompting the restructure of Bethlehem may be seen in the opinion stated by Hans Hermann von Damnitz, head of the *Administrationskollegium*:

> 18. It is clear that Pennsylvania per se, from its communal and family-like household, contributes nothing to the debt-recovery fund, which is well understood on the one hand, because they have nothing left there, but everything goes from hand to mouth; but on the other hand is worthy of some consideration, because in Europe the family of late disciple [Zinzendorf] sets another example, and contributes 2,000 Reichstaler annually as debt recovery compassion to the whole.
>
> 19. [. . .] Therefore, I conclude with the heartfelt wish that the business in particular and a household corresponding to congregational settlements [. . .] may also be established in Pennsylvania soon and completely, so that one has [something] to give to the poor in Europe.[39]

Damnitz's conclusions follow an assessment of the economic state of Bethlehem and its industries, and points out that a restructure would free up means to contribute to the poor in Europe, thus contributing towards 'the whole' instead of focusing on its own circuit.[40] The way to do this, says Damnitz, is to establish a household corresponding to congregational settlements. The Moravian term for congregational settlements is *Ortsgemeine*, a settled community. This indicates a Moravian village, such as Herrnhut, or a distinct Moravian part of a larger town, such as Zeist in the Netherlands. These were organized according to a Moravian 'constitution', in other words, rules of both civic and spiritual life.[41] In the discussions concerning the restructuring of Bethlehem, this settlement type was

---

[39] Hans Herman von Damnitz, Concerning the Pennsylvanian Issues Herrnhut, 8 February 1761, 18. Man sieht also daß Pensilvanien per se von seiner gemeinschafftlichen und familien-mäsigen Haußhaltung zur Mitleydenheit nichts beyträgt, welches auch zwar einestheils wohl zubegriffen, weil sie da nichts übrig haben, sondern alles aus der Hand in der Mund geht, jedannoch anderntheils um deßwillen einiger Betrachtung würdig ist, weil in Europa die Familie des seeligen Jüngers ein ander Exempel darstellt, und jährlich 2000 Reichsthaler als Mitleydenheit zum Ganzen beytragt. 19. [. . .] Also schliese ich mit dem hertzlichen Wunsch daß die Wirthschafft in particulier, und orthsgemein-mäsigen Haußhaltungen [. . .] auch in Pensilvanien bald und gantz eingerichtet werden möge damit man habe zu geben den Dürfftigen in Europa.' UA R.4.UVC.I.41, 135.
[40] In his notebook, Johann Arbo also notes that one of the reasons for restructuring the Single Brothers' Choir was 'that they can contribute to the debt recovery fund and, in case of need, also to other extraordinary Unity and community expenses, according to their means'. Johann Arbo's Memorandum book MAB BethSB 7: The Projects and Suggestions to the coming change of the Bethlehem Economy, especially concerning the Single Brothers' House. Dated 16 December 1761.
[41] Paul Peucker, *Herrnhuter Wörterbuch. Kleines Lexikon von Brüderischen Begriffen* (Herrnhut: Herrnhut Unitätsarchiv, 2000), 43. Herrnhut was established as such in 1728 with the seigneurial precepts signed and agreed upon, and which included a wide range of rules and regulations at both spiritual and civic levels. See Peucker, *Herrnhut 1722-1732*.

proposed as preferable to the communal household, because the congregational settlement is based on an 'everyone earns their own bread' model, freeing up, as it were, surplus funds, which could then be redirected elsewhere.

As we will see, this economic restructuring would become an ongoing process, witnessed also in St Thomas. But the first large-scale restructure took place in Bethlehem.

Transition towards waged labour

Engel, who has carried out a highly comprehensive analysis of this transition from communal economy towards a more private economy, argues the main shift was the introduction of wage labour, or working for cash. This transition was smooth, she argues, because it slipped, like hand into a glove, into the market-oriented behaviour in the surroundings. Working for cash may mean either working in one of the industries owned by the church,[42] from which the labourer then received a percentage of the profits as a wage, or labouring as an independent artisan in one of the privatized trades.[43] The newly independent artisans had to pay 6 percent interest on their tools and supplies, rent for the workshop and wages. The church thus earned a steady income, without having to worry about liabilities. In regard to labour in the church industries, the leaders now had to determine the worth of the labour of each of their employees and then pay the labourers from the profits of the business.[44]

The single household of the General Economy was broken into many smaller households, which aligned more or less with what we today call nuclear families.[45] The Single Brothers and Sisters' choirs also had to be restructured into independent economic units, paying their own way, as was the mode of operation in Europe.[46] These were the first steps to incorporating market relations into the community fabric of Bethlehem. And once the community was separated from its missionary activity, the forces of production contained in this small

---

[42] Suggestions as to which industries to keep were provided by Herrnhut, namely 'the farms with the mills, taverns, and the processing of their products, be that mowing, brewing, baking, slaughtering, candle making, tanning and tawry work, distilling, and brickmaking, also linen weaving, the store, the apothecary, the bookstore, the pottery house, the dye house, and the farrier and blacksmith, also builders and carpenters.' Engel, *Religion and Profit*, 173.
[43] The artisans who could be set up by themselves included 'the glovemaker, cooper, hat maker, furniture maker, tinsmith, nail smith, locksmith, gun stocker, stocking weaver, cobbler, tailor, turner, wagoner, saddle maker, haberdasher, watchmaker, silversmith.' Engel, *Religion and Profit*, 173.
[44] Engel, *Religion and Profit*, 173.
[45] Beverly P. Smaby, *The Transformation of Moravian Bethlehem: From Communal Mission to Family Economy* (Philadelphia: University of Pennsylvania Press, 1988).
[46] See Uttendörfer, *Alt-Herrnhut*, 83–97.

town could be unleashed and led to an economic 'boom' until the end of the eighteenth century, by which time others had caught up with their industrial practices. After this transformation of the Bethlehem General Economy into a Moravian settlement or town (*Ortsgemeine*), only missions were permitted to run communal households.

Introducing a 'free economy'

In one of the letters communicating the impending change, Johannes von Watteville writes that if Zinzendorf's original plan had been followed, according to which Bethlehem had remained a pilgrims' house where missionaries could rest and dry their equipment, while the neighbouring Nazareth had been the home of the trade and industry, then perhaps Bethlehem could have remained as such until the end of time. He continues,

> But now Bethlehem is a complete community with all the choirs, with all the professions, the entire trade and industry has moved there, you have built such large and varied houses and workshops; however, in house-holding it is not in the form of a settled community (*Ortsgemeine*), but rather a communal economy, which is an abnormality or at least something extraordinary among all our communities and can be linked with nothing but unmistakable difficulties.[47]

Here, the general, or communal, economy is depicted as an abnormality within all the various Moravian settlements and communities. At this time, in 1761, this was an accurate assessment. However, as mentioned earlier, Paul Peucker has shown that the very idea of a communal economic system was not limited to Bethlehem in Moravian history, in that earlier settlements, such as Savannah in Georgia, Pilgerruh in Holstein, Heerendijk in the Netherlands and Bethabara in North Carolina, also had communal economic systems.[48] That this type of organization now no longer was acceptable may be gleaned from a passing comment in the minutes of the Central Council meeting from 28 November 1760, where it is mentioned that the communal economy is not to be tolerated

---

[47] 'Nun aber ist Bethlehem eine vollständige Gemeine mit allen Chören, mit allen Professionen, das ganze Commercium hat sich dahin gezogen. Ihr habt so grosse und mancherley Häuser und Werkstätte gebaut, nur daß es in der Haushaltung nicht die Form einer Orts-Gemeine, sondern einer gemeinschaftlichen Oeconomie hat, welches ein Anomalon oder doch was Extraordinaires unter allen unsern Gemeinen ist und nicht anders als mit unübersehlichen Difficultaeten verknüpft seyn kann.' Johannes von Watteville to Spangenberg, 11 June 1761. MAB BethCong 637, 2.
[48] Peucker, 'A Family of Love'.

anywhere, and where it does exist, the communities must be changed step by step to *Ortsgemeinen*.[49]

While the first steps towards reorganization were taken in 1760, the decision to dismantle and reorganize was finally made in 1761 and brought largely to completion by the end of the decade. The reasons for this decision are many. Some argue that it was to redirect funds to cover the debts which began to be called in after Zinzendorf's death.[50] Others suggest it was to curtail Bethlehem's independence.[51] Paul Peucker argues that it was due to the theological mainstreaming that took place after Zinzendorf's death and so Bethlehem's communal economy seemed unpalatably radical.[52] As these studies indicate, the Bethlehem common household has already been analysed from several different angles, but my emphasis is that Bethlehem should not be regarded as an independent entity.[53] Instead, its restructure is understood as part of a general restructure of the whole Unity in line with the ideological changes after Zinzendorf's death.[54] As we will see in the coming chapters, this meant an increase in attention to economic organization and, in the case of the Danish West Indies, a change in household practice, in that the outer sphere became detached from the inner. While the Greenlandic mission had little in the way of an independent economy, it was still influenced by this restructure, in that it became much more accountable in respect to its economic practice. In Bethlehem, where economic development was high, we will see a similar situation to that of the Danish West Indies, namely an unleashing of the forces of production and the separation of inner and outer, generating a distinct economic sphere. While this process in the Danish West Indies meant an increase in plantation production, in Bethlehem it meant the breaking up of the household into a more privatized structure, moving from the General Economy to what was called the 'European model' of separating the economy from the organism.

Projects and suggestions for the new organization

In October 1761, twenty-five single brothers and sisters arrived in the Moravian community of Bethlehem, Pennsylvania, from Herrnhut in Saxony. The men

[49] Directorial Board minutes, 28 November 1760. p. 212. UA UVC.P.6.2.
[50] Engel, *Religion and Profit*; Smaby, *The Transformation of Moravian Bethlehem*; Erbe, *Bethlehem, Pa*, 131–3.
[51] Engel, *Religion and Profit*.
[52] Peucker, 'A Family of Love'. Peucker, *A Time of Sifting*, 148.
[53] In 'Family of Love' Paul Peucker places Bethlehem within a wider Moravian context, providing very interesting results.
[54] As also indicated by Erbe, *Bethlehem, Pa*, 124.

arrived on 25 October, the women a couple of days later. Among the single brothers was one Johann Arbo (1713–72)[55] and among the women was Elisabeth Kannhäuser (1723–64), from Ebersdorf. Both had been selected by lot, in Herrnhut on 16 July 1760, to travel to Bethlehem and would facilitate the transition from a communal economy to a European model. Elizabeth Kannhäuser died a year and a half after her arrival, at the age of forty years, but Johann Arbo became a very important figure in this new community structure. His notebook, outlining the fundamentals of the transition, gives us a good insight into the ideas and intentions behind the plans (Figure 2).

The first entry in Johann Arbo's notebook is entitled 'The Projects and Suggestions to the coming change of the Bethlehem Economy, especially concerning the Single Brothers' House'.[56] The Single Brothers' House, with a ready workforce of more than 100 men,[57] was clearly the economic engine of the community. It is thus no surprise that the Single Brothers' House was a priority.

Arbo states that as long as the choir system is in place, it is necessary to ensure that the choir houses are fully functioning so that they can look after their members. Currently, he notes, they are not running at – in today's language – full capacity, due to unnecessary restrictions. By freeing up the business ventures and entrepreneurial activities, the choir house will be in an even better position to take care of its members. However, he ensures, this will not have any impact on the collective nature of the community as a whole. In short, the keywords are 'freedom' and 'common purpose'.

'Freedom' is here qualified as *not* seeking enrichment but being allowed to develop unrestricted. This means, as will become clear as the book unfolds, to unleash the profits and sending them to Herrnhut instead of channelling them back into the specific community. The question of 'common purpose' is also emphasized, in that it is not, Arbo says, a matter of going solo. He mentions that

---

[55] Johann Arbo(e) was born on 6 June 1713 in Flensburg, Holstein. After an early career as a teacher, he took contact with Abbott Steinmetz and the Brethren. In 1742, he was admitted into the congregation in Herrnhut. The following year he met Zinzendorf in Gnadau and became bookbinder and secretary for Zinzendorf in the Pilgergemeine. In 1749 he became leader of the Scriptorium (*Schreiberstube*) and assistant to brother Vieroth. In 1756 he came to Herrnhut, as registrar and secretary for the *Administrationskollegium*. In 1758 he became the assistant of the manager of the single brothers and the following year took over the leadership. On 16 July 1760, he was called to Pennsylvania, as the warden of the Single Brothers' Choir. After being ordained as Diaconus, he left for Bethlehem in February 1761 and arrived eight months later, on 25 October 1761. He remained in Bethlehem until his death in on 11 December 1772. He is buried in the Moravian cemetery, the Gottesacker or God's Acre in Bethlehem.

[56] 'Die Projecte und Vorschläge zur künftigen Veränderung der Bethlehemischen Oeconomie ins besondere aber das Ledige Brüder Haus betreffend'. MAB BethSB 7. Dated 16 December 1761.

[57] Arbo's notebook has a list of 144 men arranged in 24 rooms, before the restructure. MAB BethSB7, March.

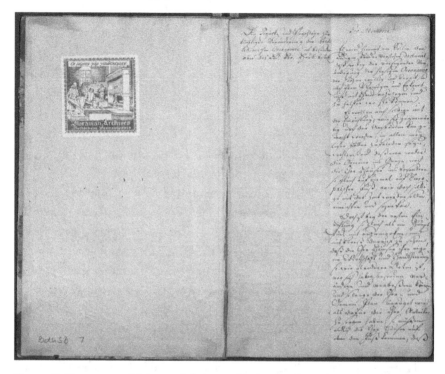

Figure 2 First page of Johann Arbo's notebook regarding the restructure of the Oeconomy of the Single Brothers' House. Reproduced with permission from Moravian Archives, Bethlehem.

they all constitute, together, the household of the Saviour and must help each other in carrying out the works of the Saviour.[58] This impending change is not to change the unity of the community, it is actually for the *good* of the community, because the better the choir houses perform, the better will it be for everyone.

After this follows a chapter on the 'Oeconomic Choir- and community- plan of the Single Brothers' Choir in Europe', in four main sections: A. Choir-Matters (*Gelegenheiten*), which refers to inner issues, such as liturgies and pastoral care; B. On the Outer Oeconomie in General; C. On the Masters and the Trades; and D. On the Apprentices and Boys. From these distinctions we can already see a new way of understanding the relation between 'inner' (choir circumstances)

---

[58] 'For although the congregation must be separated into different divisions, branches and choirs, we are all together, and are to be seen as an Oeconomie of the Saviour, where one helps, serves and supports the other wholeheartedly where it is necessary and possible'. ('Denn obgleich die Gemeine in verschiedenen Abtheilungen, Branchen und Chöre separirt seyn muß, so sind wir doch alle zusammengenommen als eine Oeconomie des Heilandes anzusehen, da eins das andere hilft, dient und von ganzem Herzen unterstüzt wo es nöthig und möglich ist.') Die Projecte und Vorschläge MAB BethSB 7.

and 'outer', when compared to the earlier organization of the General Economy as it was expressed by Cammerhof (see previous discussion). Here I will focus on section B, 'On the Outer Oeconomie in General', in order to emphasize a number of points.

Arbo begins this section by sharply distinguishing between the tasks and jurisdiction of the helper (*Pfleger*) and the warden (*Vorsteher*): 'Just as the choir-helper is only concerned with the hearts of the brothers and that they can have a blessed life in the house, so it is the warden's business to take care of the outer progress and existence of the brothers as far as possible.'[59] Nevertheless, he adds, the warden and the helper work together and manage their household as children of one father, as one family of God.

As mentioned earlier, the separation between these two spheres has different repercussions in areas of restricted economic development (Greenland),[60] restrained economic development (Europe)[61] and unfettered economic development in the colonies. While there is no difference in principle, the scale of surplus is dramatically different (see further Chapters 5 and 7). Before, the surplus generated from the various industries in Bethlehem went to fund the missions as the singular purpose of the industries in town; now, they were to be directed to (i) the choir house (their own household and industry, which they take care of all by themselves, arrange and change and improve according to the circumstances), (ii) the debt recovery fund (*Mitleidenheit*) and in case of need, (iii) also to other extraordinary Unity and community expenses, according to their means. The latter two were to be centrally managed, and every year, the warden would send a summary of the accounts to the Directorial Board for assessment.

With this new organization, the finances of the Single Brothers' House, and Bethlehem in general, would be overseen by the leadership in Herrnhut and would henceforth contribute to debt recovery and other sudden expenses. In exchange for this loss of independent household management, Arbo lists the many freedoms that accompany this new organization:

> Each choir house also has the freedom to provide for its own Oeconomie, cloth, linen, meat, grain, milk, tobacco, coffee, sugar, and all other foodstuffs and

---

[59] Die Projecte und Vorschläge MAB BethSB 7, section B.
[60] The Moravians were kept firmly on the outside of economic development in Greenland by the Danish-Norwegian colonial powers. We return to this in chapters 6 and 7.
[61] By restrained economic development, I mean that there still were a host of social and cultural circumstances which meant that the economy in Europe could not develop as rapidly as it could in the colonies.

goods, whatever they may be called, to buy themselves where it wants and can best have them.

Not only is this freedom to be enjoyed by the choir houses but also by all the individual brothers, as well as by every citizen or family in the community, so that they now are free to buy and order goods through the merchants.

Thus, the restructure meant that the common household of Bethlehem was broken up and its outer dimension placed within a circuit that was governed centrally by Herrnhut. At a local level, this liberated outer dimension could now be used for personal and communal satisfaction. The end of the General Economy was seen as so momentous for the Single Brothers' Choir that their diary begins a new volume with the introduction of the new household in 1762. The first entry, from 19 April, writes:

> After the previous communal economy, which had been conducted here for over 20 years, had finally come to an end, we began our own economy and housekeeping today in the name of our Lord with the watchword: 'He is the author of faith [Hebr 12,2], as soon one can no longer live without Him.'[62]

There is no similar disruption in the Single Sisters' Diary, which merely notes on 18 April that 'in the evening our choir had a lovefeast for the leave-taking of the Oeconomie' and the following day, 'She [A. Rosel] sang [in our morning gathering] apt verses to our commencing to work for ourselves today.'[63] In a letter from Spangenberg to Herrnhut from 9 May 1762, he writes: 'The Oeconomie in Bethlehem has at the end of April really been reduced. On 18th April, the Brothers as well as the Sisters had lovefeasts, and then they commenced their own industries.'[64]

The communal household of Bethlehem had come to an end. However, the communal household as such would continue in another form. In a circular letter from 1770 sent to all the European brothers and sisters working in the

---

[62] Diary of the Single Brothers, 19 April 1762: 'Nachdem die bisherige und schon über 20 Jahr hier geführte gemeinschaftliche Oeconomie endlich ein Ende genommen hatte, so fingen wir heute an mit der Gemein Losung: "Er ist der Anfänger des Glaubens, alsbald kan man ohne Ihn nicht mehr leben" im Namen unsers Herrn unsere eigenen Oeconomie und Haushaltung vor uns an'. MAB BethSB.2.
  As is common with the watchwords, the first is a biblical verse, in this case Hebrews 12,2 (Looking unto Jesus the author and finisher of our faith) and a verse from a Moravian hymn, here from Herrnhuter Gesangbuch 966, verse 5: at once I could no longer live without him (alsbald kont ich ohne ihn nicht mehr leben).

[63] Diary of the Single Sisters, 18–19 April 1762: 'Und Abends hatte unser Chor die Abschieds Agapen von der Oeconomie [. . .] Die A. Rosel hielt den Morgensegen. Sie sang in denselben besonders passende Verse zu unsern heut angehenden Anfang vor uns selbst zu arbeiten'. MAB BethSS.2.

[64] UA R.14.A.20, 36. Spangenberg to Johannes von Watteville. Bethlehem, 9 May 1762. Quoted in Erbe, *Bethlehem, Pa*, 123 as letter number 35.

missions, the Mission Deputation asks for donations to a newly established hardship fund. In connection with this, the Deputation mentions that since the brothers and sisters in the missions mostly live and work in communal households (Oeconomien), they thus do not generally have the opportunity to earn or save money for themselves and thus might find it difficult to donate to this fund.[65] It is this communal household which we investigate more thoroughly in the following chapters, because it becomes a crucial point of reorganization and remained a central feature of most Moravian missions until the close of the nineteenth century. In German East Africa and Suriname, the communal household was not abolished until 1900,[66] as a result of a resolution of the synod in 1899.

Conclusion

This chapter has focused on Oeconomie and household, seeking to explain the difference in Moravian terminology from our current economic system. Money was in the process of becoming a primary indicator of wealth; 'economy', while still connected to household management and thrifty organization, was taking on a more external role in the Moravian community. The notion and practice of the 'household' would undergo corresponding changes. Through the historical and indeed paradigmatic experience of Bethlehem, I have been able to introduce a number of core concepts and practices that will be explored in further detail in the following chapters.

---

[65] Letter from the Mission Deputation to Johann Arbo 'to all our dear messengers among the heathen in North America', Herrnhut, 24 January 1770, MAB PHC.140. The letter is quoted in Peucker, 'A Family of Love', 130, note 18. Thank you to Paul for providing me with the full letter.
[66] In the South African mission the transition to private households began in 1897. See the suggestions for managing in MD 1897, 27 January.

3

Change in leadership and organization
The case of Bethlehem's General Economy

Introduction

In this chapter, the focus turns to the crucial organizational changes that took place in Herrnhut, and thus the whole Moravian Unity, after the death of Zinzendorf in 1760. The decade of the 1760s deeply shaped the Unity, so grasping what – as far as possible – and how changes were implemented is vital. The first section concerns the transformations in organizational structure, which moved from the role of a charismatic leader to a collective and centralized leadership, embodied in a central council in Herrnhut. This council and other subsidiary bodies – such as the Mission Deputation – were extraordinarily busy. This leads into the second and major section of the chapter: the decisions concerning the ending of the General Economy in Bethlehem, Pennsylvania. Why Bethlehem? This was to be the first and paradigmatic case of a transition to a new economic and organizational model. Exactly what this entailed is the concern of the chapter.

Moravian leadership restructured

When Zinzendorf died on 9 May 1760, followed by his second wife, Anna Nitschmann, on 16 May, the Moravian community was shocked, though not organizationally unprepared. Nevertheless, the power vacuum left behind by such a significant presence should not be underestimated. Furthermore, it is important to emphasize that the death of Zinzendorf not only meant the death of the head of the Moravian Brethren, 'the disciple', their beloved and eccentric 'Papa'; it was also the death of a particular world view that had governed the movement from the beginning. This world view, or ideology, was rooted in

Zinzendorf's aristocratic background and had not been without its detractors, especially in the last seven or eight years of his life. As Gunthram Philipp put it, Zinzendorf was a class-conscious aristocrat, rooted in the values of the *ancien régime*. This meant, following Philipp, that he was governed by the notion of his responsibility to secure adequate provision for each community member — a notion which became increasingly problematic in the dissolution of the estate-based society and the emergence of industrial society. These problems emerged in the ongoing and unsolvable problems of the organization of the community and its private and collective industries.[1]

Earlier attempts at organization

While this is indeed a good definition of *some* aspects of Zinzendorf's person, we should also take note that there were other aristocratic members in Herrnhut, who were more willing and able to adapt to the new world and its ways. The aristocracy was not and is not *inherently* conservative, but often extraordinarily adaptable, as analyses of this transition period have demonstrated.[2] One of these supple nobles was Friedrich von Watteville (1700-1777), who came from a Swiss Patrician banking family in Bern and attended the *Paedagogium Regium* in Halle between 1713 and 1716, where he met Zinzendorf.[3] Watteville had been part of Herrnhut since its beginning and had taken an active role in its developments.[4] In 1754, he wrote a letter to Zinzendorf (who was in London) after a synod in the Oberlausitz region of Saxony. Watteville complained about the ongoing mismanagement of Herrnhut, which had wasted the fortunes of many of the wealthy brothers and sisters (*bemittleten Geschwister*) and left the community in serious trouble.[5] These were the years where the Herrnhut leaders were assessing the lessons learned and the staggering losses after the dissolution of the major

---

[1] Guntram Philipp, 'Halle und Herrnhut. Ein wirtschaftsgeschichtlicher Vergleich', in *Reformation und Generalreformation. Luther und der Pietismus*, ed. Christian Soboth and Thomas Müller-Bahlke, Hallesche Forschungen 32 (Halle: Verlag der Franckesche Stiftungen Halle, 2012), 125–205, here 201–2.
[2] Carl Brinkmann, 'Die Aristokratie im kapitalistischen Zeitalter', in *Grundriss der Sozialökonomik IX: Das Soziale System des Kapitalismus. 1.Teil : Die Gesellschaftliche Schichtung im Kapitalismus*, ed. G. Albrecht, G. Briefs and C. Brinkmann (Tübingen: J. C. B. Mohr, 1926), 23–34; Grunewald, *Politik für das Reich Gottes? Der Reichsgraf Christian Ernst zu Stolberg-Wernigerode zwischen Pietismus, Adligem Selbstverständnis und europäischer Politik*.
[3] Gerhard Reichel, 'Der "Senfkornorden Zinzendorfs." Ein Beitrag zur Kenntnis seiner Jugendentwicklung und seines Charakters', in *Erster Sammelband über Zinzendorf*, ed. Gerhard Meyer and Erich Beyreuther, 1 (Hildesheim: G. Olms, 1975), 141–372; Teigeler, *Zinzendorf als Schüler in Halle*.
[4] Peucker, *Herrnhut, 1722-1732*.
[5] Friedrich von Watteville to Zinzendorf, 21 June 1754. UA. R.2.A.34.3.

community of Herrnhaag in 1753.[6] Watteville's general complaint was that brothers and sisters of means were pouring money into various ventures, and no effort was being made to make use of such wealth wisely, such as the establishment of foundations to secure future funds. This not only meant an 'unreasonable strain' on the wealthy members but also generated laziness and complacency. Watteville's protests were echoed by another local nobleman, Hans Hermann von Damnitz (whom we discussed in the previous chapter), protests which led to the establishment of a board of trustees, the *Administrationskollegium*, at the significant synod in Taubenheim in 1755.[7] At the synod, the financial planning of the Unity was structured, and Zinzendorf was given a less prominent role in managing financial affairs.[8]

In these years, a further number of bodies arose to cope with various branches of the Moravian project and their finances, the precise nature of which has not yet been adequately researched.[9] A representative body, the *Collegium Advocatiae*, had been in place since 1753 and dealt with representations to local governments and agents. The chancellor, Abraham von Gersdorff, was also responsible for the archive and in charge of issuing official documents on behalf of the Unity.[10] This body devolved into the Directorial Board, a college of directors established in 1757, which constituted a board in charge of the estate of the Unity and its representations. Attached to it were a number of subordinated bodies which dealt with the children's institutions, the choirs and the Zinzendorf family estate. The *Missionsdiakonie*, established in 1755 and in charge of the biannual collections to support the missions, was placed under the auspices of the Directorial Board.[11]

This organization, which was necessary due to rapid expansion, increasing financial issues and general logistics, also meant that when Zinzendorf died

---

[6] Herrnhaag in Isenburg-Büdingen was established in 1738 and along with the adjacent castle of Marienborn quickly became the new centre for Moravians after Zinzendorf's expulsion from Saxony in 1736. It was dissolved due to the new count's insistence that the Moravians swore allegiance to him as lord instead of Zinzendorf (Peucker, *Time of Sifting*, 53). Marienborn remained in the ownership of the Moravian Unity until it was finally sold in 1773.
[7] The members of the *kollegium* were von Damnitz, Heinrich von Zeschwitz, Julius von Seidliz, Anthony von Lüdecke, Charles von Schachmann, Johann Friedrich Köber and two secretaries: Weinel and Johann Gotthold Wollin. Peucker, *Herrnhuter Wörterbuch*, 11. Peucker notes that the Administrationskollegium was dissolved after the death of von Damnitz in 1761.
[8] For a penetrating analysis of Zinzendorf relationship to money, see W. R. Ward, 'Zinzendorf and Money', in *Church and Wealth*, ed. W. J. Shiels and Diana Wood (Oxford: Blackwell, 1987), 283–305.
[9] But see the recent excellent article by Heidrun Homburg, 'Gläubige und Gläubiger: Zum "Schuldwesen" der Brüder-Unität um die Mitte des 18. Jahrhunderts', in *Pietismus und Ökonomie (1650-1750)*, ed. Wolfgang Breul, Benjamin Marschke and Alexander Schunka, Arbeiten zur Geschichte des Pietismus 65 (Göttingen: Vandenhoeck & Ruprecht, 2021), 301–35.
[10] Peucker, *Herrnhuter Wörterbuch*, 35.
[11] Peucker, *Herrnhuter Wörterbuch*, 22.

there were structures in place that would be able to continue the work. Of greater interest is the way they were reorganized and managed in the years after his death.

The establishment of Central Council (*Ratsconferenz*) and Inner Council (*Enge Conferenz*)

On 30 May 1760, twenty leading men in the Moravian Unity met for the first time since Zinzendorf's death three weeks earlier. Zinzendorf's son-in-law, Johannes von Watteville,[12] stated that the present body would continue the work of Zinzendorf and that the departments, 'already established by the late Papa (Zinzendorf), would proceed as usual'.[13] For almost a year, this council, called the *Ratsconferenz*, met every other day and discussed matters ranging from managing gossip in Herrnhut to restructuring the General Economy, from the need for providing a baker in Neuwied to ensuring a shoemaker for St Thomas and so on. This jumble of topics indicates that while there *were* a couple of subordinated bodies, this council was the main trunk, as it were. The *Ratsconferenz* understood itself as taking the place of Zinzendorf without any clear plan as to what leadership would emerge or continue.

In January 1762, the *Enge Conferenz*, the narrow or Inner Council, was established, most probably at the initiative of Johann Friedrich Koeber. Having studied law at the University of Leipzig, Koeber had been part of the leadership circle since the mid-1750s and had become an increasingly crucial figure in helping the Unity through periods of financial difficulties.[14] In a candid letter to the *Ratskonferenz*, Koeber urges the matter of leadership to be resolved. He maintains that the leadership of the Unity resides in this college, as the representative of the general synod, rather than in any individual.[15]

---

[12] Johannes von Watteville, born as Johann Michael Langguth (1718–88), had become a central figure in the Moravian community in the late 1730s and was adopted by abovementioned Friedrich von Watteville in 1745, securing him a noble title in order to marry Zinzendorf's oldest daughter, Benigna, in 1746.

[13] Minutes of the Central Council 1760-1, 30 May 1760. The leading men were in the order given in the minutes: Johannes von Watteville, Heinrich [XXVIII Reuß-Ebersdorf], Leonhard Dober, Ignatius [Heinrich XXXI Reuß-Ebersdorf], Johann Nitschmann [Ebersdorf], Johann Nitschmann [Herrnhut], David Nitschmann, Jonas Paul Weiss, Andreas Grassmann, Friedrich von Watteville, Ernst Julius von Seidlitz, Johann Georg Waiblinger, Johann Friedrich Koeber, Nathanael Seidel, Albert Anton Vieroth, Paul Eugenius Layritz, Carl Heinrich von Peistel, Joachim Heinrich Andresen, Johann Töltschig and Friedrich von Marschall (UA R.3.B.4.c.1, pp. 2–3).

[14] His memoir gives a good indication of his importance for the direction of the Unity. GN 1786, VIIIa, appendix to week 32.

[15] This letter is transcribed and translated in Christina Petterson, 'Governing the Living Community of Jesus: Johann Friedrich Köber's Letter on Leadership', *Journal of Moravian History* 21, no. 2 (2021): 143–62.

In urging a centralized and collective leadership, Koeber was also seeking to curb Johannes von Watteville's influence in the Unity at large. Watteville is mentioned several times as acting as an individual and in his own interest,[16] to which Koeber calls attention and wishes to end. He indicates that the charismatic leadership form which characterized Zinzendorf's leadership cannot be continued by any person within the community.

In 1762, then, both the Inner Council and the Mission Deputation are established and proceedings formalized. Below we will return to the significance of this, but before we do, we need to consider the events of 1760-1. The sources are minutes from the council (*Ratsconferenz*) and the Directorial Board (*Direktorial Conferenz*). Our focus is on the restructure of Bethlehem, which, as mentioned earlier, epitomizes many of the changes which took place in the years following Zinzendorf's death. In other words, the changes to Bethlehem and the changes within the Unity were closely entwined. Both have to do with centralizing and redistributing as we will see in the present chapter.

The meetings discussing these important changes were held in both the interim leadership council, Central Council (*Rathsconferenz*) and the Directorial Board. The relationship between the two bodies is important in order to understand their respective tasks and roles in this decision. The *Rathsconferenz* is the group that took the place of Zinzendorf and which delegated tasks to the various subordinated groups, of which the Directorial Board is a crucial one. The *Rathsconferenz* thus is a more overall governing structure, while the Directorial Board is much more organizational, dealing with the various tasks given to them by the council. There is also a significant overlap in membership between the two groups, and so the formal distinction between them is not always completely clear. But it is important to understand where the decision to end the General Economy is made.

---

[16] Paul Peucker cites a personal letter from Heinrich XXXI, Count Reuss ('Ignatius') to Nathanael Seidel in Bethlehem which shows this conflict between personal interest and collective will: 'We do not hear or see very much of Johannes. He is going through the mill. The plan of the interim administration is "we", and they strongly object to his usual word "I". Regarding the management of affairs it has got to the point that he is not allowed to make a resolution [by himself] but the conference has to do it.' ('Von Johannes hört und sieht man nicht viel. Er hat eine eigene Schule. Der Plan der Engen Conferenz ist *wir* und da arbeiten sie stark auf das ihm so gewöhnliches Wörtlein *ich*. Das extendirt sich denn auf die Besorgung der Affairen, daß er nicht mehr eine Resolution geben darf, sondern die Conferenz muß es thun, das ist in sich schön, aber die Menschlichkeit mengt sich denn doch vieleicht nein, und wir Alten gehen denn ein bisgen zu weit. Du verstehst mich und du kenst Leonhard.') Heinrich xxxi. Reuss (Ignatius) to Nathanael Seidel, Zeist, 28 September 1762, PP SNath 6, MAB. Translated and cited in Peucker, *A Time of Sifting*, 160.

End of the General Economy: First steps

On 7 July 1760, one of the many items of the day's meeting in the council (*Ratskonferenz*) concerned Bethlehem. It was decided, as noted by Katherine Carté Engel,[17] that after Nathanael Seidel's departure to Pennsylvania, it would be useful if Spangenberg were to return from Bethlehem to Herrnhut to serve the Unity at large. It was also discussed that someone from the General Directory and senior council should be sent to Bethlehem, and here Friedrich von Marschall's name came up – a possibility already mentioned during Zinzendorf's lifetime. The following week, on 16 July 1760, the discussions began, which would in the course of less than a year communicate the decision to end the General Economy to the leadership in Bethlehem and a directive to reshape Bethlehem into a so-called *Ortsgemeine*, a congregational town.

The transformation itself has been thoroughly analysed by Engel, but I will follow a different path in terms of the decision-making process. The reason is that I have a different reading of a passage in the archival material, and this changes how we understand the developments. Engel assumes the decision to end the General Economy was made by the *Ratskonferenz* on 16 July:

> Two weeks later, 'much was discussed about the outward affairs of Bethlehem, and the necessity of bringing it in order, and finally deciding it through [the Lot].' Though they did not state it outright, the 'it' was the dissolution of the Oeconomy.[18]

I would like to propose a different reading, namely that the minutes should be transcribed and translated as 'much was discussed about the outward affairs of Bethlehem, and the necessity of bringing it in order, and finally decided through * [the Lot]: Marschall goes with Nathanael to America to the proposed Bethlehem post'.[19] What was decided was indicated by the colon (:), namely that Marschall and Nathanael go America.[20] This was the decision made and not the decision by lot to end the General Economy in Bethlehem. This point is very important,

---

[17] Engel, *Religion and Profit*, 162.
[18] Engel, *Religion and Profit*, 162–3.
[19] 'Es wurde bey dieser Gelegenheit vieles vom äußeren Statu von Bethlehem gesprochen, und von der Nothwendigkeit damit in Ordnung zu kommen, und endlich durchs * decidirt: Marschalls gehn mit Nathanael nach America zu dem vorgeschlagenen Bethlehemische Posten.' Minutes of the Central Council, 16 July 1760. UA R.3.B.4.c.1.
[20] Similar constructions may be seen on UA R.3.B.4.c.1, 14 July 1760, point 9: 'To replace Jaschkens in Nieska, H.H. Thiels was suggested, and in his place in Berthelsdorf, Lampaders, and it was decided: It is according to the heart of the Saviour, that H.H. Thiels goes to Nieska, and Lampaders to Bethelsdorf *'

because it casts a different light on subsequent communication and decisions. For example, Engel downplays the emphasis on Friedrich Koeber and neglects the role of Friedrich von Marschall.[21] Both of these men were instrumental in providing suggestions for reshaping the General Economy into an *Ortsgemeine*. Furthermore, it seems that the decision to end the General Economy is made *not* by lot but by the leadership, in particular Koeber.[22]

Second, Engel argues that the decision to end the General Economy was made because the creditors had begun to call in their debts, and sharp eyes in Herrnhut saw that the enormous surplus created by the industrious brothers and sisters in Bethlehem could be redirected into the black hole of debt,[23] instead of going, as Danmitz put it, 'from hand to mouth'.[24] While this is clearly one substantial reason for breaking up the communal household, it is also important to see this move within the overall restructure of the Moravian community in terms of theological direction, administration and economic management. As such, it is then possible to see the dissolution of the General Economy as one element in the entire restructuring of the Moravian global community, its socio-economic premises and its ideological reshaping. In this, Koeber and Marschall were prominent architects. Thus, the two quibbles I have with Engel's argument are connected. Let us now follow events as they unfolded.

July 1760: Communicating the impending change to Bethlehem

As mentioned earlier, the first steps were taken in July 1760, where it was decided to bring Spangenberg to Europe and send Marschall to Pennsylvania. The position Marschall was to fill was that of attaché, in the sense that he had to represent the leadership of the Moravian Church over against the colonial government, ensure that the outer matters of Bethlehem were in line with government regulation and be in charge of external correspondence and negotiations. Along with this decision, the various new leaders of Bethlehem were selected by lot, among others Johann Arbo, who would be the new warden of the Single Brothers' Choir.[25] This was all communicated to Spangenberg in a

---

[21] Engel writes that Erbe overplays Koeber's role in the proposed restructure and in turn emphasizes Spangenberg's concerns with the developments in Bethlehem. Engel, *Religion and Profit*, 288–9, note 4. Friedrich von Marschall is only mentioned once as author of a letter. Engel, *Religion and Profit*, 281, note 27.
[22] Smaby, *The Transformation of Moravian Bethlehem*, 33.
[23] Engel, *Religion and Profit*, 32, see also Erbe, *Bethlehem, Pa*, and Dietrich Meyer, *Zinzendorf und die Herrnhuter Brüdergemeine* (Göttingen: Vandenhoeck & Ruprecht, 2009), 63–4.
[24] See Chapter 2, page 49.
[25] Minutes of the Central Council, 16 July 1760. UA R.3.B.4.c.1.

letter written by Johannes von Watteville, dated 15 July.[26] In his usual unctuous style, Watteville asks that since Bethlehem had grown and expanded beyond its original purpose (a mere pilgrim house), 'whether it wasn't according to the heart of Jesus and according to the nature of the circumstances the best and most blissful that Bethlehem would be set up as a local settlement like Herrnhut?' He notes that Zinzendorf, Papa, had been an eager proponent of a change, so long as it were possible without harm to the soul or to the whole structure. Watteville believes he has found a way to make it work:

> The workers', pilgrims' and children's institutions, including those members who were reluctant to leave the Oeconomie, continue in the common household and they would have the entire agricultural and livestock farming in Bethlehem, the shop, mills, tanneries, dye works, forests, inns, ferry, and other similar industries, from where all costs, interest, and the like would be taken care of. If the Oeconomie also employed members in these branches who live by themselves as local members, then it would be arranged with them beforehand how much they should have annually or weekly, and this would be arranged in such a way that they could survive well and properly. All other members would be paid for their work as is customary in the country, and they do the same, when they buy something from the Oeconomie. The choir houses are set up on European footing, with their own Oeconomie, which also pays for everything they receive from the household, and the brothers pay [the household] for what they drink and eat, and board. Apart from gardens, members will not get involved in agriculture, and the orchard remains within the Oeconomie. The choir houses take over capital according to the value of their houses and generate an interest from it and set it up with the professions on the German footing, for this purpose Nathanael will bring along designated choir-deacons.[27]

---

[26] The date on the letter is thus one day before the meeting where these various positions are decided by lot which means that either it is a mistake, or the letter was deliberately antedated. The letter was presented to the council meeting on 18 July, where it was read through. Minutes of the Central Council, 18 July 1760. UA R.3.B.4.c.1.

[27] Johannes von Watteville to Spangenberg. Herrnhut, 15 July 1760: Die Arbeiter und Pilger und Kinder-Anstalten desgleichen auch solche Geschwister, die aus der Oeconomie ungerne gingen, continuirten in der gemeinschafftlichen Haushaltung und die hätte zu ihrem Soutien die gantze Land- und Viehwirtschafft in Bethlehem, den Laden, Mühlen, Gerberey, Färberey, Waldung, Gasthöfe, Ferry und andere dergleichen Branchen, davon auch alle Unkosten, Interessen und dergleichen ins Ganze besorgt würden, wenn die Oeconomie in diesen Branchen auch Geschwister employirte, die vor sich als Orts-Geschwister leben, so würde mit ihnen zum Voraus[ein Ab]kommen getroffen, was sie jährlich oder wöchentlich haben sollen, und das würde so eingerichtet, daß sie wohl und ordentlich bestehen könnten; allen anderen Geschwistern würde ihre Arbeit landüblich bezahlt, und so thäten sie auch wieder, wenn sie etwas von der Oeconomie kauffen. Die Chorhäuser richteten sich auf den Fuß ein, wie in Europa, hätten ihre eigene Oeconomie, die auch alles bezahlte was sie von der Haushaltung kriegte und die Brüder bezahlten ihr wieder, was sie vor Essen und Trincken, Wohnung von dem Chorhauße genößen. Die Orts-Geschwister ließen sich außer Gärten nicht mit Ackerbau ein, und der Baumgarten bliebe ganz der Oeconomie; die Chorhäußer übernehmen nach

Watteville is suggesting a mixed structure, where the Oeconomie retains the heavy industries, in which some could work according to the old way; others could work according to the new privatized way, where they receive wages for their labours in the privatized industries and at the wage level of the area. In between are members who want to be independent of the Oeconomie but work within its industries. These will be given an allowance or income agreed upon beforehand. The choir houses will be decentralized and be independent households, with their own expenses and industries, the establishment of which is to be paid for by capital loans. The members will pay for food and board. As Engel has described, this suggestion will in the end be the one largely adopted. Spangenberg received Watteville's letter in late autumn and responded to it with counter-suggestions dated 11 November 1760. His main suggestion, as we will see, is to move the industry to Nazareth, reduce Bethlehem and keep the General Economy.

November–December 1760: The appointed committee sets to work

In the meantime, the discussions in Herrnhut continue. After the council's remark, on 28 November 1760, that general economies are not to be tolerated and that wherever they are they must be gradually dismantled, a committee was established on the following day to assess the state of Bethlehem and make suggestions as to what may be done to bring it back on its feet. The Board appointed Jonas Paul Weiss, Nathanael Seidel, Friedrich von Marschall and Koeber to assess the current state of Bethlehem and present a final resolution to the Directorial Board. Less than a week later, on 2 December, Koeber indicated eight points on which the conference should focus.[28] Two are of interest here, namely the third and seventh items on the agenda. The third point was to examine carefully the whole 'status economicus' of Pennsylvania, 'to set all economic sections apart, to provide a more specialized and proper method of accounting, so that all creditors

---

dem Werth ihrer Häußer ein Capital und ver-interessiirten es und richteten es mit den Professionen auf den deutschen Fuß ein, um weswillen auch Nathanael geschickte Chor-Diaconos mitnehmen will. UA R.14.A.20.7.31

[28] Namely: property titles and transfer thereof (1-2); to clarify and the economic organization of Pennsylvania, update the accounting practices and separate Bethlehem from Lititz and North Carolina (3-4). Another item on the agenda is to authorize previous demands to Pennsylvania by the previous General Diacony and the present *Administrationskollegium* to discuss and to bring about an appropriate agreement and to reach an equal agreement concerning the actives that the Pennsylvania brothers and sisters have with the *Administrationskollegium* (5-6). The seventh item is to consider whether there is anything to take note of about the present mode of administration governing in Bethlehem, and whether and to what extent it would be beneficial to change the communal Oeconomie. Finally, it should be considered whether the Oeconomate and Diaconate Collegium at Bethlehem should be given a kind of constitution and instruction on behalf of the Unity leadership?

and debtors, all assets and liabilities, all funds and needs, all income and expenses appear in their proper light and true nature.'[29] The purpose was, as Erbe also notes, to get a full insight into the financial health of a given community, so as to better assess how much they should contribute to the debt recovery fund.[30]

The second point of interest is item seven, which notes that it should be considered whether there is anything that should be kept in mind about the 'modem administrationis', as it has so far been carried out in Bethlehem, and whether and to what extent the communal Oeconomie, which has been in place until now, should be changed.[31] Item seven, then, is a discussion of how Bethlehem up until now has been administered, whether there was anything in this way worth keeping and, finally, whether it should be changed. This is then the first official mention of the step taken to consider a transition from the practice hitherto in place. As with the first point, this is also connected to a certain administrative practice, or perhaps more precisely, a departure from an older and more integrated mode of administration, the inherent value of which is called into question.[32] Weiss, Nathanael, Marschall and Koeber were given this task and to present their assessment to the Directorial Board to make a resolution. The results were presented at the meeting on 10 January 1761.

Plans

January 1761: Results are presented to the Directorial Board

On 10 January, Jonas Paul Weiss presented the Directorial Board meeting with the results from the committee's work.[33] The minutes record thirteen

---

[29] Memorandum on the Conference on the Pennsylvanian Oeconomies. Herrnhut, 2 December 1760: Der ganze Status Oeconomicus von Pensylvanien wäre hiernechst gründlich und deutlich zu examiniren, alle oeconomische Abtheilungen auseinander zu setzen ein mehr specialisirter und ordentlicher Rechnungsmethodus an Handen zu geben, damit alle Creditors und Debitores, alle Activa und Passiva, alle Fonds und Bedürfnuße, alle Einnamen und Ausgaben in ihrem behörigen Lichte und wahrer Beschaffenheit erscheinen. UA R.14.A.41.b.6.

[30] Erbe, *Bethlehem, Pa*, 131–2.

[31] Memorandum on the Conference on the Pennsylvanian Oeconomies. Herrnhut, 2 December 1760, point 7. 'Zu überlegen, ob über den Modem Administrationis, wie selbiger bisher zu Bethlehem geführet worden, nichts zu erinnern und ob auch in wieferne die bisherige gemeinschafftliche Oeconomie abzuändern, gut gefunden werden möchte.' UA R.14.A.41.b.6.

[32] In the Oeconomie, the accounting, or bookkeeping, had been integrated in the sense that none of the industries or the farms had individual accounts. The new accounting system would ensure transparency into the different branches of industry through separated balance sheets, so that is was possible to discern 'whether this or that place brings about usefulness or damage'. Erbe, *Bethlehem, Pa*, 142, citing Marschall's report on the status oeconomicus from 1766 in UA UVC.X.145. Erbe notes that this decentralization also manifested itself in the independence of the choirs which was completed in 1766 (142–3), the beginning of which we saw in the previous chapter.

[33] Minutes of the Directorial Board, 10–13 January 1761, pp. 233–47. UA UVC.P.6.2.

points, discussed on 10 January, and fifteen points discussed in the following meeting, on 13 January. They include considerations as to the future focus of Bethlehem and Nazareth, namely the professions, rather than farming (anyone with that proclivity should go to [North] Carolina instead), the fortune of the community (all included 10.000 £), that the plan to change to *Ortsgemeine* should be undertaken in one hit, and not step by step, because the expenses may be shared between the established brothers and sisters, rather than falling on the Oeconomie. The discussions regarding the committee's work on America continued at the following meeting on 13 January. Because families had not lived together under the communal economy, it was necessary to build houses for families. They would begin with two families in one house, sometimes even four families in one house if there were no children at home. The children were to be kept in the various institutions, unless they demonstrate a certain skill in a profession. The first reorganization is to establish the choir house of the Single Brothers according to European parameters, which would make the families want to establish themselves. The Oeconomie will continue to bear most of the burden, which is why certain branches of professions and services must remain within the Oeconomie. As to which ones, this would be better determined in Bethlehem rather than in Herrnhut. The report also notes that it was a shame that settlements (*Ortsgemeinen*) were not established from the beginning, because then there would at present have been ten settlements instead of the Oeconomie and 'thus the benefit for the whole would have been indescribably bigger'.[34] Here, the 'benefit' is in purely financial terms. Bethlehem's crucial and central role in expanding and supporting the missions in the Americas for twenty years has been effectively dismissed.

February 1761: Blueprint for the restructure in place

In early February 1761, the comprehensive plan for the restructure of Bethlehem had been drawn up by Marschall, Koeber, Jonas Paul Weiss and Nathanael Seidel.[35] This is, in essence, the blueprint for the 'reduction' of the communal household, and the verdict is expressed as follows:

> The communal economy that has existed up to now has, on the one hand, something astonishingly worthy, and has, in fact, with a few working hands, also accomplished a great deal in the outer things [...]. Yes! If one could imagine that

---

[34] 'so würde der Nuz fürs Ganze unbeschreiblich größer seyn'. Minutes of the Directorial Board, 10 January 1761, p. 236. UA UVC.P.6.2.
[35] Partially transcribed in Erbe, *Bethlehem, Pa*, appendix 7 (179–82).

the private individuals would be so convinced of the whole plan that they would gladly remain within it, and that people would be able to direct such an economy without others suffering through its weakness, it would be very desirable.

But since this is not to be expected, it is probable that this too perfect economy has often stood in the way of the growth of the community as well as of the outer things, that the surrounding brothers and sisters have admired this family more from afar than they have yearned to be within it, so that not many of them could have been moved in, but most of them were brought over from Europe at great expense, even if it was only for the worst manual labour.

[...]

Pennsylvania must therefore be judged as it is, and what its present circumstances can or need, and not as one would like it to be or imagines it should be.[36]

The General Economy then, while extraordinary, has inhibited economic growth. It was, they claim, admired more from the outside as an ideal rather than considered as an actual option.[37] The task, then, is to assess and reshape it according to 'present circumstances' rather than according to ideals. And according to the debt situation, it was deemed necessary that Bethlehem was to be drawn into the debt recovery fund and thus become part of the whole rather than, as it seemed, an independent entity.

---

[36] Friedrich von Marschall's Report on the Oeconomicum, February 1761. Chapter 3 (III Bisherige Haushaltung), page 15: Die gemeinschaftliche Oeconomie, welche bisher gewesen, hat auf der einen Seite etwas Erstaunenswürdiges, und hat in der That mit wenigen arbeitenden Händen auch im äußeren außerordentlich viel praestirt [...] Ja! Wenn man sich vorstellen könte, daß die Privati von dem ganzen Plane so überzeugt wären, daß sie gern darinnen blieben, und daß Menschen im Stande wären, eine solche Oeconomie zu dirigiren, ohne daß andre durch ihre Schwachheit litten, so wäre sie sehr zu wünschen.

Allein da dieses nicht zu erwarten stehet, so ist wahrscheinlich, daß eben diese zu vollkommene Oeconomie, sowohl dem Anwachs der Gemeinen, als dem Äußern öfters im Wege gestanden, daß die Land-Geschwister, diese Familie mehr von weitem admiriret, als sich hinein gesehnet haben, daher nicht viele von ihnen haben zugezogen werden können, sondern die meisten sind von Europa mit großen Kosten hinübergebracht worden, wenn es auch nur zur schlechtesten Hand-Arbeit gewesen. [...]

Pennsylvanien muß also beurteilt werden, wie es ist, und was seine jetzige Umstände praestiren können oder bedürfen, und nicht wie man es gerne hätte oder sich vorstellet, daß es werden solle. UA UVC.X.141

[37] This was also an issue in Heerendijk, where a possible solution to the economic difficulties of the community was proposed by Spangenberg, who suggested that would ease its requirements on residents and allow members to settle in Heerendijk without submitting to the common household. Spangenberg was hoping to attract wealthy Moravians in Amsterdam, who wanted to live in a Moravian community but were less enthusiastic about communal household. This proposal was rejected by the lot, however. Peucker, 'Family of Love', 131. Engel has examples of proppertied people permitted to settle in Bethlehem without joining the communal household. Engel, *Religion and Profit*, 58–61.

Spangenberg's letter (November 1760) with suggestions arrives from Bethlehem

In the meantime, Spangenberg's suggestions for the restructure had arrived in February. His concerns, expressed in an eight-page letter that was sent 11 November 1760 on behalf of the Bethlehem leadership,[38] were as follows:[39]

While acknowledging the necessity for some change, he is concerned with how one can change the Oeconomie so that no harm is done to 'the souls'. Spangenberg raises various practical objections to changing Bethlehem into a congregational settlement, such as Herrnhut or Gnadenfrei.

First of all, the infrastructure was based on a different socio-economic system and was not designed for this purpose.[40] Indeed, Spangenberg asks, who will establish the people who want to live for themselves (as citizens, *Bürger*)? Who will build the necessary houses? Who will give them the necessary advance and give collateral for the debts they will make? Half-hearted people who care little or not about 'the Lord's cause' will rejoice in such a change and make an effort for themselves. However, a question arises that bedevils the Quakers, Mennonites, separatists and Swenckfelders, namely becoming rich and full and deviating from the (Saviour's) plan. Spangenberg reminds Johannes that it is not the same in the Americas as it is in Herrnhut, Gnadenfrey and so on, where a citizen must struggle honestly to survive with his family, whereas in the Americas one usually becomes rich, after which the desire to give and help where it is necessary usually ceases.

In terms of a proposal for Bethlehem, they list a number of concrete issues, such as care of the dependents,[41] capital interests, quit-rent and taxes, as well as repairs to houses, mills, barns, stables and other buildings, along with necessary new constructions. Their concrete suggestion is to make Nazareth the settlement and those who wanted to work for themselves could set up there. Bethlehem would remain as the missionaries' rest-stop and provision-centre

---

[38] Peter Böhler, Andreas Lawatsch, Gottlieb Oertel, and Mathäus Schropp. See the list drawn up by Schropp, which suggests a number of suggestions as to a disintegrated household in MAB BethCong 610.1: Vorschläge wenn die Oeconomie solte auseinander gesezt werden 31 October 1760 (suggestions for separating the Oeconomie. 31 October 1760).
[39] August Spangenberg to Johannes von Watteville, 11 November 1760. UA R.14.A.20.7.33.
[40] See, for example, the problems with the mill-stream and its maintenance in the privatized economy, Engel, *Religion and Profit*, 175.
[41] They had been through the membership catalogue and found 144 missionary children, 62 orphans or quasi-orphans, 133 children of citizens, 61 people who because of age and weakness cannot live on their own, for example, old widows. Thirty-seven girls, who are also not yet able to earn their clothes or necessary sustenance, even if they can partially work, and 228 pilgrims (not including those in North Carolina or the West Indies). The provision of these 665 people falls to the common economy. August Spangenberg to Johannes von Watteville, 11 November 1760. UA R.14.A.20.7.33.

(pilgrims-seat), with a number of semi-'privatized' industries. One suggestion was that the income from the industries remain in the General Economy. As for the question of paying the members who work for the common economy – as artisans, or on the plantations, in building and other jobs – but who are not accounted for in the General Economy, they suggest: they should be paid a 'representative amount', with which they can provide for themselves and their children, as they themselves see fit. However, it should not be regarded as a wage, because the Oeconomie was not able to provide competitive wages if it were to have anything left.

Spangenberg's letter demonstrates that it was not merely a reorganization but a fundamental rethinking of a community structure, its members, organization and social relations. His suggestion to establish a settlement in Nazareth was put before the lot at the meeting in Herrnhut on 26 February and rejected.[42] At this meeting, they also state that the Oeconomie will not be abolished (*aufgehoben*) but merely placed on a better footing and that the expression abolishing the Oeconomie should be avoided both internally and externally. Consequently, the letter from the Directorial Board to Bethlehem speaks of 'reducing' the Oeconomie.

Execution

March–April 1761: Decision sent to the leadership in Bethlehem

In the Board meeting on 31 March, Koeber's response to Spangenberg was read and approved.[43] The twenty-six page missive presented to the leadership in Bethlehem the decisions made concerning the future of their General Economy and lays out, in twenty-one points, the issues raised by Koeber in December the preceding year.[44] The document is formulated in such a way that the most contentious topics are introduced incrementally, so that once one has agreed

---

[42] Minutes of the Directorial Board, 26 February 1761. UA UVC.P.6.2, p. 295.
[43] Draft of Directorial Board to Spangenberg et al. Herrnhut, 31 March 1761 is in UA R.14.A.41.b, 3. The clean copy sent to Bethlehem is in MAB BethCong 637, 4.
[44] Namely, the transfer of property titles from the deceased David Nitschmann to Nathanael Seidel to ensure that it remains property of the Unity (1-3); moratorium on land-purchases and what the already acquired land is to be used for (4-6); the debt recovery fund, the debts incurred by Bethlehem and the necessity of Bethlehem to contribute to this fund for the continuance of the Unity as a whole (7-10); the funds for children, Native Americans and mission in general (11-13); jurisdiction and claims of the *Administrationskollegium* (14); introduction of a more specialized accounting system (15); the reduction of the communal household and the estimated expenses (16-17); moratorium on agriculture (18); establish statutes for the settlement (18); and the separation of Bethlehem from Lititz (20) and North Carolina (21).

to the necessity of 1–15, that it is necessary to safeguard the property of the Unity,[45] that the debts should be brought down to ensure the survival of the Unity, ensuring that the missions are taken into account, and that we need to provide a more transparent accounting system and so forth, then point 16 on reducing the communal economy is not such a big step.[46]

The missive states that the Directorial Board has considered all incoming reports and letters concerning Bethlehem with the assistance of the brothers Nathanael and Friedrich Marchall, not only by a committee specially appointed for this purpose but also in repeated meetings of the Board. What follows is a general outline of what has to happen, leaving the specifics and manner of arrangement to the leadership in Bethlehem. Both Nathanael and Marschall 'are well informed about the contents and process and are in a position to give our warmly beloved brothers in Bethlehem sufficient information'.

After dealing with the issue of transfer of property and land purchase, the document raises the first sensitive topic, namely, that of the debt recovery fund. Point 7 begins by acknowledging the hard work, diligence and prosperity 'of our dear brothers and sisters in Pennsylvania'. In spite of the various complaints over economic hardship and numerous expenses (such as that of Spangenberg), it cannot be denied 'that this economic status is proportionately more advantageous, according to the funds and means of acquisition belonging to it, than the economic condition of some of the Moravian establishments, as well as of the entire Unity and its settlements in Europe'.[47] Thus, in order to allow the Unity to continue, Bethlehem must contribute its fair share.

---

[45] The immense amount of energy put into bringing this about suggests that there was a worry that some individuals may make claims on the property. The minutes from the Board meeting on 12 February mention that certain sharp-witted people have to be handled with care, since they might easily get the idea, and that anyone who belongs to the Oeconomie and works can make claims on the assets. Minutes of the Directorial Board, 12 February c.2. UA UVC.P.6.2, p. 268. Erbe mentions that this danger was pre-empted in Spangenberg's 1754 reforms, where according to the 'brotherly agreement,' stipulated that all assets belonged neither to the individual nor the whole. Erbe, *Bethlehem, Pa*, 141. In the Bethlehem archives, there are a number of yet unprocessed declarations which are, in effect, contracts between a new member and the community. Here it is emphasized that a given individual waives any claim to reward for his work, on his own behalf and on the behalf of his inheritors, and agrees to being entitled to clothes, food and board, and in the case of leaving, only taking his possessions, such as clothes. It is clear that the individual member has no claims to the property or wealth of the community. That the matter would be a different one with the dissolution of the economy seems to be at the bottom of the reference to sharp-witted people.
[46] A similar practice can be seen in Koeber's letter to the Inner Council pertaining to the new leadership structure. See Petterson, 'Governing the Living Community of Jesus', 146–7.
[47] Directorial Board to Spangenberg et al. Herrnhut, 31 March 1761: 'kann aber doch nicht an Abrede stellen, daß dieser Status oeconomicus nach den dazu gehörigen Fonds und Erwerbungsmitteln nach Proportion vortheilhafter situiret sey als der oeconomischer Zustand einiger Brüder-Etablissements, so wohl auch des gesamten Theils der Unität und ihrer Gemein-Plätze in Europa.' MAB BethCong 637, 4.

And then we reach point 16, on 'one of the most important affairs of the General Directorate', namely the prudent reduction of the communal Oeconomie and the implementation of a European-style settlement in Bethlehem.

While Spangenberg's suggestion of creating the settlement in Nazareth was rejected by lot,[48] the Directorial Board states its agreement with Spangenberg in that several industries[49] must be kept within the communal household to support the dependents of the Oeconomie, its missionary work and its debts. The remaining professions and labourers can be established by themselves and paid a fixed income.[50] Engel notes that these suggestions were reflected in subsequent accounting books.[51]

As Erbe points out, this transition was a long process. The new type of bookkeeping was not successfully introduced until 1766[52] and not until 1770 was the transition complete. The ten-year period also meant a phasing out of the 'old communal household spirit' and normalizing new social relations.

Since Engel and Erbe have demonstrated what exactly the restructure entailed, I see little need to repeat their points here, but instead conclude this chapter off by looking at the implications of the transition.

Implications of the restructure: Market economy and mission work

Erbe suggests that the struggles over the economic and social organization of Bethlehem were a symptom of the increasing *Bürgergeist* in the Moravian Church of the 1760s, which was particularly embodied in someone like Koeber. While commonly translated as civic spirit, *Bürgergeist* is more precisely translated as bourgeois spirit, with all of the connotations of liberal ideology and the entrepreneurial individual.[53] Erbe sees this as a contrast to the older pilgrim

---

[48] This is the only reference to a lot-decision in respect to Bethlehem that I have been able to find.
[49] Namely: the farms with their mills, taverns and the processing facilities, such as malting, brewing, baking, slaughtering, candle making, white and red tanning, distilling, brick burning, linen weaving, the store, the apothecary, the bookshop, the pottery-workshop, dye house, the blacksmiths and iron smiths, the masons and carpenters.
[50] Mentioned here are the coopers, hatmakers, plumbers, nail smiths, locksmiths, gunsmiths, weavers, crockery makers, tailors, turners, wainwrights, saddlemakers, trimmers, watchmakers, silver smiths.
[51] Engel, *Religion and Profit*, 173.
[52] Erbe, *Bethlehem, Pa*, 142–3.
[53] In the missive to Bethlehem, it is explicitly stated that the focus of Bethlehem is to be on the trades, and the way of the Moravians should be more *bürgerlich* and with more *bürgerliche* enterprises than peasantry and agriculture. MAB BethCong 637, point 4. Under point 18, it is repeated that those families who have the proclivity towards farming rather than bourgeois enterprise should go to North Carolina.

and fighter spirit (*Pilger- und Streitergeist*) embodied in the earlier Spangenberg (1740s and 1750s).[54] It cannot be denied that Koeber played a significant role in the restructure of the Moravian Unity after Zinzendorf's death, not only in relation to Bethlehem but also in his push for a less feudal and charismatic leader of the Unity in the future (see Conclusion). He was also instrumental in ensuring that the Moravian organization and administration were more focused on growth and profit following liberal economic principles. In terms of the restructure of Bethlehem, we now turn to two significant implications: the increase of the market and the diminishing of the missions, both of which are analysed by Engel.

Market

As mentioned earlier, Spangenberg understood that the proposed transformation was a fundamental restructure of the communal household's basic community structure, its organization and its social relations. He mentions the concern that it will provide attraction and opportunities for people who care for their own enrichment, which will have a detrimental effect on the larger and, above all, shared purpose. The American context, he noted, was particularly conducive to rapid wealth and ensuing egotism.

Engel's analysis has demonstrated how the transition meant that the reorganized community would fit comfortably into the market-oriented behaviour of the surroundings. The change in labour to working for wages or earning income from the profits of one's independent business also meant that money was introduced as a mediator between individuals, between the community and those who work for the community. Every item of work became valued as labour, and everything was assessed according to its market value and ability to generate profit. Establishing individual waged households, choir houses which functioned as independent economic units and individual labourers who worked for wages meant that the new Bethlehem no longer had a shared purpose for its industry, but that each and every person, and his or her labour, became the end in itself. This did not mean, of course, that there was no religious community or community spirit. As a congregational settlement, it was a religious community and its members were members of this community. Before, its industry and enterprise had not been a distinct sphere of action but

---

[54] Erbe, *Bethlehem, Pa*, 133–4. Spangenberg would go on to be one of the chief representatives of the conservative turn of the Moravian Church after Zinzendorf's death.

completely and organically integrated with its religious purpose. Now, this unity had been disrupted, and the town's economic activity was separated from its original raison d'être.[55]

Mission

What distinguishes Engel's analysis from other studies of the end of Bethlehem's General Economy[56] is her attention to the consequences of the dissolution for the missions. As she points out, the change to Bethlehem was twofold: 'by 1765 Bethlehem's pilgrim congregation had been eliminated, the house congregation dissolved, and the town stripped of almost all its ties to missionary work'.[57] For Bethlehem, the General Economy and missionary work were integrated, and by missionary work is meant the missions to not only the Native Americans in Pennsylvania but also the Cherokee in North Carolina, as well as managing and supporting the missionaries and missions to the slaves in the Danish and British West Indies. In the aforementioned report to the Directorial Board, which was discussed on 10 and 13 of January 1761, it is mentioned that Bethlehem has 'demanded' assistance from the European Heathen Diacony to the missions, because not only do they have many 'heathens' to serve there (i.e. in Bethlehem), but also in other 'heathen places' such as St Thomas, at great expense. The comment in the minutes is that 'once it is properly organised there [i.e. Bethlehem], and, as here [in Europe], properly pulled together throughout the whole country, it will be fine'.[58] Likewise, the very large expenses for [North] Carolina are unsurmountable and Bethlehem will not be able to sustain such an expense in the future. This issue is deferred to at a time when it can be discussed at greater leisure.[59]

The letter requesting this assistance had been sent by Spangenberg in January 1759, before Zinzendorf's death, and addressed the issue of whether Bethlehem should or could contribute to the debt recovery fund.[60] In other words, it was written before the changes to the communal household of Bethlehem. So, in

---

[55] Thank you to Paul Peucker for pressing me on this point.
[56] Such as Erbe, *Bethlehem, Pa* and Smaby, *The Transformation of Moravian Bethlehem*.
[57] Engel, *Religion and Profit*, 161–2. Erbe, *Bethlehem, Pa*, points out that this new regulation of the Mission Plan, as well as the partial hiatus on child care, meant that the greatest financial burdens of Bethlehem had been lifted, 139.
[58] Minutes of the Directorial Board, 10 January 1761. UA UVC.P.6.2, p. 237, point i: 'wenns dort recht eingerichtet, und wie bey uns durchs ganze Land ordentlich dazu colligirt würde, es schon gehen werde'.
[59] Minutes of the Directorial Board, 10 January 1761. UA UVC.P.6.2, point k, p. 237.
[60] See full discussion in Engel, *Religion and Profit*, 156–57. The letter from Spangenberg is mentioned in footnote 41 on page 288, and the archival reference is UA UVC X.145.

view of the dissolution of the General Economy, how, then, could the missions be supported henceforth?

In the resolution sent to Bethlehem, the Directorial Board resolved to constitute a renewed 'Heathen Diacony' to serve the mission and to this end appoint seven diaconates, two of whom should be in Bethlehem. Because of Bethlehem's duties in respect to St Thomas, St Croix and St John, as well as Antigua and Jamaica, the Directory envisioned that everything that Bethlehem uses for this purpose (travel, sending workers and their maintenance, as well as advances made and remittances and remunerations received) should be properly accounted by the two appointed Deacons. Further, whatever cannot be covered by the general mission of by biannual collections may be claimed from the Heathen Diaconia in Europe.[61] The Native American mission, however, is to be financed completely from Bethlehem and rely solely on voluntary donations. Nathanael suggested that implementation of this new approach should wait a couple of years and so the Directorate followed this advice.[62]

There is a suggestion here that the West Indian mission is a different priority than that of the Native American mission, which is treated more like the European Diaspora – that is, friends of Moravians living and gathering outside Moravian settlements.[63] In other words, already here we see a separation of the West Indian mission from the North American mission. The seven-deacon scheme mentioned here would not be realized, but in 1762 the Mission Deputation was established, which would oversee the Moravian missions and provide limited structural support. As we will see in the following chapter, this restructure would eventually mean that the West Indian mission would be removed from Bethlehem's supervision. This was formally decided by lot in an Inner Council meeting in April 1764, namely that the missions in the West Indian Islands from now on should be managed by Europe and not Bethlehem.[64] However, already in 1762, the founding documents of the Mission Deputation list the following

---

[61] This is already raised in Marschall's report, UA UVC.X.141, chapter IV, point 3, p. 20.
[62] Directorial Board to Spangenberg et al. Herrnhut, 31 March 1761, MAB BethCong 163, 4, point 13. See also the minutes from the Directorial Board, 12 February 1761. UA UVC.P.6.2, point g. pp. 269–70.
[63] 'Die Indianer-Sache hingegen bliebe davon gänzlich abgesondert und ein Incumbens speciale für Bethlehem, so wie die Besorgung der Diaspora für die deutschen und europäischen Gemeinen.' (The Indian issue, on the other hand, would remain entirely separate and a special responsibility for Bethlehem, just as the provision of the diaspora [is] for the German and the European congregations). Directorial Board to Spangenberg et al. Herrnhut, 31 March 1761, MAB BethCong 163, 4, point 13.
[64] Minutes of the Inner Council, 10 April 1764, UA R.6.A.b.47.d, pp. 184–6. Both the reassignment of the missions and the founding of the Mission Deputation are reported at the Marienborn Synod as a fait accompli: UA R.2.B.44.1.c.1, 135–7.

missions: New-Herrnhut and Lichtenfels in Greenland; the Danish West Indies (St Thomas, St Croix and St John), Antigua and Jamaica; several outposts in Dutch Guiana, such as Paramaribo in Suriname, Saron on the Saramacca river (Suriname), Ephrem on the Courantyne river (on the border between Suriname and Guyana), Pilgerhütten in Berbice; and finally, Tranquebar in the East Indies. As Katherine Engel has pointed out, there is no mention of the North American missions in this list.[65] Furthermore, the missions to the Danish and British West Indies are mentioned as distinct missions under the auspices of the Mission Deputation.

Breaking up the General Economy also meant breaking up the mission organization and reorganizing the relationships between the various parts to a new whole. This is the topic of the following chapters.

Conclusion

This chapter has focused on the restructure of the General Economy in Bethlehem as part of a general restructure of the Moravian Unity after the death of Zinzendorf and Anna Nitschmann in May 1760. The reason for this specific concern with Bethlehem is that this was the first and paradigmatic case of breaking up an integrated, organic whole into smaller pieces in order to release the surplus in the Moravian Unity. As we will see in Chapter 5, this process would happen again in the Danish West Indies. This is important for understanding the direction of the Unity after 1760 and how it pursued a liberal economic practice. This would have a profound effect on the missions in the colonies, in that the economic focus would become much more pronounced, leading to greater participation in the extraction and plunder of resources in some contexts.

---

[65] Engel, *Religion and Profit*, 169. Engel also points out that the restructure and its demands as well as the ongoing conflicts of the Seven Years' War (1756–63) had taken its toll on Bethlehem.

New-Herrnhut in St Thomas, the Danish West Indies

4

Time of transition and change in mission 1760–4 in the Moravian Unity

Introduction

This short chapter is transitional, in the sense that it sets the broader context for the analysis of the Danish West Indian mission of St Thomas in the next chapter. At the same time, the chapter follows the analytical structure of my discussion of the changes that took place in Bethlehem, Pennsylvania (Chapters 2 and 3): these changes cannot be understood without considering both what was happening in the central leadership in Herrnhut and on the ground in Bethlehem. So also with St Thomas. In this case, the crucial matters of central leadership concern the initial and ad hoc impulse to missions during the period of Zinzendorf's leadership, the establishment of a 'Mission Deputation' soon after his death and then the all-important Marienborn Synod of 1764, where major decisions were made to reshape the material foundations of the missions. These are the topics of the present chapter, which set the context for the analysis, in the next chapter, of the mission in St Thomas and its slave-holding economy.

The earlier missions: 1730s and 1740s

The missionary zeal had been part of Zinzendorf's childhood dreams since his schooldays in Halle. Here, at August Hermann Francke's dining table in 1715, he met the missionaries of the Danish-English-Halle mission to Tranquebar, Bartholomäus Ziegenbalg, Heinrich Plütschau and Johann Ernst Gründler, during their furlough.[1] This missionary zeal was to lie dormant for some years, until 1731, in this year, Zinzendorf was attending the coronation of

[1] Hutton, *A History of Moravian Missions*, 7.

King Christian VI of Denmark, and here his aristocratic machinations went to work. At the Danish court, Zinzendorf encountered and was enraptured with Anton, the Black slave belonging to the Privy councillor and director of the West India and Guinea Company, F. A. Danneskiold-Laurvig. After Anton's visit to Herrnhut, where he told the Moravian brothers and sisters of his siblings on St Thomas who longed to hear about Christ, the community was ready to begin a new chapter in this Danish colony. The mission to St Thomas began, as did the mission to the Kalaallit in Greenland. These were followed by the missions to the Indigenous and enslaved people in Suriname and the Native Americans of Pennsylvania. The early missions, then, were the results of Zinzendorf's connections with the Danish court, his cultivation of networks in England and Spangenberg's connections in the Netherlands. Through these connections, the Moravians gained access to the Danish colonies in the Caribbean and North Atlantic, and then to Dutch Suriname, and British colonies in the Americas, initially Georgia, Pennsylvania, North Carolina, and the British West Indies.

While the establishment of these missions all demanded negotiations with the colonial powers, the missions themselves were much less prepared and planned – especially in the first years. They were mainly ad hoc affairs, with actual instructions for missionaries in specific locations only produced by Zinzendorf in 1736 and in 1738, as well as a general text to all 'heathen messengers' in 1738.[2] The 1740 synod in Gotha then agreed on a text on Moravian missionary work among 'the wild, slaves, and other heathen'.[3]

On their ways to their respective destinations, the missionaries to St Thomas and Greenland stopped over in Copenhagen where they met with a Pietist sympathizer, the Lord Chamberlain Carl Adolph von Plessen. He asked both parties how they were going to make a living in the various places. David Nitschmann, en route to St Thomas, stated that he and Leonhard Dober were going to work among the slaves. When told that this would never be permitted for white people, he then proposed that they would live off his trade as a carpenter – and proceeded to acquire tools before sailing from Copenhagen.[4]

---

[2] 'Instruction an allen Heyden-Boten', in Uttendörfer, *Die Wichtigsten Missionsinstruktionen Zinzendorfs*, 19–20. In her article on Zinzendorf's ideas about mission, Carola Wessel notes that Zinzendorf was hesitant about giving instructions due to his lack of experience and knowledge as to what the messengers were to encounter and also that the very nature of a general instruction could impede a brother in a given and very specific circumstance. See Wessel, 'Zinzendorfs Überlegungen zur Mission', 163–73, here 165.
[3] These are all gathered in Uttendörfer, *Die Wichtigsten Missionsinstruktionen Zinzendorfs*. For an analysis of these local instructions, see Wessel, 'Zinzendorfs Überlegungen zur Mission'.
[4] The documents pertaining to this early stage of the Danish West Indian mission are published in Rüdiger Kröger, *Johann Leonhard Dober und der Beginn der Herrnhuter Mission*, Schriften aus dem Unitätsarchiv 1 (Herrnhut: Comenius Buchhandlung, 2006).

Christian David, who was bound for Greenland, had the following interchange with the Lord Chamberlain:

> Pleß asked how we imagined nourishing ourselves in Greenland. I said: from the work of our hands, and the blessing of God; also, we want to grow something and bring all kinds of seeds from the soil, as well as cultivate. Added to this a house, so that we will not trouble anyone. He said: there is no wood there, how will you build? And I said, we will dig ourselves into the earth and live there. He said: no, take wood with you, and build a wooden house, I will give you something towards that, and he gave me 50 Reichsthaler on the spot.[5]

These two instances tell us that the first missionaries had very little knowledge of the types of societies to which they were heading and that they were assuming that their skills were directly applicable. This was not the case, as we shall see. The possibility of earning their own bread was completely contingent upon a range of factors in the various locations. As Jan Hüsgen notes, geographical, climatic, personal and political factors all had an impact on the development of economic activities in the various missionary territories. In late eighteenth-century Labrador this meant trade; in late eighteenth-century Suriname, bakery and agriculture.[6] In the Danish West Indies, they entered into the plantation enterprise.[7] The individual mission settlements had thus grown and developed in different ways to support the task of evangelization.

In the late 1750s, the time had come for an assessment of the assets of the various missions, and steps had been taken to gather this information. Thus, on Nathanael Seidel's visitation of the mission in the Danish West Indies in April 1759, he brought with him Jens Korn, who was to be placed in charge of Oeconomie matters. At the request of the Directorial Board, Korn's first task

---

[5] Christian David to the Brothers and Sisters in Herrnhut, 4 April 1733: 'Pleß fragte, wie wir uns in Grönland zu nähren gedächten, ich sagte von unserer Hande-Arbeit und Gottes Seegen. Wir wolten uns was anbauen und allerley Saamen von Erdgewächßen mit hinein nehmen, und den Acker bauen, darzu ein Hauß, damit wir niemand beschwärlich wären. Er sagte, es wäre ja kein Holtz, von was wolten wir den bauen. Ich sagte wir wolten in die Erde graben und in der Erde wohnen. "Nein", sagte er, "nehmet itzt Holtz mit, und bauet ein hölzern Hauß, ich will euch dazu was schencken", und gab mir gleich 50 Reichsthaler.' UA MDF 1874.1.3.
[6] Jan Hüsgen, *Mission und Sklaverei: Die Herrnhuter Brüdergemeine und die Sklavenemanzipation in Britisch- und Dänisch-Westindien*, Missiongeschichtliche Archiv 25 (Stuttgart: Franz Steiner, 2016), 44.
[7] Apart from Hüsgen, *Mission und Sklaverei*, see Jon F. Sensbach, *A Separate Canaan: The Making of an Afro-Moravian World in North Carolina, 1763-1840* (Chapel Hill: Published for the Omohundro Institute of Early American History and Culture, Williamsburg, Virginia, by the University of North Carolina Press, 1998); Jon F. Sensbach, *Rebecca's Revival: Creating Black Christianity in the Atlantic World* (Cambridge, MA: Harvard University Press, 2005). For an older more apologetic study, see Oliver W. Furley, 'Moravian Missionaries and Slaves in the West Indies', *Caribbean Studies* 5, no. 2 (1965): 3–16.

was to draw up an inventory of possessions.[8] Spangenberg had also sent an inventory of assets from Bethlehem and Nazareth in 1759.[9] The background to this step is most certainly to be found in the issue of *Mitleidenheit* (compassion, co-suffering), the fund established in 1757 to bring down the debts of the community, discussed in the previous chapter.[10] For our purposes here, it is significant that the Directorial Board would receive a number of reports from the missions pertaining to their assets in the years when the restructuring would commence.

As Karl Müller pointed out almost a century ago, the support of the missions went from serendipitous offerings from friends in the first twenty-five years to the establishment of the Heathen-Diacony in 1754, a move that accounted for the various donations.[11] However generous and substantial the donations were, it was not enough to support the expenses of travel or the provisions required in remote regions. Further, how the missionaries coped in their various locations depended on the opportunities granted within the parameters set by the colonial powers.

Missions in 1760 and 1761: A period of transition

At the time of Zinzendorf's death in 1760, the Moravian community had grown to encompass the mission to the Danish West Indies, Greenland, Pennsylvania, Suriname, and taken the first steps in Labrador and the British West Indies. Added to this was an extensive number of communities in the German states and the UK, the Netherlands and Switzerland.[12] There was, as mentioned earlier, no overall organization of the Moravian missions in place. The correspondent with the missionaries was, and had been since the 1750s, Zinzendorf's son-in-law, Johannes von Watteville, who had been in charge of the collection box for the missions. During the Central Council meeting on 1 December 1760, Johannes

---

[8] Nathanael Seidel's visitation (Inhalt einiger Conferenzen welche bey dem Aufenhalt unsers lieben und theuren Nathanaels in Neuherrnhut auf St. Thomas von Zeit zu Zeit gehalten worden), session 2, 5 April 1759: 'Zugleich wurde resolvirt, daß ein Inventarium gemacht werden soll von unsern Plantagen, Negern, vom Vieh und allem, was zu unsere Oeconomie gehört' (Furthermore, it was resolved that an inventory should be made of our Plantation, Blacks, of cattle and everything which belongs to our household). UA R.15.B.a.12.127.
[9] Bethlehem leadership to Directorial Board. 13 January 1759. MAB BethCong 425.
[10] Engel, *Religion and Profit*, 155–60. See discussion in the minutes of the Directorial Board, 7 February 1761. UA UVC.P.6.2.
[11] Müller, *200 Jahre Brüdermission I*, 317–18.
[12] See the list of settlements and societies compiled by Gisela Mettele in *Weltbürgertum oder Gottesreich*, 277–9.

reminded everyone of the establishment of a 'college' to manage the missions and wanted it to commence already from the new year. The matter was to be taken up in the Directorial Board and would eventually result in the establishment of the Mission Deputation in January 1762. A year was to pass between this early call and the implementation. In this year, the Directorial Board was busy with a number of matters, of which the most time-consuming item on the agenda was dismantling the communal economy in Bethlehem. As we saw in the last chapter, this was an incredibly detailed process, which took a year to plan, a year to implement and many more years to come to completion. In the year it took to plan the restructure of Bethlehem, Koeber and other financially astute brothers (Marschall, Jonas Paul Weiss) were able to flex their administrative muscles, which came to influence the overall restructure of the Unity missions.

While the Directorial Board was concerned mostly with money matters in relation to the restructure of Bethlehem, the Central Council (*Ratsconferenz*) was more concerned with overall organizational matters pertaining to the mission. At the same time, the Central Council was also keen to establish a mission body to oversee certain aspects of the missions. After Johannes' first flagging of the establishment of a college to manage the missions, the minutes of the council show continuous attention to mission-related questions and mention several times that this or that will be a matter for the future mission body. We are, in other words, still in the planning phase. One matter discussed twice is the difference between the settlements (*Colonien*) and the mission (*Heydenmission*):

> In the first case, every one lives from his own basis (*Fond*); in the second case everyone lives in one household (*Oeconomie*), and even he who works only physically does so for the best of the mission and is thus to be considered an envoy to the heathen (*Heidenbote*) because he does it for the Heathen cause.[13]

This characterization of the mission is an important one, in that the division of labour into missionaries and support workers describes positions in the making. On the one hand, it sounds like the organization of work and mission as it was in the Bethlehem General Economy, where the itinerant *Pilgergemeine* worked as missionaries among the Native Americans. As explained in Chapter 2, this

---

[13] Minutes of the Central Council 1760-1, 3 December 1760, 175: 'In ersteren lebt jeder auf seinen eigenen Fond; in letztern lebt alles in Einer Oeconomie, und wer auch nur leiblich arbeitet, thuts doch zum Besten der Mission, und ist als ein Heydenbote zu consideriren, weil ers für die Heyden-Sache thut' (UA R.3.B.4.c.1, point 11). The other mention is in the meeting on 1 December 1760, point 10 (p. 190), where it is mentioned that a discussion arose as to the difference between missions (*Heyden-plätze*) and the settlements (*Colonien*) such as North Carolina without mentioning the contents.

transient community was materially supported by a *Hausgemeine*, a house community, which worked for this purpose in Bethlehem. In the Danish West Indian mission, as we shall see in Chapter 5, this was also the case: In 1736–7 Friedrich Martin evangelized, while Matthäus Freundlich and Johann Bönicke worked to support the three of them. Because the mission/labour organization in St Thomas was born out of necessity rather than conscious planning, it also indicates a significant feature of the society in which such a division of labour makes sense, and this in turn influenced the Unity itself. In the missions in Greenland, however, this was not how the mission was organized, and this is undoubtedly due to the fact that there were no means of income as such, and so all the missionaries shared in the various tasks of subsistence, to which the congregation made the major contribution. In Chapter 1, I referred to these household organizations and their distinct labour organizations as models, namely, the Greenlandic model, which I characterized as a community based on subsistence economy supplemented with some trade skills and annual food provisions from Europe. Then, there was the Bethlehem model, where the house congregation ensured self-sufficiency and supported the missionaries. The third model, that of St Thomas, was more of a profit, or plantation, model, where the profits generated from sugar production were used to fund other missionary activities on the islands. The dissolution of Bethlehem meant shifting it more towards the St Thomas model in that the profits were now to be distributed away from Bethlehem and contribute to a larger economic plan. At the very time when the Central Council was characterizing a mission settlement as one household (Oeconomie), with some evangelizing and others labouring to support this cause, the General Economy in Bethlehem was under restructuring.

Another fascinating point in the minutes concerning the founding of the Mission Deputation is the mention of the separation of the Diacony and what is called *Credit-wesen*, or 'credit matter'. The minutes note that this separation is the case in the settled communities (*Gemeinen*), and in future it would be a good move if this separation could also take place in the mission posts where there are so-called establishments, that is, businesses. It continues: 'The Diacony deals only with the upkeep of the missions, just as the other [the credit-matter] with the increase in revenue of the establishments and plantations.'[14]

---

[14] Minutes of the Directorial Board 28 January 1762: 'In Zukunft wird gut seyn, daß auch auf den Heiden-Posten, wo Etablissements sind, so wie in den Gemeinen, die Diaconie und das Credit-Wesen auseinander zu halten. Die Diaconie hats blos mit dem Unterhalt der Missionen zu thun, so wie das andre fürs mehrer Aufkommen der Etablissemens und Plantagen.' UA UVC.P.6.2.

In other words, the mission upkeep and business ventures should be kept separate, just as daily upkeep and business are separated in European congregations, for example, Kleinwelka or Herrnhut. In extension of the models mentioned earlier, this indicates that the Bethlehem model is *not* one to be followed, in that the Bethlehem model is based on the unity of these spheres that were inseparable. As we saw in the previous two chapters, the restructuring of Bethlehem after 1760 is explicitly mentioned as making it follow a European way or model.

Apart from these economic considerations, the Central Council also dealt with numerous smaller and larger issues concerning the missions in the East Indies,[15] Greenland,[16] the Danish and British West Indies,[17] and Suriname and Berbice.[18] And while the economic matters after 1762 would be dealt with by the Mission Deputation, internal matters – both practical and spiritual – would be dealt with by the Inner Council, and then later by the UAC, the Unity Elders' Conference.[19] It was not until the 1789 synod in Herrnhut that an independent department for mission affairs (*Missionsdepartement*) was established under the auspices of the UAC.

The Mission Deputation: Establishment and tasks

On 28 January 1762, the Directorial Board founded the 'Mission Deputation in charge of the Mission Diacony', in short, the Mission Deputation (*Missionsdeputation*). This body was part of the overhaul of the missions already flagged in 1760-1 and regarded as a necessity for a number of reasons. One reason was that Johannes von Watteville, who had until now managed

---

[15] For example, Minutes of the Central Council 1760-1, 30 June 1760; 27 August 1760; 3 September 1760; 15 October 1760; 19 January 1761. UA R.3.B.4.c.1.

[16] For example, Minutes of the Central Council 1760-1, 17 October 1760; 12 November 1760; 24 November 1760; 3 December 1760; 9 February 1761; 18 February 1761; 7 March 1761. UA R.3.B.4.c.1.

[17] For example, Minutes of the Central Council 1760-1, 25 June 1760; 12 July 1760; 25 July 1760; 24 November 1760; 1 December 1760; 3 December 1760; 13 February 1761; 23 March 1761. UA R.3.B.4.c.1.

[18] Minutes of the Central Council 1760-1, 18 August 1760; 8 October 1760; 13 October 1760; 15 October 1760; 20 October 1760; 22 December 1760; 19 January 1761; 4 March 1761; 23 March 1761. UA R.3.B.4.c.1.

[19] The UAC was established at the General Synod in Marienborn in 1769 as the leadership body governing the Unity between the general synods. In 1764, the synod had established this body under the name *Unitätsdirektorium*, which in 1769 was changed to UAC. This remained, with numerous modifications, the leadership of the Unity until 1899, where it was replaced by the *Unitätsdirektion*. See Peucker, *Herrnhuter Wörterbuch*, 53-5 (*Unitätsältestenkonferenz*, *Unitätsdirektorium*, *Unitätsdirektion*).

the oversight of and communications with the ever-increasing domestic and overseas missions, wanted to devote his time to his other duties. Another reason was that circumstances within the community at large had also changed, and the eagerness among the members to serve as missionaries was no longer as immediate as it had been in the past; members had started asking questions about 'external matters', that is, material support, instead of simply being willing to set off and serve the Saviour in far-flung 'heathen' places. Thus, it was regarded as necessary to ask the Saviour to restore this older sense of brotherhood among 'our people' (Figure 3).[20]

The Deputation consisted of three brothers (Leonhard Dober, Jonas Paul Weiss and Paul Eugenius Layritz), who were appointed to oversee the finances of the sprawling and growing overseas missions in the name of the Unity, with Johannes Friedrich Lucius as bookkeeper and accountant. The Mission Deputation had three corresponding agents in Zeist/Amsterdam, London and Copenhagen, capitals of the three colonial powers in whose territories the Moravians were operating.[21]

On the following day, the document confirming the establishment of the Deputation and its instructions was signed by the Directorial Board. The instructions have eleven pages and contain an extensive amount of detail. Here, however, I want to draw attention to two points. First, the instructions begin with the purpose of the missions:

> 1. The purpose of all missions so far organized by the Unity of the Brethren is to bring to the poor Heathens the great message from their Creator and Redeemer concerning their salvation and preservation in the grace they have received. For this purpose, it is not only necessary that the messengers and witnesses of Jesus, who have been decreed to do so, are provided with the necessary equipment and sufficient travel money to see them to their destination, but also to provide them

---

[20] Minutes of the Directorial Board, 28 January 1762: 'Jene sind dermalen nicht mehr so willig, und diese wollen immer gern alles vollauf haben, und wir finden genug, den Heiland zu bitten, daß er auch in dem Theil den ehmaligen Brüder-Sinn unter unserem Volk wieder herstelle, da man nur darauf am meisten dachte, daß man für den Heiland an die Heiden-Örter gienge, und nicht viel Notiz von dem äußeren Durchkommen im Voraus nahm.' UA UVC.P.6.2.

[21] The missions are New-Herrnhut and Lichtenfels in Greenland, the Danish West Indies (St Thomas, St Croix and St John), Antigua and Jamaica, several outposts in Dutch Guiana: Paramaribo in Suriname, Saron on the Saramica river (Suriname), Ephrem on the border between Suriname and Guyana, Pilgerhütten, Berbice and, Tranquebar, the Danish trading post on the south-east coast of the Indian subcontinent. As Engel notes, the North American missions are left out from this list. Engel, *Religion and Profit*, 169. A possible explanation could be that Bethlehem and Nazareth in North America were in the process of being transformed into a settlement and thus no longer regarded as a mission, as discussed in Chapter 3.

Time of Transition and Change in Mission

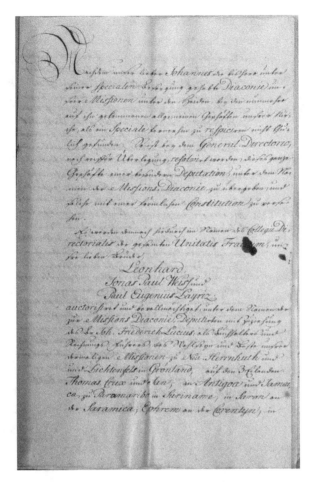

Figure 3 The first page of the constitution of the Mission Deputation in 1762. UA R.15.4A.7a. Reproduced with permission from the Unity Archives, Herrnhut.

with a place to stay, and a roof for preaching the Gospel as well as providing for their necessary upkeep.[22]

Here it is written, sealed and signed that the responsibility of this newly established body was to oversee the material needs of the worldwide missions and to manage and distribute funds, the transportation of missionaries to and

---

[22] Instruktion für die Deputation zur Missionsdiakonie 1762: '1.Der Zweck aller Missionen, die von der Unität der Brüder bishero veranstaltet worden, ist, daß den armen Heiden die große Botschaft von ihrem Schöpfer und Erlöser, zu ihrer Rettung und Bewahrung in der empfangenen Gnade, gebracht werde. Zu diesen Zweck ist nicht nur erforderlich, daß die dazu verordneten Boten und Zeugen Jesu mit der nöthigen Ausrüstung und zulänglichem Reisegeld biß an Ort und Stelle versehen, sondern ihnen auch ein Plaz zu ihrem Aufenthalt, und ein Dach zur Predigt des Evangelii wie auch ihre nothdürftige Unterhaltung besorget werde.' UA R.15.4A.7a.

from their posts, and equip them with the necessary goods to sustain them and their work. While the objective of the Deputation was to 'restore' the sense of brotherhood, we see here that they actually did make improvements at the material level, in that they committed to furnishing missionaries with the necessary equipment, travel funds, a place to stay and provisions for upkeep.

The specifics of this responsibility are presented in the first six pages. The instructions then go on to explain the source of this money. Three sources are mentioned: first, from biannual collections among the members on Epiphany (6 January) and the nativity of John the Baptist (24 June); second, from 'the establishments' erected to house the missions; third, from the commercial society, which was an investment society established in 1758 and lasted for ten years.[23]

My interest is in the second source, the 'establishments', by which is meant businesses, such as the bakery in Paramaribo and the plantation in St Thomas, in the Danish West Indies. The instructions note that in order for these 'establishments' to be utilized in the best possible way, the Deputation will collect notes on what belongs to which mission, gather all necessary documentation (proof of purchase, value, measurements and surveys of the lands in possession, etc.). Based on this information, the Deputation will then assemble a complete inventory of all the houses that have been built, the chattels in stock, supplies – in short, a complete and clear understanding of the economic state (*Statu Oeconomico*) of every mission. It will assess which lands and houses are usable or useless, what is necessary for more culture and utilization, what is counterproductive, and offer council.[24] It is, in other words, a full economic assessment of the individual missions, their assets and their potential for growth.

---

[23] Peucker, *Herrnhuter Wörterbuch*, 36. *Kommerzensozietät*.
[24] Instruction for the Deputation to the Mission Diacony 1762: 9: 'Der zweyte Fond der Missions-Diaconie sind die bereits hie und da zum Dach der Missionen errichteten Etablisemens. In Absicht auf dieselben wird die Missions-Diaconie zuförderst alle nöthige Notizen einziehen, was vor Ländereyen (seigneury) zu einem jeden Etablissement gehören, von wem und wie hoch sie erkauft worden, richtige Copien der Kaufbrieffe und aller dazu gehörigen Documentorum einschicken, und aus den Archiven, worinnen dergleichen zu finden seyn möchten, sich communiciren lassen, wo möglich die nöthigen Risse und Ausmessungen herbeyschaffen, und darauf genau sehen, wie überall der Titulus possessionis beschaffen, auch wo sich ein Scrupel darüber ereignet, davon in Zeiten gehörige Anzeige beym General-Directorio thun und um Verfügung ansuchen. Nechstdem wird die Missions-Diaconie von allen Etablissemens ein vollständiges Inventarium von allen erbaueten Häusern, angeschafften vorräthigen Mobilien, Vorräthen, aussenstehenden Activis sowol als contrahirten Passivis, kurz, eine völlige und deutliche Nachricht von dem Statu Oeconomico einer jeden Mission einziehen, was von den Ländereyen und Häusern brauchbar oder unbrauchbar, was zur mehreren Cultur und Nuzbarmachung erforderlich, oder derselben entgegenstehe, zum Aufnehmen oder Schaden gereiche, untersuchen und nach Befinden der Umstände mit Rath und That die Förderung derselben und Abwendung alles Schadens beaugen.' UA R.15.4A.7a.

These profits, which are to be used to finance the missions, will in future be a feature of the Mission Deputation's list of incomes from 'our establishments'.

Here, then, we have the emergence of the organization and centralized financialization of the Moravian worldwide mission. As Gisela Mettele noted in her important book on the Moravians as global actors:

> [T]he economic development of the Moravian Brethren was subject to the planning and governance of the community leadership. With the missionary spread of the Moravian Brethren from the 1730s, it was no longer only about ensuring the economic survival of the individual settlements, but also about the financing and organisation of a worldwide mission and evangelisation-campaign.[25]

As Mettele notes, the missions had been underway since the early 1730s. However, as discussed earlier, the central administration thereof did not take place until thirty years later. This then raises a number of questions: How were the missions managed and financed earlier, what happened to eventuate this centralization, and finally, how significant was this change? These are questions which will be addressed in the remainder of this book. Before we do, I want to take a look at the assessment of missions at the first General Synod of the Moravian Church, held in Marienborn in 1764. This would be the central governing body of the Moravian Church after Zinzendorf's death.

First General Synod in Marienborn, 1764

At the first General Synod in Marienborn, the 'heathen-cause' was debated in a number of sessions. Reports on the work of the Mission Deputation were received and the Deputation was reconstituted. This would come to be an agenda item at every subsequent synod. I discuss this material to close the chapter, because this is where the new chapter of the Unity formally begins. As mentioned earlier, the Mission Deputation dealt with economic matters after 1762, the practical and spiritual matters were dealt with initially by the inter-synod board (from 1769 the UAC, the Unity Elders' Conference). This synod at Marienborn is thus the first time that the mission is discussed in a synod setting, and we can see how the inner and outer issues are separated.

---

[25] Mettele, *Weltbürgertum oder Gottesreich*, 65.

There were three sessions at the synod. The first summed up the various missions and provided a good overview of the state of affairs of the missions, the second session dealt with current problems and the final session reconstituted the Mission Deputation for the next five years and discussed a couple of problems specifically relating to economic issues in St Thomas.

Session one: Assessing specific missions

The first mission mentioned is Greenland, which is praised as a 'wonder of grace' (*Wunder der Gnade*), in that the community had been so well organized into choirs. It is reported that one of the missionaries, Jens Haven, has been eager to visit the 'Esquimaux' in Labrador, where it was assumed that the inhabitants had the same language as the people of Greenland. Since the Saviour had approved this venture, Haven was already in Labrador.[26] Next came the North American missions, which were managed by the missionaries in Bethlehem, and consisted of three Native American missions: Pachgatgoch, Nain and Wechquetank. The members of the latter two were at the time of the synod removed to Philadelphia and placed under protection in barracks, because of the battles of the French and Indian War. While the belief of the leadership was that the worst had passed, the situation was still regarded with some apprehension.[27]

Then there is the Danish West Indian mission, which was seen to be progressing 'with great blessing' (*in grossen Seegen fortgegangen*), since the congregation was growing rapidly, especially in St Croix.[28] Jamaica, however,

---

[26] For a full presentation of Haven's background and desire, see Olsthoorn, 'Cranz's Greenland as a Stepping Stone to Labrador: Tracing the Profile of the Inuit'.

[27] Studies on Moravian missions in Pennsylvania include Katherine Faull, 'Masculinity in the Eighteenth-Century Moravian Mission Field: Contact and Negotiation', *Journal of Moravian History* 13/1 (2013): 27–53; Katherine M. Faull, 'From Friedenshütten to Wyoming: Johannes Ettwein's Map of the Upper Susquehanna (1768) and an Account of His Journey', *Journal of Moravian History* 11 (2011): 82–96; Rachel M. Wheeler, *To Live upon Hope: Mohicans and Missionaries in the Eighteenth-Century Northeast* (Ithaca: Cornell University Press, 2008); Katherine M. Faull, *The Shamokin Diaries 1745-1755: The Moravian Mission to the Iroquois* (University Park: Pennsylvania State University Press, forthcoming).

[28] Studies on the Moravian mission include Heike Raphael-Hernandez, 'The Right to Freedom: Eighteenth-Century Slave Resistance and Early Moravian Missions in the Danish West Indies and Dutch Suriname', *Atlantic Studies* 14/5 (2017): 457–75; Frank Marquardt, '"Distinguishing Ourselves from the Other Religions": Confessional Conflicts and Their Influence on the Early Moravian Danish West Indies Mission', *Journal of Moravian History* 19, no. 2 (2019): 133–55; Frank Marquardt, '"Konnexion durchs ganze Land". Die Herrnhuter Brüdergemeinde im kolonialen Sozialraum Dänisch-Westindiens 1739-1765' (PhD thesis, Oldenburg, Carl von Ossietzky Universität, 2022); Michael Leemann, '"Weiße" und "schwarze Schafe". Versklavung, Rassismus und Religion in Berichten zur Herrnhuter Mission in Dänisch-Westindien', in *Verglichene Körper. Normieren, Urteilen, Entrechten in der Vormoderne*, ed. Cornelia Aust and Claudia Jarzebowski, Studien zur Alltags- und Kulturgeschichte 35 (Stuttgart: Franz Steiner Verlag, 2022).

was not progressing as rapidly as was hoped, and the mission in Antigua now had a house and chapel.[29] The missions to Berbice had ceased for a while because of the slave rebellion in 1763, and the remaining missionaries had been sent to Suriname. The mission in Suriname was improving, mentioned as being one which has caused them much distress, but they hoped that the Saviour would see them through.[30] A second group of missionaries had been sent out to the East Indies (Tranquebar and Nicobar Islands); the mission, however, was in some danger, in that there had been conflicts with the Halle missions, problems which Koeber had tried to solve by travelling to Halle to discuss in person, but nothing had come of his visit.[31] Then, the mission to Guinea was mentioned, and it was noted that it had been an ongoing wish of Zinzendorf's, but the time was never right according to the lot. Finally, it was at this session that the future of the management of the West Indian missions was cemented. It was asked whether the missions in the West Indian Islands should be managed by Europe or continue to be managed by Bethlehem. The Inner Council had already asked the Saviour (through lot), who decided that it should be managed from Europe henceforth.[32]

Session two: Particular problems

The second session of the synod considered various particular circumstances. The session summed up the number of 'heathen' congregations, of which there were ten overall: two in Greenland, two in North America (exiles in Philadelphia

---

[29] For the mission to Jamaica, see Katharine Gerbner, '"They Call Me Obea": German Moravian Missionaries and Afro-Caribbean Religion in Jamaica, 1754–1760', *Atlantic Studies* 12/1 (2015): 160–78. For Antigua, see John Catron, 'Slavery, Ethnic Identity, and Christianity in Eighteenth-Century Moravian Antigua', *Journal of Moravian History* 14/2 (2014): 153–78. For Antigua (and Barbados) albeit in the nineteenth century, see Winelle J. Kirton-Roberts, *Created in Their Image: Evangelical Protestantism in Antigua and Barbados, 1834–1914* (Bloomington: Authorhouse, 2015).

[30] For work on Suriname, see Jessica Cronshagen, 'Owning the Body, Wooing the Soul: How Forced Labor Was Justified in the Moravian Correspondence Network in Eighteenth Century Surinam', in *Connecting Worlds and People: Early Modern Diasporas*, ed. Dagmar Freist and Susanne Lachenicht (London: Routledge, 2016); Jessica Cronshagen, '"A Loyal Heart to Go and the Governor". Missions and Colonial Policy in the Surinamese Saramaccan Mission (c. 1750-1813)', *Journal of Moravian History* 19, no. 1 (2019): 1–24; Jessica Cronshagen, 'Herrnhuter Diaspora, Erinnerungskultur und Identitätsbildung "in Abwesenheit". Briefnetzwerke zwischen Europa und Surinam', in *Religion und Erinnerung. Konfessionelle Mobilisierung und Konflikte im Europa der Frühen Neuzeit*, ed. Dagmar Freist and Matthias Weber (Oldenburg: de Gruyter, 2015); Jessica Cronshagen, 'Contrasting Roles of Female Moravian Missionaries in Surinam Negotiating Transatlantic Normalization and Colonial Everyday Practices (Eighteenth Century)', in *Das Meer. Maritime Welten in der Frühen Neuzeit*, ed. Peter Burschel and Sünne Juterczenka (Köln: Böhlau Verlag 2020).

[31] The most extensive analysis of the competition between the missionaries in Tranquebar is Thomas Ruhland, *Pietistische Konkurrenz und Naturgeschichte: Die Südasienmission der Herrnhuter Brüdergemeine und die Dänisch-Englisch-Hallesche Mission (1755-1802)*, Unitas Fratrum Beiheft 31 (Herrnhut: Herrnhuter Verlag, 2018).

[32] Minutes of the Marienborn Synod. UA R.2.B.44.1.c.1, 112–37.

and the other in Pachgatgoch), three in the Danish West Indies and one each in Antigua, Jamaica and Saron in South America. The minutes observe:

> The difference between the heathen congregations is the same as between the Christians; we have some in Nain and Wechquetanck and in two places in Greenland where the separation of the sexes and supervision of the children is maintained as in the settlements; also no one has permission to live there, except members, and those who want to become members. In contrast, in [St.] Thomas etc. it does not work like that. There the house community consists of our brothers and the Blacks in their service, the rest of them are scattered over more than 100 places on the island, so also in St. Croix and [St.] John, and if we didn't have such fine helpers there, it would hardly be able to work thus.[33]

The matters discussed were based on questions posed by synod delegates. For example, there were questions on the continued wearing of native dress by the Native American converts, the extent of teaching and evangelization in respect to Native peoples and the extent to which living together is an obstacle or a resource for evangelization in various settings – I will return to this final issue in the following chapters.

Session three: Reconstitution of the Mission Deputation

The final mission session of the synod was the one in which the Mission Deputation was reconstituted. Two issues of note were discussed in this session. The first concerned the provision of care for brothers and sisters who had risked life and health in the mission fields, and were now no longer able to support themselves – in other words, the question of retirement. This matter had earlier been the charge of the *Heiden-Diakonie*, but the synod resolved to ensure that this burden would be shared with other funds.

The second matter concerned commercial trade (*Handel*) in the missions: the synod determined that *Handel* was to be avoided. The matter of commercial

---

[33] Minutes of the Marienborn Synod. UA R.2.B.44.1.c.1, 696–702: 'Der Unterschied der Heiden Gemeinen ist ebenfalls wie bey den Christen; wir haben welche z.E. in Nain und Wechquetanck des gleichen an 2 Orten in Grönland, wo es mit der Separation der Geschlechter und in Absicht auf die Kinder gehalten wird, wie in Gemein-Orten, es hat auch niemand als Geschwister, und solche die es werden wollen, Erlaubniß da zu wohnen. Hingegen in Thomas pp gehts nicht so. Daselbst besteht die Haus-Gemeine aus unsere Brüdern und denen in ihrem Dienst befindlichen Negern, die übrigen sind in 100 und mehr orten auf der Insel zerstreut so auch in St. Crux und Jan, und wenn wir da nicht so hübsche Helfer und Helferinnen hätten, so würde es kaum gehen.'

trading and the profits therefrom would come to preoccupy the Unity for years to come.[34] The Marienborn synod minutes state:

[C]are must be taken to prevent our brothers from engaging in business deals. No soldier [i.e. of Christ] should entangle himself in the trade of nourishment. It makes the local inhabitants jealous and we may easily be reproached with the fact that we go to such areas not just for the sake of the salvation of the souls, but for the sake of commerce and profit.[35]

The minutes continue by observing that if missionaries had followed the apostolic calling in its strictest (mendicant) sense there would have been no need for funds, but because they need houses and chapels, an income is necessary. However, there have been no problems with industries such as milling, shoemaking and tailoring, which have kept the entire mission afloat. Indeed, such work is part of the old simplicity.[36]

In light of these deliberations, the West Indian mission posed a problem. The synod observed that 'trade is of a particular nature in the West Indies'. In terms of the 'simile of a sugar mill': it is observed that 'once it grabs the tip of a finger, it continues to pull and then rips off the whole arm'. The minutes observed that this simile 'is apt here'.[37] However, it was also noted that what the brothers in the West Indies are doing, namely procuring the necessary materials and paying for it in products of the land, is not to be regarded as commercial trading. In the next chapter, I will analyse in more detail the Moravian enterprise in St Thomas, but here it needs to be noted that the synod discussed whether it would make sense to appoint a brother to manage only 'the outer things', that is, matters of

---

[34] See the excellent analysis of the case of Labrador by Thomas Dorfner in '"Commercium nach dem Sinn Jesu". Überlegungen zum Marktverhalten der Herrnhuter Brüdergemeine am Beispiel des Labradorhandels (1770–1815)', *Jahrbuch für Wirtschaftsgeschichte* 61, no. 1 (2020): 39–66. See also Engel, *Religion and Profit*.

[35] Minutes of the Marienborn Synod. 'Bey unsrer Mission ist sorgfältig zu vermeiden, daß unsere Brüder sich nicht in Handlungs-Geschäfte einlassen. Kein Kriegs-Mann soll sich in Händel der Nahrung flechten. Es macht bey denen Landes-Einwohnern Jalousie und kann uns leicht den Vorwurff zu wege bringen, daß wir nicht allein um der Seelen-Heil, sondern des Commercii und des Gewinstes willen in solche Gegenden gehen.' UA R.2.B.44.1.c.2, 1493.

[36] Minutes of the Marienborn Synod. 'Hiebey wurde erinnert: Wenn freilich das Apostolat in stricten Sinne bey uns noch statt fände, so hätten wir alles das nöthig. Da wir aber Häuser und Capellen haben müssen, so ist der Casus anders. Wir haben auch nicht gesehen, daß es Schaden gehabt, daß unsere Brüder z. E. die Mühlbauerey, Schusterey und Schneiderey etc. getrieben und dadurch ihrer Hände Arbeit sich nicht nur genähret, sondern auch die ganze Mission mit erhalten haben, dabey aber doch großentheils legitimirte und gesegnete Knechte Gottes geblieben.' UA R.2.B.44.1.c.1, 1495.

[37] Minutes of the Marienborn Synod. Es ist in dem West-Indien mit dem Commercio ganz besonders beschaffen, und das Gleichniß von einer Zucker-Mühle, die, wenn sie einmal die Spizze eines Fingers ergrifft, immer weiter zieht, u hernach den ganzen Arm wegreißt, paßt sich hierher. Marienborn Synod Protocol, vol. 2: UA R.2.B.44.1.c.2, 1494.

industry and household management. To this the response was that it is often difficult to get people to agree to such a posting and that it also often requires that such brothers are used for 'soul-work' anyway. After this discussion, the synod proceeded with the constitution of the Mission Deputation for the coming five years.

Conclusion

The importance of the Mission Deputation and its sources of income cannot be underestimated. What this indicates is the separation of the inner and the outer spheres. As before, the outer, economic, sphere would be in service of the missions. But in the post-Zinzendorf period, this outer sphere was given a life of its own because it had to contribute to the missions in general and not just each mission to which it was connected. Because the 'establishments' or industries of the missions had to finance other missions, the Danish West Indian establishments, namely sugar plantations, had to be separated from the Danish West Indian missions. From this location outside the immediate sphere of the mission in question, the profits of the 'outer' realm came to be used for financing not merely the Danish West Indian mission itself but also all the missions. The founding of the Mission Deputation to oversee the economic activities and assets of the missions is also an indication of this separation. The externalized sphere is what we today would call economy, but such an abstract entity was not a clear-cut entity at the time.

Another point of interest is the change in leadership, which was connected to the new developments. This was a move from the charismatic, individual authority vested in the person of Zinzendorf to a more institutional and collective authority. Such a collective authority meant the active influx of a broader influence of people with different economic ideas, such as those of Johann Friedrich Koeber and Friedrich von Marschall. The push for different economic thinking was already underway during Zinzendorf's lifetime, as we saw in the gathering of documentation of mission assets, but due to his continued authority these economic approaches could only really be unleashed after his death.

Another change concerns the expectations of missionary work. At first, missionaries to the Danish West Indies and Greenland were mainly Moravian (*mährische*) artisans who were severely put to the test and put their lives at risk. Not a few failed the test. For example, the mission to the Danish West Indies claimed many Moravian lives. The risks, as far as we can tell, were faced willingly and eagerly. However, at the time of Zinzendorf's death, this eagerness seems to have abated, the disposition was no longer so and the unquestioning submission to the will of the Lamb had shifted.

We can see that changes took place at a number of levels. These changes ran all the way from the top, with transformations in the executive body of the Unity and centralized financialization of the mission, down to the more pragmatic and slightly less obedient missionary on the ground. With the creation of centralized mission boards and financial bodies, the Moravians were increasingly drawn into the world at large and forced to think within its terms and conditions. Massaging multiple missions into a large complementary whole, smoothing out wrinkles centrally, orchestrating the economics, was most certainly a shift, albeit a necessary one away from the ad hoc structures of yore. Interestingly, these issues were not discussed in great detail at the 1764 synod, which instead focused on a general assessment of the missions, along with concerns over theological, cultural and economic issues.

With these developments in the central administration of the missions in mind, and especially the changes implemented, we are now able to turn to the developments in the mission in the Danish West Indies, where these changes made a considerable difference in the organization of the mission.

5

'Plantation disposition'

The 'outer' sphere and the accumulation of riches in the Danish West Indies

Introduction

The material conditions in the Danish West Indies[1] meant that the Moravian mission developed in a fundamentally different way than from what we will see in Greenland. In St Thomas, the ruling authority structure was different, the economic matters were relatively highly developed and the possibilities for organization, settlement and evangelization were notably conditioned by these factors. The Danish West Indies were, as the Americas in general, part of the 'New World' and here the Moravians would meet challenges on a scale they had not experienced in Europe. They were confronted with what Marxists call the 'unleashing of the forces of production', that is, the extreme and rapid economic development of early capitalism, and so-called primitive accumulation, or the appropriation of 'unowned' wealth and land.[2] The challenge faced by the

---

[1] The Danish West Indies consisted of St Thomas (seized in 1671), St Croix (bought from the French in 1733) and St John (seized in 1718). The islands were initially colonized by the West India and Guinea Company, and in 1755 these were sold to the Danish crown. In their visitation instructions to Christian Heinrich Rauch in 1755, the leadership in Bethlehem asked him to find out whether St Thomas still belonged to the company or belonged fully to the crown. See visitation reports of Christian Heinrich Rauch, MAB MissWI 154. Point 26 on the first list, point 28 on the second list. The islands were sold to the United States in 1917 and are today known as the US Virgin Islands.

[2] In Marx's own words: 'The discovery of gold and silver in America, the extirpation, enslavement and entombment in mines of the aboriginal population, the beginning of the conquest and looting of the East Indies, the turning of Africa into a warren for the commercial hunting of black-skins, signalised the rosy dawn of the era of capitalist production. These idyllic proceedings are the chief momenta of primitive accumulation. On their heels treads the commercial war of the European nations, with the globe for a theatre.' Marx, *Capital*, 739. I write 'un-owned' in citation marks because the land and labour power which was violently appropriated was claimed as private property, a mode of ownership which was unknown in the seventeenth century, and thus regarded as legitimate plunder. Hugo Grotius, the lawyer in service of the Dutch East India Company (VOC), has the clearest indication of this shift in property relations from 'those distant days' to now in his *Commentary on the Law of Prize and Booty*, 316–17. Grotius describes ownership of yore as to be understood in a

Moravians was how to negotiate this volatile context: Was it possible to be part of these settler societies and not be consumed by the acquisition of wealth? Katherine Carté Engel's book on the Moravians in Bethlehem clearly demonstrates the struggles of the Moravian leadership concerning these issues in Pennsylvania,[3] which I discussed in Chapters 2 and 3. In this chapter, the focus is on the developments in St Thomas and the Moravian mission's slow but steady incorporation into the socio-economic structures of the Danish West Indies. The interest and focus of this chapter, then, is on the 'outer' issues of the St Thomas mission, how this developed in the eighteenth century and how the rapid changes after 1760 in the central leadership and the decisions made affected the St Thomas mission. As noted in Chapters 3 and 4, the years 1760-4 saw a number of fundamental and far-reaching changes in the organization of the Unity, and we saw what this meant for Bethlehem. We will now take a look at how this manifested itself in St Thomas, where there was plenty of scope for economic development. Inevitably, the accelerated development following Zinzendorf's death and the restructuring of the economic organization would have repercussions for the missionary work and the nature of the household. In the following chapters we will look at the effect of some of the changes on the mission in Greenland. But because Greenland never became an economically high-gain territory for the Moravians, in the sense they never gained a foothold in the commercial aspects of colonization there, the changes in Greenland manifested themselves in a rather different way: the 'inner' sphere became more pronounced.

While there have been important studies into the Moravian missions among enslaved people in the Caribbean and North Carolina, the focus has been on what we might call the cultural aspects of slavery and its contributions to historical conceptions and discussions of race. Katherine Gerbner's 2018 study of supremacy,

---

universal and indefinite sense. 'For God had given all things, not to this or that individual, but to the human race; and there was nothing to prevent a number of persons from being joint owners, in this fashion, of one and the same possession.' Private property arises, says Grotius, through use in three steps. The first is food consumed, which becomes part of the human body. This act of claiming property, says Grotius, was then transferred to the second class of property, 'moveables' such as clothing. This is then transferred to immovables, such as land. Above all, land is the topic of interest, in the sense that land is used to grow crops, orchards and produce fibres for clothes. Grotius' here foreshadows the doctrine of *terra nullius* of European colonialism, which designates lands not tilled and thus not used, and thus to be 'legitimately' seized. Hugo Grotius and Martine Julia Van Ittersum, *Commentary on the Law of Prize and Booty*, Natural Law and Enlightenment Classics (Indianapolis: Liberty Fund, 2006). See also Christina Petterson and Roland Boer, 'Bible at the Origins of Capitalist Theory' in *Cascade Companion on Bible and Economics 5: Bible in an Age of Capital: Reading Scripture in Capitalist Contexts*, Matthew Coomber ed. Forthcoming 2023. Martin Schermaier, 'Res Communes Omnium: The History of an Idea from Greek Philosophy to Grotian Jurisprudence', *Grotiana* 30 (2009): 20–48.

[3] Engel, *Religion and Profit*, see especially chapter 4: 'The Moral Parameters of Economic Endeavor'.

whiteness and Protestantism analyses the issue of slavery and conversion among the Quakers, Anglicans, and Moravians and the missionary tactics deployed in the Atlantic context.[4] Although certainly provocative in terms of its overall argument, its lack of attention to the economic aspect renders it less useful here.[5]

Instead, my analysis in this book as a whole owes much to the important study by Jan Hüsgen, *Mission und Sklaverei* from 2016, which deals with slavery as a means of financing the Moravian mission in the West Indies. However, while my study is interested in changes in Moravian economic practice, Hüsgen's overall concern is with slavery and emancipation in the British and Danish West Indies. Such a difference in scope will invariably affect focus points, interests and questions. An important methodological difference is that Hüsgen rarely distinguishes between different periods in the Danish West Indian mission but collapses together earlier and later material. He thus seems less concerned with the historical *development* of slave-ownership.[6] The present book, as you know by now, does see a significant change after Zinzendorf's death in 1760 and thus a difference in Moravian practice in most fields between the earlier and later periods of the eighteenth century. The significant change is that a distinction

---

[4] Katharine Gerbner, *Christian Slavery: Conversion and Race in the Protestant Atlantic World*, Early American Studies (Philadelphia: University of Pennsylvania Press, 2018).

[5] Other studies with a similar cultural focus include Claus Füllberg-Stolberg, 'The Moravian Mission and the Emancipation of Slaves in the Caribbean', in *The End of Slavery in Africa and the Americas*, ed. Ulrike Schmieder, Katja Füllberg-Stolberg and Michael Zeuske, Slavery and Postemancipation 4 (Münster: LIT Verlag, 2011), 81–102; Jon F. Sensbach, 'Race and the Early Moravian Church: A Comparative Perspective', *Transactions of the Moravian Historical Society* 31 (2000): 1–10; Sensbach, *Rebecca's Revival*; Louise Sebro, *Mellem afrikaner og kreol: Etnisk identitet og social navigation i Dansk Vestindien 1730-1770* (Historiska institutionen: Lunds Universitet, 2010).

[6] This also explains why he is so relaxed about using Oldendorp as a central source. However, as is the case with the use of David Cranz's *History of Greenland* as a reliable source to the Greenland mission, a similar warning also applies to Christian Georg Oldendorp's *Historie der caribischen Inseln*, which was completed in 1776. Building on the tremendous success of David Cranz's book, Oldendorp was commissioned to carry out a similar study of the mission in St Thomas, St Croix and St John. The completed manuscript was more than 6,000 pages long and was based on a seventeen-month sojourn in the Danish West Indies, between 1767 and 1768, as well as five months of subsequent archival research in Bethlehem, Pennsylvania. The General Synod in 1775 commissioned Johann Jakob Bossart, the archivist in Barby, to revise and prepare the manuscript for publication. The heavily redacted result of about 1,100 pages was published in 1777 and is the foundation of the English translation from 1987: C. G. A. Oldendorp and Johann Jakob Bossart, *C.G.A. Oldendorp's History of the Mission of the Evangelical Brethren on the Caribbean Islands of St. Thomas, St. Croix, and St. John*, trans. Arnold R. Highfield and Vladimir Barac (Ann Arbor: Karoma Publishers, 1987). The full text of Oldendorp's manuscript was published in 2000. Oldendorp, *Historie der caribischen Inseln*. See also the accompanying commentary published by Gudrun Meyer et al., *Christian Georg Andreas Oldendorp: Historie der caraibische Inseln Sanct Thomas, Sanct Crux und Sanct Jan. Kommentarband*, Beiheft Unitas Fratrum (Herrnhut: Herrnhuter Verlag, 2010). For comparisons between the original text and Bossart's revision, see Anders Ahlbäck, 'The Overly Candid Missionary Historian. C. G. A. Oldendorp's Theological Ambivalence over Slavery in the Danish West Indies', in *Ports of Globalisation, Places of Creolisation. Nordic Possessions in the Atlantic World during the Era of the Slave Trade*, ed. Holger Weiss (Leiden: Brill, 2016), 191–217; Leemann, '"Weiße" und "schwarze Schafe"', 137–60. Because there are larger gaps in the archival material for the Danish West Indies, Oldendorp is a valuable source, but again, as with Cranz, must be used with care.

emerges in St Thomas between the Moravian slave congregations and the slaves owned by the Moravians. While the first are the aim and results of the mission activities, the Moravian-owned slaves produced the surplus that paid for these missions. These were separated spheres of concern and *how* these became separated spheres of concern is my focus. In other words, I am concerned with the 'outer circumstances' of the mission and how the Moravians adapted to and participated in the social and economic conditions at hand. The outcome was that in St Thomas they successfully manoeuvred within the emerging structures of a capitalist system and subordinated the mission in the process.

Rude awakening in the Danish West Indies

The economic foundation of St Thomas in the eighteenth century was sugar production based on plantation slavery. Labour was firmly tied to the plantation economy, and any means to make a living fed into this, whether it was building sugar mills on other plantations, making shoes for slave-owners or pounding iron to make slave-chains. One was either a slave or an upholder of slavery. Some, like Domingo Gesoc,[7] were both, but to be neither was not an option. The Moravian mission to the slave population of the Danish West Indies was the very first of the Moravian missions.[8] It began in 1732, with the arrival of Leonhard Dober and David Nitschmann (Bishop) on St Thomas.[9]

First years (1732–8)

Very soon after their arrival, it became apparent that Dober and Nitschmann could neither survive by means of their own labour nor act independently of

---

[7] Domingo Gezoe or Gesoc, known as Mingo, was a slave of Johann Carstens and a member of the Moravian community. He was a slave as well as a plantation owner. Also, his wife Joanna owned slaves, as is clear from the minutes of the Helpers' meeting on 10 September 1761, where it is noted that Joanna Gesoc's Fiba is suggested to the lot as candidate for baptism. See UA R.15.B.b.20.b, p. 33. In her will, Joanna Gesoc also provides instructions for her slaves and conditions for their manumission. See Rigsarkivet 697, St. Thomas Byfoged. 1755-1827 Testamentprotokoller for Notarius Publicus 1781-1796, pp. 151–3. Thank you to Josef Köstlbauer for making me aware of this document.

[8] The sources to these earliest years are published in Kröger, *Johann Leonhard Dober und der Beginn der Herrnhuter Mission*.

[9] Among the first-generation Moravians there are several people named David Nitschmann. Two David Nitschmanns became important figures in the history of the community, David Nitschmann the Bishop and David Nitschmann Syndicus. David Nitschmann the Bishop (1695–1772) became the first bishop of the Moravians in 1735, when he was consecrated by Daniel Ernst Jablonski. He was one of the founders of Bethlehem, as well as chief negotiator in establishing a number of settlements in Northern Europe. He returned to North America and died in Bethlehem.

David Nitschmann Syndicus (1703–79) was more of a scribe and secretary. He became part of the leadership of the Unity after Zinzendorf's death and was the first archivist of the Moravian Church. It is thus common to indicate which David Nitschmann to which one is referring.

external influences; rather, they were entirely dependent on connections with and support of the colonial society.[10] In spite of their aristocratic support network in Copenhagen and some of the planters on the island itself, the Moravian presence in St Thomas was full of troubles in the first decade. They had to deal with petty bureaucrats, hostile planters, unfriendly governors and zealous pastors from other churches. For example, as the result of a series of unrelated charges[11] brought to the governor by the Reformed pastor on the island, a number of Moravians were imprisoned in 1738. They were released only when Zinzendorf made a surprise visit to the island later that year.[12]

The economic structures also created problems in terms of employment and making a living. In comparison with Greenland, where the missionaries initially were able to act outside the colonial network, the colonial society in the West Indies was heavily developed with a booming frontier economy and an established plantocracy. This was the context into which Nitschmann and Dober set foot. Labour was semi-monopolized, in the sense that the labour from which they were expecting to make a living, namely their skills and trade, was being carried out by skilled slaves.[13] In a letter to the Moravian Isaac Lelong in Amsterdam, Spangenberg offered this assessment of West Indian society:

> He who is rich in the West-Indies, is truly rich, and often lives royally. He who is poor, however, is also so poor that he cannot help himself, where he doesn't want to be the servant of the rich and tyrannise their slaves.[14]

This position, being servant to the rich and tyrannizing their slaves, was that of the so-called *Meisterknecht*, chief or master servant, and was in fact one of the only employments available for the brothers. For a short period, Dober was even

---

[10] Hüsgen, *Mission und Sklaverei*, 41.
[11] Timotheus Fiedler, one of the survivors from St Croix, who had stayed in the plantation business on St Croix rather than continue as a missionary, had been arrested for theft. While he was no longer part of the mission, he was still regarded as a Moravian, thus causing a scandal. Friedrich Martin, Rebecca and Matthäus Freundlich were arrested for refusing to take an oath when called to testify against him. Furthermore, Martin was accused of acting without proper credentials and that his 'copulation' of Rebecca (a free woman) and Freundlich was thus null and void. Oldendorp has a full account of this in his *Geschichte*, 2/1: 275–306. See also Jon Sensbach's book on Rebecca and her story. Sensbach, *Rebecca's Revival*.
[12] See Oldendorp, *Historie der Caribischen Inseln*, 2/1: 325–6.
[13] In his memoir, Böhner writes that Mingo had helped him gain employment in building a sugar mill, then followed another commission from Carstens and from there it gathered speed. This had helped 'their very poor housekeeping'. Memoir German original and English translation available at the Bethlehem Digital History Project: http://bdhp.moravian.edu/personal_papers/memoirs/bohner/bohner.html (accessed 24 September 2020).
[14] August Gottlieb Spangenberg to Isaac Lelong, Skippack, 9 June 1738. UA R.15.B.a.10, 80. See Christina Petterson, 'Spangenberg and Zinzendorf on Slavery in the Danish West Indies', *Journal of Moravian History* 21/ 1 (2021). See page 45 for the German original.

employed at the estate of the notorious Governor Gardelin as estate manager.[15] In 1733, twelve brothers were contracted by Lord Chamberlain von Plessen to clear and survey land for his six plantations.[16] Minding slaves for plantation owners did not present the missionaries with the desired access to the slaves, and this approach was abandoned. From 1736 onwards, the missionaries settled into a household mode, where one would act as the primary breadwinner in trades where the Moravians could make inroads, especially shoemaking and tailoring, and the two others were able to supplement these earnings with smaller tasks, alongside the necessary evangelization. Even then, it was a fragile construction, and the frequent illnesses threw the delicate balance into disarray several times.

Purchase of a plantation

On 10 July 1738, Danish Creole planter Johann Carstens bought Dorothea Salomon's plantation on behalf of Friedrich Martin and Matthäus Freundlich. Initially named Deknatel or Teknatel, after its financial backer the Mennonite preacher Joannes Deknatel,[17] Zinzendorf renamed the plantation Posaunenberg, from where the trumpets would call the true believers to the Saviour. In 1757 it became known as New-Herrnhut.

The plantation was a practical solution to a number of problems facing the missionaries in St Thomas. Its purpose was to serve as a centre for the mission,

---

[15] Philip Gardelin was governor of the St Thomas and St John, 1733–5. Not only was he in charge of brutally striking down the slave rebellion on St John in 1733, he was also the author of the slave code of 5 September 1733, the rules for the employees of the West India and Guinea Company that applied to the punishment and disciplining of slaves. See summary in Neville Hall, 'Slave Laws of the Danish Virgin Islands in the Later Eighteenth Century', *Annals of the New York Academy of Sciences* 292, no. 1 (1977): 174–86, here 174–5.

[16] Jan Hüsgen argues that through these employments as overseers, as well as through their regular visits on plantations, the Moravian knowledge of plantation management accumulated. He draws attention to the anonymous and undated document in the Herrnhut archives on 'The best and surest means regarding the form in which a sugar plantation must be started and how it should be worked on, as well as what is needed and required for its establishment', as an indication of possessing this knowledge and thus being able to implement it in establishing their own plantation. Hüsgen, *Mission und Sklaverei*, 44–5, see footnote 96. The document (UA R.15.B.a.3, 10) is divided into two parts. The first part is the one mentioned earlier and concerns the establishment of a plantation and what equipment is required, tools, weapons, iron and so on ('Die besten und sichersten Mittel, welcher Gestalt eine Zucker plantagie angefangen und bearbeitet werden muß, desgleichen was zu deren Einrichtung gebraucht und erfordert wird'). The second part is an example of instructions to the person placed in charge or the inspector ('Die Instructiones derer Gevollmächtigten oder Inspecter könte etwa folgender maße lauten').

[17] The debt for the purchase was taken over from Carstens by Deknatel and two members of the Mennonite congregation in Amsterdam, Daniel Almonde and Susanna van Almonde. The debt was finally paid out in full by 1761. The archival material for this sale is found in the Moravian Archives in UA MDF 1027 (1-4). As these documents show, this was an urgent matter to be resolved after Zinzendorf's death, because the Unity was afraid of losing the plantation as part of claims made on the properties because of the unresolved debts.

a quiet and safe place where the slaves could gather when they came for instruction, instead of meeting in small and not readily accessible rooms in the town of Trepus, where the missionaries had their expensive lodgings. Another hope for the plantation was to obtain some means of sustenance and income. The nine slaves (Peter Bomba,[18] Jeffery, Claas, Cesar, Jantje, Anna, Magdalena, Marianna and a girl, May) that came with the plantation were meant to help and support the missionaries on the plantation.

As today's Moravian Church in St Thomas demonstrates, the first objective was manifestly achieved. The plantation-based mission created a community for people forcibly removed from their own communities and surroundings. The African people enslaved in the West Indies came from a host of different nations, with no given bonds apart from what had been formed on the slave ships and the plantations on which they worked.[19] The Moravian mission enabled a community formed along different lines. By 1749, there was already a flourishing congregation in St Thomas. As the catalogues drawn up during Johannes von Watteville's visitation in 1749 demonstrate,[20] there were 276 members from 80 plantations and owners, and a number of helpers strategically placed on several plantations to monitor the members there.

In terms of upkeep, however, the missionaries were still not able to manage. Their plans for sustenance were not successful, their cotton did not produce as much as hoped and other ways of earning a living were meagre. Then, in 1743, after a meeting to discuss their economic circumstances, they decided to plant sugar on advice from the Suriname missionary, Jean-Francois Reynier, who was staying in St Thomas on his way through to Europe.[21] From the first crops, they had to give half of the processed sugar to Limberg at the neighbouring plantation in exchange for the processing. It was also from Limberg that they acquired the initial seedlings. Once they had established their own processing equipment in 1747, the full end-product was theirs to sell (see Figure 4).

---

[18] A Bomba was a slave appointed as foreman, and his tasks were to oversee and punish the other slaves on the plantation – it was thus the highest rank within the slave-group and had a number of privileges attached thereto. https://en.natmus.dk/historical-knowledge/historical-themes/danish-colonies/the-danish-west-indies/slavery/ (accessed 18 May 2023).
[19] Seidel's visitation report MissWI 175, 4 lists a number of African nations. See also Oldendorp, *Historie der caribischen Inseln*, vol. 1.
[20] Catalog of members on St Thomas, St Croix and St John. MAB MissWi 179.
[21] Letters and remarks to the diaries of St Thomas, Croix, and John. UA R.15.B.a.14. Jean-Francois Reynier was of Hugenot background, and with his wife, Maria Barbara Knoll, had worked as missionaries in Suriname. See Aaron Spencer Fogleman, *Two Troubled Souls: An Eighteenth-Century Couple's Spiritual Journey in the Atlantic World* (Chapel Hill: University of North Carolina Press, 2013). Fogleman's presentation of the visit to St Thomas and its significance is on pages 163–4.

As indicated in Chapter 2, the turn to producing sugar generated a controversy with Bethlehem in 1747. In Oldendorp's version, the leadership in Bethlehem feared that the brothers in St Thomas would be led astray by profit-hunger, by concerns with sustenance, by harsh treatment of the slaves and so on. These were all seen as elements that 'stick to' such a form of production. In other words, these temptations would counter the very reason for the Moravian presence in St Thomas and cause damage to the mission as well as to their own hearts. Furthermore, the leadership noted, it was not desirable that they have so many slaves, but should rather proceed as far as possible without slaves and using their own trades.[22] The response from the missionaries in St Thomas was, according to Oldendorp, based on their experiences and the insights therefrom.

> The sugar-production was, when considered in and of itself, regarded as an innocent means of nourishment, similar to agriculture in Europe, and indeed the most innocent means in the West Indies. [. . .] In terms of tradesmanship, apart from carpentry and mill-construction, they had always led a miserable life and were only just able to support themselves, whereas the necessary building-works, travelling between islands, and other expenses required by the mission could not be supported [by this labour].[23] [. . .] They thus did not regard the sugar-production as damaging, or as countering their calling, but indeed as a useful matter, and one which the Lord had given in their hands for the sake of persisting in the missionary work, which they had no intention of giving up now that they were there.[24]

It has not been possible to find this exact sentiment expressed in one document, but rather it seems to be a collation of opinions expressed in person during visitations or visits to Bethlehem. Echoes are found in various sources, as we will see further.

Challenges to the ideal household

Johannes von Watteville arrived in St Thomas on visitation in 1749, the first visitation since the establishment of the sugar works.[25] In his first communications

---

[22] These concerns are presented in the visitation reports of Christian Heinrich Rauch, MissWI 154, to which we return later.
[23] Nathanael Seidel's visitation in 1753 notes how much the income from the sugar contributes towards their upkeep and travels between the islands, thus also showing some understanding of the enterprise. MAB MissWI 175.5, Relation von Bruder Nathanael's Besuch in den Caribischen Inseln.
[24] Oldendorp, *Geschichte der Mission*, 2/2: 682–3. My translation.
[25] According to Oldendorp, Josef and Mary Shaw were dispatched from Bethlehem in May 1747 'to examine the brothers' plantation issue and to abolish the sugarplants'. They never arrived, however, and it was assumed, says Oldendorp, based on information from a pirate who had sailed out in the

Figure 4 View of the plantation Bethel and the surroundings of New-Herrnhut on St Thomas. Drawing by Oldendorp, 1770. UA TS.Bd.23.58. Reproduced with permission from Unity Archives, Herrnhut.

back to Cammerhof in Bethlehem after his arrival (and not his visitation diary as such), he notes that the plantation is a pleasant place, with good air and well managed: 'the brothers have a good house-holding.'[26]

Slaves and slave-owners in the mission

However, on 30 April 1749, soon after arriving, he held a conference with the brothers and sisters concerning the mission and their work, the minutes of which were sent to Bethlehem. The last item in the minutes note:

> Finally, I discovered that of the 23 Blacks on our plantation, only 3 were baptized, I then recommended to our brothers and sisters that our plantation should be a model above all others, and that in St. Thomas it should become what Gnadenhütten is among the Indians and what the settlements (*Ortsgemeinen*)

---

same group, that their ship capsized near Bermuda during a cyclone. Oldendorp, *Geschichte der Mission*, 2/2: 686–7.

[26] Johannes von Watteville to F. Cammerhof. St Thomas, 27 April 1749. MissWi 129.15: Man siehts, daß Brüder da wohnen, und eine ordentliche Haushaltung haben.

are in the countries. Therefore, it would be desirable that all the Blacks of our plantation were brothers and sisters.[27]

Gnadenhütten was an outpost mission station established in 1746 on the Lehigh River and was the most significant one in the Moravian mission at the time.[28] Bethlehem, while originally a missionary settlement, was, as we saw, transformed into an *Ortsgemeine* after 1760. Herrnhut was also an *Ortsgemeine*. The ideal was, as Hüsgen also notes, that all the slaves on New-Herrnhut should be part of the Moravian community. The community itself should be organized along Moravian lines, by which is meant living together according to choirs and being a community unto oneself.[29] New-Herrnhut in Greenland was mentioned as another example of such a desirable settlement at the Marienborn Synod (see Chapter 4).

In other words, the Moravian plantation in St Thomas should be a model for others to follow, rather than, as seems to have been the case, to have followed the patterns of other plantations with their slaveholders and slaves.[30]

The extent to which this was remedied, however, is questionable. In 1753, the numbers of slaves owned by the Moravians had risen to 34, valued at 2,400 Reichsthaler.[31] A catalogue of the baptized slaves from 1736 to 1753 lists slave-ownership, and here we see that out of the 1,079 baptized slaves, 29 are noted as belonging to the brothers. Another list was drawn up in 1755 (see Figure 5), and it notes 'The Black men and women as well as Children which are our property'.[32]

Here we find the following information: the names of fifteen men and twelve women, three named boys, and nine unnamed girls and four boys. The list in question concerned the settlements at Deknatel (New-Herrnhut), Crumbay

---

[27] Johannes von Watteville's visitation in St Thomas, St Croix and St John. MAB MissWi 173, 4: 'Zulezt fand sich, daß unter den 23 Negers auf unserer Plantage nur 3 getaufte waren, da ich denn unsern Geschwistern ans Herz legte, daß unsere Plantage ein Muster vor alle andere seyn, und das in St. Thomas werden solte, was Gnadenhütten unter den Indianern ist, und was die Ortsgemeinen in den Ländern sind; es wäre darum zu wünschen, daß alle Negers unserer Plantage Geschwister wären'.

[28] Engel, *Religion and Profit*, 141–2. In 1755 it was attacked by the Delaware, and eleven members were killed.

[29] Hüsgen, *Mission und Sklaverei*, 85. See also Mettele, *Weltbürgertum oder Gottesreich*, 49–58, for an outline of Moravian settlement practice in Europe.

[30] A point also raised by Winelle Kirton-Roberts in her paper 'Did You See My Chains? An Inquiry into the Moravian Mission at Sharon in Barbados and Its Justification for Shackled Africans, 1795-1834' at the symposium *Race, Slavery, and Land. Moravian Legacies in a Global Context, 1722-2000* held at Moravian University, 4–5 November 2022.

[31] Diaries of Nathanael Seidel's visit to the West Indies. MAB MissWi 175, 2. In this note in the folder containing the documents from Nathanael Seidel's visitation in 1753, we see an estimate of the possessions of the brothers from 1753 notes that their debts were around 4500 Reichsthaler, 'made through the purchase of their [34] Blacks and some pieces of land'. A copy, written by Georg Weber, is in Herrnhut (UA R.15.B.a.3, 31): 'Unserer Geschwister Schulden belaufen sich auf 4500 Reichsthaler, die sie gemacht durch Ankaufung ihrer Neger und einiger Stücke Landes'.

[32] Black men and women and children which are our property. July 1755. MAB MissWI 180.7.

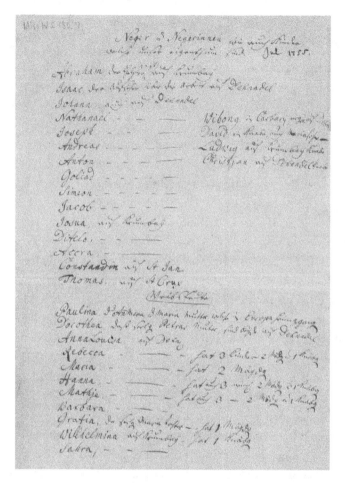

Figure 5 List of slaves and their children owned by the Moravians, July 1755. MAB MissWI 180.7. Reproduced with permission from Moravian Archives, Bethlehem.

(Niesky), St Croix and St John. A comparison of the two lists reveals that of the ten men who are at Deknatel, five are baptized (Isaac, Johann, Nathanael, Josef, Andreas) and five are not (Wibong, Anton, Goliath, Simeon and Jakob). Of the women at Deknatel, six are baptized (Paulina, Dorothea, Anna Louisa, Rebecca, Maria and Hanna) and four not (Petra, Mathje, Barbara and Gratia). This suggests that in 1755 it was still not a regular practice that the slaves owned by the Moravians were also a member of the congregation. There is thus a distinction between 'enslaved Moravians' – that is, slaves who were members of the Moravian community – and slaves of the Moravians – that is, slaves owned by the Moravian missions. This question requires further examination.[33]

[33] Hüsgen, *Mission und Sklaverei*, 102, 107.

'Inner' and 'outer'

The very fact that the Moravian mission owns slaves that are not baptized indicates a division of the inner and outer, which is a departure from what was regarded as proper household practice. Returning to the 1747 letter by Cammerhof discussed in Chapter 2, we recall that he used the term 'outer' (*äußerlich*) several times as a term that denotes work, money and so on, as separated from and set over against the inner, spiritual issues of the mission. This problem, of responsibly balancing mission and economy, had already been an issue earlier; indeed, as Hüsgen has demonstrated, it was a problem from the beginning of the mission. Already in 1733, Zinzendorf had been approached by the Chief Chamberlain at the Danish court, Carl Adolph von Plessen, who requested the service of twelve brothers to establish six plantations and manage his slaves on the newly acquired St Croix.[34] Zinzendorf had been concerned that the brothers would be caught up in the needs of daily upkeep and be taken away from their actual purpose. However, the proposal was generally supported and the plan proceeded.[35] One of the twelve, Timotheus Fielder, indeed ended up 'straying' from the actual purpose in 1736, when he opted to stay in the service of von Plessen on St Croix, rather than return with the remaining Moravians to join the mission on St Thomas. As Oldendorp observes, Fiedler 'disappeared into the world.'[36] In a letter to Fiedler in 1736, Christian David wrote: 'The matter is not to cultivate the land in order to nourish oneself there, but rather to preach the gospel of Jesus Christ.' He continues: 'And to that end two or four, at the most six, which constitute a small community, is enough.'[37] Christian David drew from first-hand experience in Greenland, as we will see in the next chapter. The question of balance was also prevalent in the conflict about sugar, as we saw previously. However, instead of being resolved, this distinction – between 'inner' and 'outer' – grew ever sharper, as the Moravian economic organization was reshaped according to the structures of an emerging capitalist system.

---

[34] The documents are found in UA R.15.B.a.3 and include the correspondence as well as the contracts. The contract between Plessen and the brothers is also transcribed and printed in Oldendorp, *Historie der caribischen Inseln*, 2/3: 2163–5.
[35] Oldendorp, *Historie der caribischen Inseln*, 2/1: 71.
[36] Oldendorp, *Historie der caribischen Inseln*, 2/1: 202.
[37] Christian David to Thimotheus Fiedler, 17 November 1736. 'Denn nicht das Landt anbauen, ist die Sache, sich alda zu nehren, sondern das Evangelium Jesu Christi zu verkündigen, und dazu sindt 2 oder 4, auf das meiste 6, die ein Gemeinlein außmachen, genug.' UA R.15.B.a.10, 30. Christian David's letter is referred to in Oldendorp, *Geschichte der Mission*, 203, but Oldendorp does not include archival references, so his sources must be sought through the information he provides. Thank you to Olaf Nippe for finding this particular letter for me.

Expansion of the sugar industry

In 1760, it appears that there was a desire to expand the sugar industry in St Thomas. In a letter from Johannes von Watteville to Brother Jens Korn in St Thomas, Watteville noted that he has 'real misgivings about the proposal to buy a sugar plantation with Blacks and to gradually pay for the same from the production'. 'There is always a great risk', he writes, 'because if the Blacks die, or years of failure come, or other unfortunate events occur, the whole work of the Saviour in St. Thomas could come into great distress.' He emphasizes that he is 'not at all personally against our brothers being involved with sugar production' and that he does not regard it 'in any other way than agriculture and cattle herding in Europe and North America'. Nevertheless, he prefers as a way forward to continue to grow sugar on their land, and gradually buy more land, as they have been doing already. If they want to increase production, Watteville suggests they use some of the land they already possess.[38]

Two years later, on 29 December 1763, the missionaries bought a plantation from Christian Cornelius Rebhun,[39] a doctor in St Thomas for whom the Moravians had processed sugar previously.[40] The inventory of the purchase shows that 7,000 West Indian dollars were exchanged for land, sugar works (mill, boiler-house and still), livestock and a single slave, by the name of Israel. The ostensible purpose of purchasing the plantation was to provide the slaves with wood and land to grow food.[41] The plantation was known as both Rephun's plantation and Bethel, the latter being the Moravians' name.[42] Bethel was only ever intended as an economic supplement to the main plantation of New-Herrnhut, which

---

[38] Johannes von Watteville to Jens Korn. Zeist, 6 September 1761, MissWi 129.24: '6. Bey dem Vorschlag, eine Zucker-Plantage mit Negern zu kauffen und dieselbe aus den Producten derselben nach und nach zu bezahlen, habe ich richtige Bedenken. Es ist allemal ein grosses Risico dabey, denn wenn die Neger sterben, oder Mißwachs-Jahre kommen, oder andere Unglücks-Fälle geschehen, so könte das gantze Werck des Heylands in S. Thomas in große Noth kommen. Daher bin ich nicht davor, so was zu wagen, ob ich gleich gar nicht vor meine Person dagegen bin, daß unsere Brüder sich mit dem Zucker-Bau abgeben; ich sehe denselben nicht anders an, als daß er dort das ist, was in Europa und North America Ackerbau und Viehzucht.'

[39] Rebhun had been a surgeon with the Danish troops in St Thomas and left the island in March 1769. He died 20 February 1772 and is buried in what was at the time the German church, Christianskirken. Kristian Carøe, *Den danske lægestand. Doktorer og licentiater 1479-1788* (Copenhagen: Gyldendalske Boghandel Nordisk Forlag, 2021), 103; 'Christians Kirke. Frederik's Tyske Kirke', in *Danmarks Kirker 4*, (1973): 75–287, here 228.

[40] Visitation reports of Christian Heinrich Rauch, 28 May 1755. Here it is mentioned that the request to process sugar was granted after much discussion. MAB MissWI 154.

[41] This is stated in Böhner's letter to the Deputation, where he also explains that they want to sell the still and the mill to bring down their debts. Johann Böhner to the Mission Deputation, New-Herrnhut, 1 February 1764. MDF 1911, 35. In a letter written after his arrival, Johann Peter Schwimmer notes that the more than half of the plantation is barren and uncultivated, and could, if more slaves were acquired, be rather profitable. Johann Peter Schwimmer to the Mission Deputation. St Thomas, 6 November 1766. MDF 1911, 66.

[42] The name 'Bethel' was decided by the Mission Deputation, see 9 June 1765, pkt 3.

housed the church and missionary accommodation. It is presumably for this reason that Bethel has never drawn much attention – except for Hüsgen's study.[43]

However, for my argument and its concern with the economic sphere, Bethel is vitally important. This is not least because when it was put up for sale in 1797, the inventory included sixty-five slaves, the youngest being a three-month-old called Jacob.[44] Note carefully: when the Moravians purchased what became known as Bethel, there was one slave. When they sold the plantation more than three decades later, it had sixty-five slaves – quite an increase. We will return to this matter below, for now I wish to consider some of the visitations to St Thomas undertaken by the Moravian leadership. While we have already seen the results of Johannes von Watteville's visitation in 1749, we will consider some of the subsequent visitations and their focus on the household.

Visitations to St Thomas

Visitations were a means of securing conformity with the theological and practical organization of the global Moravian community, as well as communicating and implementing leadership decisions and planning.[45] Until the early 1760s, the leadership and oversight of St Thomas were undertaken by Bethlehem in Pennsylvania. It was from Bethlehem that Nathanael Seidel and Christian Heinrich Rauch travelled to St Thomas, and it was to Bethlehem that they reported. We also see this pattern with Johannes von Watteville, who reported back to Cammerhof.[46] After 1760, when the mission in the Caribbean came under Herrnhut's leadership, it was the leadership there that appointed the person who was to be in charge of overseeing the mission.

Visitation of 1753: Early distinction between inner and outer duties

After Johannes von Watteville's visitation in 1749, the next one was that of Nathanael Seidel, one of the elders of the Moravian community. In 1753, he travelled from Bethlehem via New York to the Danish West Indies. He arrived in

---

[43] Hüsgen, *Mission und Sklaverei*. See also Harald Lawaetz, *Brødremenighedens Mission i Dansk-Vestindien 1769-1848: Bidrag til en charakteristik af Brødrekirken og dens gerning og af den farvede races stilling til christendommen* (Copenhagen: O.B. Wroblewski, 1902), 134–9.
[44] Inventory of the Plantation Rephun. UA MDF 1027, c. 9 June 1797. In the assessment from 16 January 1799 (UA MDF 1027, d), the number of slaves included in the sale is seventy-four.
[45] Mettele, *Weltbürgertum oder Gottesreich*, 139–45.
[46] The first visitation to the Danish West Indies was Spangenberg in 1736, followed by David Nitschmann (bishop) in 1742.

St Croix and then made his way to St Thomas, where he stayed for seven weeks.[47] In his report on the organization of the mission, he notes that St Thomas is the undisputed centre of the Caribbean islands and that the brothers and sisters have organized themselves reasonably: 'They now have Deknatel, where they have established a sugar-plantation worked by their own Blacks, and is reasonably in order, whence they are able to obtain annually a good deal towards their economy and sustenance, and also to provide for their necessary travels to St. Croix and St. John, and other expenses.'[48] The organization of the missionaries and their tasks mentions the individual missionaries and their tasks in both Deknatel and Crumbay (Niesky).[49] The leader is one Georg Weber, who lived on Deknatel, and directed the mission as a whole. Further through his visits to St Croix and St John, Weber 'has to direct the outer Oeconomie'. The other missionaries are mentioned as being useful in both inner and outer duties (Brother and Sister Böhners, Handschens and Romers) and some only in terms of their outer usefulness: Brother Masser is a helper in the outer Oeconomie, Matt. Kremsner is a helper of Brother Böhner in building mills and where else he can be put to use. Brother Michler is used in the cobbler's workshop in service to the Oeconomie.

We see here that the term 'Oeconomie' is used in two ways. There is the Oeconomie as such and then there is the outer Oeconomie. Outer Oeconomie seems closer to our later understanding of economy, as a separate sphere of financial circulation. The Oeconomie as such is then the household of the mission. We will revisit this question when we can compare the usage in later documents.

In relation to the 1753 visitation, I would like to note one final item. In November of the following year, Spangenberg penned a letter to Zinzendorf. Spangenberg writes:

> Surely Nathanael's visitation was from the Saviour. He came at a time when he was most needed. But shouldn't there be one Oeconomus in St. Thomas, Croix and John? I do not mean in opposition to that of Brother Weber, but under him, or with him.[50]

---

[47] The documents from his visit are held in MAB and consist of two versions of the report and sixteen pages of minutes from meetings through June and July. Diaries of Nathanael Seidel's visit to the West Indies (1753). MissWI 175, 1–5.
[48] Original draft of Nathanael Seidel's report of his visit to St. Thomas, St. Croix and St. John. MAB MissWi 175, 4.
[49] Crumbay/Niesky was purchased in 1750. This property was used for workshops rather than sugar production and would become an economic centre later in the century. Christian Degn, *Die Schimmelmanns im Atlantischen Dreieckshandel: Gewinn und Gewissen* (Neumünster: K. Wachholtz, 1974).
[50] 'Nathanaels Visitation war wol gewiß vom Heyland. Er kam zu einer Zeit, da er am allernöthigsten war, aber solte nicht ein Oeconomus seyn in St. Thomas, Crux und John? Ich meyne nicht in

Spangenberg is advocating the appointment of a person in charge of management alongside or under the leadership of Weber. This practice would be introduced in 1759.

Visitation of 1755: Addressing the question of Moravian-owned slaves

In 1755, Christian Heinrich Rauch travelled to the Danish West Indies from Bethlehem, armed with a list of forty-two points to be discussed and clarified. The first conference was held on 15 May of that year and the last on 29 July. He made sure to visit all three islands. In one of the first conferences, on 28 May, Rausch pointed out that they were the Saviour's tools and that they should not entangle themselves further into plantation and other matters, which would impede their missionary work. It was also noted that 'we' are God's people, as are 'our own Blacks' and therefore they should not be treated according to the local method, since this is not appropriate 'for us'.[51] From the discussion points, it is clear that this was an issue to be discussed more fully, and after visiting St John and St Croix, it is raised again on a meeting on 9 July on Deknatel.

This meeting concerned the 'outer' issues on St Thomas and listed fourteen points for discussion, including organization, sexual conduct and management. Some of Georg Weber's almost insurmountable number of tasks were reassigned, and Johann Böhner and Christian Friedrich Töllner were appointed in charge of the 'outer' matters and the bills (with instructions to show moderation in acquiring debts).

Rauch now moved on to the issue of slaves. He has heard, he said, that 'your Blacks' are sometimes beaten and that the brothers in Bethlehem have also heard of this and are very uncomfortable with this situation. They would like to ask whether it really is beneficial that 'our brothers in St. Thomas' hold so many slaves and run a sugar plantation, and whether it would not be better to get rid of all the slaves and manage by means of their own trades and their kitchen garden? Treating slaves according to the principles of this world, Rauch pointed out, imperils the Moravians' status as tools and servants of the Saviour. After a discussion of the matter, the St Thomas brothers convinced Rauch that it was impossible to be in St Thomas without slaves but conceded that a change had to happen in their treatment thereof. While there is no discussion of the

---

Opposition des Bruder Webers, sondern unter ihm, oder mit ihm.' Spangenberg to Zinzendorf, 27 November 1754. UA R.15.B.a.12, 112.

[51] Visitation reports of Christian Heinrich Rauch. MAB MissWI 154, 28 May 1755.

baptism of the Moravian-owned slaves, there is still an echo of the concerns of Watteville in 1749, namely that in their treatment of their own slaves, Deknatel was not readily distinguishable from other plantations with slaveholders and slaves. For example, if a slave turned out to be a seducer, Rausch notes that it be preferable that he be sold rather than beaten, since this would be the more humane punishment.[52] Bethlehem had also requested an answer to the following questions: How many Blacks do they have? What kind of insurance is there for the plantation and property? Sketches of 'our' places are requested. What do the brothers owe, and what is owed them? These items belong to what we know as an inventory and indicate an increased interest in economic issues — following on, presumably, from the establishment of the economic overseers in Herrnhut.

As we saw earlier, Bethlehem's concern with the plantation industry in St Thomas had a longer history, and it would continue to be a bone of contention between Bethlehem and St Thomas until the restructuring after the death of Zinzendorf. Thus, in a careful 1758 letter from Bethlehem, Spangenberg gently suggested that the brothers and sisters in St Thomas should perhaps plant more food and draw their Blacks into useful trades, such as shoemaker, tailor and carpenter, instead of running a plantation. In the letter, Spangenberg admits that it is difficult for white brothers to work hard in the West Indies but asks whether the plantation really yields that much that it is necessary to turn to such an approach.[53]

Visitation of 1759: Clearer distinction between two types of Oeconomie

Nathanael Seidel's second visitation took place in 1759. One of the most significant events of this visitation was the introduction of a brother, Jens Korn, to be in charge of the 'Oeconomie'. Jens Korn was Danish and so in a position to communicate with the colonial authorities.[54] Since the last visitation, Brother Böhner had been in charge of overseeing the 'outer' matters of the mission on the three islands, but now this was to be handed over to Korn. It was emphasized

---

[52] But see the visitation reports from Loretz, where on 24 April 1784, Paulus, a slave belonging to the Moravian plantation, is discovered to have fathered a child with Mary Magdalene, Colly's wife, and should, 'as was the practice among our early brothers, receive 100 lashings from the Bomba'. MDF 1920, 24 April 1784.
[53] Spangenberg to Weber, 23 January 1758. UA R.15.B.b.25, 15. Nathanael Seidel also voices this point of view in the minutes of the Central Council, 25 June 1760, pkt 3c. UA.R.03.B.4.c.1.
[54] That this was an advantage may be seen in the search for his replacement after his death in 1762, where it was noted that someone who could write in Danish would be a distinct preference.

that this did not imply a change in organization or structure but merely in personal.[55] It was decided to produce an inventory (*Inventarium*) over 'our plantation, Blacks and cattle, and everything which belongs to our Oeconomie'. This was carried out at the following meeting a couple of weeks later. Nathanael informed the brothers that the inventory was not only for their own benefit, to get a clear idea of property and debt, but that the Unity's leadership (*General-Directorium der Unitaet*) also wanted an overview of the possessions in each institution and the Oeconomie.

The inventory was drawn up by Jens Korn and included the plantation with the house, the family house, the Single Brothers' House, the kitchen and two storerooms, the carpenter's house, the church, the sugar mill, boiler-house and distillery. It also listed forty-seven slaves ('Blacks') including women and children,[56] along with livestock, and materials and tools of the trades (*Professionen*). Note carefully: the slaves are listed as part of the stock of the plantation, alongside livestock and tools of trade. As Hüsgen notes, this is the earliest example of an inventory that adopted the existing management techniques of a slave society.[57]

Interestingly, Korn's overall assessment of the management and income of the mission was that the plantation and its sugar production did not yield enough to fully support the mission because of drought and the depleted soil. The expenses to be covered by the 500 RD which the plantation brings in are

1) Daily housekeeping
2) The procurement and maintenance of plantation tools, hoes, knives/ machetes, axes and so on
3) The upkeep of the slaves, both those in domestic services and the elderly and infirm
4) The sustenance of the brothers and sisters in St Croix and St John, who have been helped from 'St Thomas Oeconomie'.

Instead, what had kept them afloat were the trades, mill-building, carpentry, building, shoemaking, and the assessment is that this will continue. The mission

---

[55] Nathanael Seidel, New-Herrnhut, St Thomas, 5 April 1759. UA R.15.12.B.a.25, 127.
[56] Jens Korn to Christian Hillmar Saalwächter. St Thomas, 20 July 1759. The slaves were listed according to men: Joseph with wife and four children valued at 600 RD, Isaac, wife and four children valued at 600 RD, Jacob, wife and three children at 500 RD, Simon, wife and five children at 600 RD, Anton, wife and three children at 500 RD, Simson at 230 RD, Nathanael and wife at 250, Suah at 100 RD, Johann at 50 RD, David, a boy, at 150 RD, Christian and Ludwig at 300.
[57] Hüsgen, *Mission und Sklaverei*, 62. For the development of accounting as originating in slave-holding management, see Caitlin Rosenthal, *Accounting for Slavery: Masters and Management* (Cambridge, MA: Harvard University Press, 2018).

on the three islands can ensure its own upkeep and does not need to burden the community in Europe or the *Heiden-Diakonie*.

The third meeting of Seidel's visitation was on 7 May 1759. On this occasion matters of Oeconomie were discussed, since Nathanael wanted to tie up a couple of loose ends. It was decided that it was imperative to have a brother in charge of 'everything that belongs to our local Oeconomie' and to carry out whatever was agreed upon in the meetings. The areas of responsibility are listed as:

1) 'Our plantation Blacks,' who must have someone to whom they are assigned, and who looks after them, takes care of and regulates their work, and on whom they depend in every way. The Brother must report everything in the house conference, all cases must be discussed there, and he must always get his instructions there. This is the main task and of high priority, because in the absence of a particular organisation (*Special-Anstalt*) they have come into disarray.
2) Supervision and care of the cattle, both in New-Herrnhut and in Crumbay.
3) Oversight of the store rooms, distributing all that is needed, keeping the keys, keeping an eye on stock and provisions, and reporting to the meetings if an item is running short.
4) All matters of some consequence must be agreed at the meetings, and, apart from small matters, the brother cannot do anything on his own account.

Nathanael had already talked with some of the more experienced brothers about this role, and they had suggested Brother Heckedorn as an intermediary until a married couple would arrive from Bethlehem to take on the tasks. The wife would take over the kitchen duties, now in the hands of Sister Verona, who is vastly overworked, and Brother Heckedorn would then return to his present duties. This suggestion was approved by the *Saviour* (i.e. by lot), and Brother Heckedorn agreed.

From the above list, Brother Heckedorn's tasks and duties were straightforward. They correspond roughly to the list of duties Rasmus Holt compiled for the house-meetings in 1782 as he was preparing to return to Europe.[58] Heckedorn and Holt's duties included the storage of provisions and wine, the running of the apothecary, the supervision of plantation work and sugar production. His wife

---

[58] Mentioned in Hüsgen, *Mission und Sklaverei*, 74, note 213. House Conference, St Thomas, UA R.15.B.b.20.a, 17a.

was in charge of kitchens, chickens, laundry and gardens. Both husband and wife were in charge of handing out provisions to the slaves in their respective areas of work.[59]

These tasks were very much practical on the ground management *within* the Moravian household (*hiesige Oeconomie*, the local economy), whereas the tasks of Jens Korn were situated on the borderline between the Moravian community and the world: that is, the 'outer' Oeconomie. As we see from his correspondence and papers,[60] Korn's tasks were to liaise with a merchant/agent in Saint Eustacius regarding goods,[61] collect outstanding debts, negotiate with the new Danish inspector on St Croix, assess which brothers can earn bread and how new arrivals may be of use to the Oeconomie.[62] His replacement, Jeppe Brøndum, came to the West Indies in 1764 and died a year and a half later. The appointment of Brøndum, a skilled bookkeeper,[63] signifies the increased administrative emphasis on external affairs that had come to prevail in Herrnhut after Zinzendorf's death. This new emphasis also had an impact on the Moravian plantation enterprise, as we will see.

The reason I have dealt with these points in some detail is that the tasks of Brother Korn and Brother Heckedorn are distinct, but both are referred to as 'Oeconomie'. The distinction between the two usages of the term was becoming clearer. Importantly, both areas of duty are regarded as requiring full-time labour: each brother was to devote himself solely to the appointed task. And since it is our task here to analyse the transformations in household organization, and in particular the development of an external economic sphere, it is important to understand how this distinction emerged and how it functioned.

---

[59] After Brother Hellert requested to retire from this duty in 1794, it was discussed whether Peter, the Bomba, should take over this task, given that the missionaries were in the process of selling the plantation and thus needed someone to take over in an interim. However, in the meeting minutes of 20 January 1796, they have received a letter from Verbeek stating that Brother and Sister Haensel are on their way to take over from Hellert, because the UAC did not think it appropriate that a stranger should manage the plantation ('wel die UAC nicht vor gut hielt, daß dieselbe [die Plantage] durch einen Fremden verwaltet würde). Minutes of the Helpers' Meeting, 22 November 1794. UA R.15.B.b.20.e.
[60] Jens Korn to Christian Hillmar Saalwächter 21 (20 July 1759); 22 (2 August 1760). UA MDF.1911.
[61] Upon his arrival, Korn had changed agent, from Frau Balsen to a Daniel Meister, with whom he was previously acquainted. UA MDF.1911, 21 (20 July 1759) Jens Korn to Christian Hillmar Saalwächter in Amsterdam.
[62] Jens Korn to Christian Hillmar Saalwächter, 24 March 1762. UA MDF.1911, 25.
[63] Jeppe Brøndum, New-Herrnhut, St Thomas to Jonas Paul Wiess, Herrnhut. 20 March 1764. Brøndum notes that he spent the first many months in New-Herrnhut getting the books and accounts in order which had been left in a mess. UA MDF 1911, 37.

Visitation of 1783-4: All eyes on the 'outer' Oeconomie

More than twenty years would pass before the next visitation. The reason for this significant gap in time was that between 1762 and 1782 the supervision of the mission in the Danish West Indies had been assigned to Martin Mack, who previously had been working as a missionary among the Native American population of Pennsylvania. His presence in the islands from 1762 and appointment as bishop in 1770 meant that no visitation took place until Johann Loretz's visitation in 1783-4. Records indicate that Martin Mack had been away from the Danish West Indian mission for three years on a visitation trip to the British West Indies. In his absence, the situation in the Danish West Indies had gotten completely out of hand, giving rise for the need to restructure. The Unity leadership, now with a seat in Barby,[64] sent Johann Loretz in 1783. While the restructure of authority in the Danish West Indian mission was a central reason for the visitation,[65] there were other pressing issues pertaining to economic organization.

First, it was decided that each mission station should henceforth be self-reliant instead of receiving assistance from New-Herrnhut. The visitation notes that Friedensthal and Friedensberg in St Croix had not relied on external assistance for several years and have prospered. A similar situation is to be expected from New-Herrnhut and Niesky in St Thomas, because the smithy in Niesky would serve the Oeconomie there. This had for some years been the most profitable trade and given higher priority in the mission as a whole because the income from carpentry and mill construction had decreased in the latter years. The two sites which are seen as being at a disadvantage are Bethania and Emmaus in St John, but plans have been set in motion to ensure their productivity and survival. The ultimate aim for this restructure was that the costs for the Mission Deputation should be lowered.[66]

One of the central tasks in the restructure as requested by the UAC was to separate the plantation Bethel/Rephun from the Oeconomie of New-Herrnhut.[67]

---

[64] The Unity shifted its main seat several times between Herrnhut, Berthelsdorf and Barby on the Elbe in Sachsen-Anhalt.
[65] Lawaetz, *Brødremenighedens Mission i Dansk-Vestindien*, 91. See also UAC letter to Mack, 10 August 1783.
[66] Loretz to Johannes von Watteville, 23 April 1784. UA R.15.B.a.21.a, 109. Loretz also mentions in his report that the main costs of the mission were borne by the Mission Deputation and only in the latter years had the so-called Missions Diakonie in New-Herrnhut shouldered a small part of the costs.
[67] In his section on Bethel, Hüsgen draws attention to this separation but attributes the decision to the mission: '1784 hatte sich *die Mission* jedoch entschlossen, die Plantage Bethel als von der Missionsstation separates Unternehmen zu betreiben.' Hüsgen, *Mission Und Sklaverei*, 53. Emphasis added.

On the first mention of this move, on 23 April 1784, the state of books and ledgers are mentioned as being in a dreadful state, so much so that there was little to report in terms of balance. A week later, on 1 May 1784, the Bethel/New-Herrnhut separation has been making progress, and Brother Reichelt, who had been given power of attorney to clarify the state of affairs, and take control thereof, was now ready to do so. Henceforth, the annual status report and invoices of the plantation as well as all items and Oeconomica would come through Brother Reichelt's hands. With his remarks added, this reporting material was to be directed to the Helpers' Conference for examination and consideration, following which the necessary resolutions and orders about were to be made. Thus, the status report was compiled by Brother Reichelt, and a general assessment was then recorded in a designated 'common book'. From the annual status reports and accounts of the plantation, as well information concerning assets, transactions and other economic items, Reichelt was tasked with compiling a general status report for the Mission Deputation for the purpose of inspection and assessment. This in turn would help them make the correct dispositions to the Helpers' Conference.[68]

These new measures meant that Brother Reichelt was placed as mediator between the local leadership council, the 'Helfer Conferenz', and the Mission Deputation in Herrnhut. His task was to watch, advise and support the 'Oeconomie' both in general and in particular, and ensure uninterrupted communication between the two bodies. This was confirmed in the transferral of authorization (*Vollmacht*) bestowed upon Reichelt by the Mission Deputation in a document signed on 12 August 1783. Here it is stated that his appointment is to ease the missionaries' burden and to enable the missionary enterprise to proceed without impediment. According to this authorization, Reichelt's tasks included facilitating the use of the plantations, houses, associated land, as well as all trades and professions, which are owned by the Unitäts-Mission-Diaconia, and to maintain them all in good condition. This would entail surveying the preservation of the buildings and erecting new buildings if this would contribute to the prosperity of the plantations and the Oeconomie, and, thus, the mission. It is also his task to 'procure Blacks, as well as the necessary livestock and other necessities'; to supervise the slaves, to employ the necessary master-servants in proper order and to dismiss their services; to maintain in good order all inventories both on the plantations and in the professions and trades; to keep

---

[68] Visitation reports from Johann Loretz, St Thomas and St Croix UA MDF 1920, 23 April 1784 and 1 May 1784.

an eye on the ebbs and flows of business; to keep an account of all income and expenses, both cash and in kind; to keep accounts and to send these accounts to the Mission Deputation every year.

This significant appointment indicates that it not only was Bethel that had to be separated and organized as a specifically economic enterprise, but all money-making ventures that then could support the mission work from the outside, so to speak. The minutes demonstrate that the Unity leadership in Barby were looking to restructure the Danish West Indian mission. This would ensure that any surplus from individual settlements would go directly to the leadership in Barby, rather than be distributed within the Danish West Indian mission itself. As Hüsgen demonstrates, the profits from Bethel were considerable.[69]

Further divisions and distinctions

In the minutes of the Helpers' Conference from 1786, we can see how this separation is to be enforced. The detail is worth recounting in detail, since it provides an insight into how far the restructuring went. Brother Belling, who took over after Reichelt's sudden death, was now placed in charge of Bethel, not only as its overseer but also as master-servant – the position of the white slave driver mentioned earlier. By this time, there was a further division of labour. Belling's tasks would no longer include income and expenses, since Brother Göttling was to take over the plantation account, as well as that of overseeing the entire *Diaconie*, while another brother, Auerbach, was to manage the Oeconomie of New-Herrnhut. Apart from overseeing the slaves and the work on the plantation, Auerbach's tasks included – under Brother Göttling's direction – the purchase and distribution of provisions. It is emphasized that the plantation has its own storeroom and that henceforth the items therein were to be kept strictly apart from the house and the Oeconomie. A brother would be appointed under Brother Auerbach's direction to manage the storeroom and provisions for New-Herrnhut, distribution among the slaves, keep an eye on their work and, in coordination with the other brothers and sisters, execute whatever would make the best use of the Oeconomie and conversely serve it the best. The separation between New-Herrnhut and Bethel was to be enforced down to the level of modes of transport, in that the Oeconomie in New-Herrnhut should preferably

---

[69] Hüsgen has a convenient table of income from 1785 to 1797 and the income from sugar and rum on page 54.

have its own cart and horse. If this was not possible, it should remunerate the plantation for the use thereof.

These comprehensive distinctions and separations naturally have repercussions for the slaves, in that Friedrich and his wife Dorothea, for example, who now belonged to the Oeconomie, had hitherto worked on the plantation. But given the repeated instructions by the UAC and the Mission Deputation to separate the Oeconomie and the plantation, this must be reinforced on the ground in St Thomas, with all the inconveniences entailed. This means, then, the slaves that belong to the Oeconomie work for the Oeconomie and the slaves that belong to the plantation work on the plantation. It is noted that the assignment of Friedrich and Dorothea to Bethel may have been the cause of their occasional displeasure, since they had been told during the discussion (presumably relating to the restructure in 1784) by Reichelt that they belonged to the Oeconomie. Finally, the separated management and finances also meant that since Belling was spending most of his time in the service of the plantation, the plantation must remunerate the Oeconomie. This was not to be regarded as a fixed salary, since Belling would supposedly have time remaining, during which he would be able to work in the watch-makery.[70]

As this detailed entry demonstrates, the separation was to be enforced rather rigidly in terms of what belonged to which Oeconomie, and if anything changed hands, monetary compensation had to follow. The plantation thus was fully separated from the mission, and while Belling could work in both Oeconomies, his tasks were restricted to the sphere of production.

Sale of the Bethel plantation

Less than a decade later, in 1793, the Moravian leadership (*Helfer-Conferenz*) in St Thomas received notice from the Missions Department that the Saviour had approved the sale of the plantation.[71] However, this was kept quiet for some time, and, when the time for concluding the sale came in 1797 the sale was an immense shock to the slaves on the plantation, in that most of them were also to be sold as part of the inventory. Of the twenty-four men and boys for sale, twelve had been with the Moravians since 1784, as had twelve of the eighteen women. They had expected to be treated differently. In a letter by missionary Matthäus Wied to Johann Renatus Verbeek, chair of the Missions Department,

---

[70] Helpers' Conference, Danish West Indies, 28 August 1786. UA R.15.B.b.20.e.
[71] Mission Department to Helpers' Conference in St Thomas. 19 October 1792. UA R.15.B.b.26.d, 121.

who at this point was in St Croix on visitation, we see that the news created an uproar, not only on Bethel but also on New-Herrnhut, where people demanded to know what would happen to their family members on Bethel. Furthermore, two of the carpenters who were working in Niesky left work upon hearing that they had been sold.[72] The missionaries, as the letter indicates, were adamant that the reason for selling was the behaviour of the slaves.[73]

> Now that they have not respected all the validity and good admonitions, and after long warnings they have brought it to the point that we are compelled to get rid of them, they tear the hair on their heads because of the unheard-of that we are doing to them, and at the same time they are happy that they are discussing with each other (as sensible brothers and sisters seem to have told us): the day it will happen, they want to start a dance with Combeé (a pagan kind of drum) on the plantation. Up to now they would have had to do it secretly and go to others, but now they want to do it publicly in front of us.[74]

---

[72] It was communicated through Christian, an enslaved helper, that they would be treated as runaway slaves if they did not return to work. Wied to Verbeek, New-Herrnhut d. 20 July 1797. MDF 2282.1, n.
[73] The sale had been discussed in correspondence back and forth between Herrnhut and New-Herrnhut since 1790, after the drought. Their friend in St Thomas, Commander Malleville, had been advising it for some time, and he emphasized that the Black people cannot be governed with goodness but needs to be kept under sharp discipline (R.15.B.b.26.d, 136. Malleville to Herrnhut, 22 May 1793). This is in response to Brother Loretz's letter from 24 October 1792 (UA R.15.B.b.26.d, 123), where he notes that the missionaries have for a long time had difficulties in the administration of the plantation and that management thereof was incommensurable with their calling as 'messengers of peace' to the Black people. In the meeting minutes from Verbeek's visitation, it is also discussed in relation to Emmaus that the harshness with which the Blacks must be treated to bring about the necessary benefit (!) is extremely difficult for the brothers, and that, therefore, all the Oeconomies sought to use as little of the same Blacks as possible (UA R.15.B.b.20.e (1797), Minutes of the Helpers' Conference, Danish West Indies 25 April-3 May 1797, here 1 May 1797). In their letter communicating the instruction to sell to the Helpers' Conference in the Danish West Indies, the Missions Department noted that Spangenberg had often said that it was not becoming of the brothers to own plantations alongside proclaiming the gospel, in that it placed them in the inevitable situation of having to treat the Blacks—or let them be treated—with harshness ['Besonders lag es unserm seligen Bruder Joseph öfters sehr im Gemüthe, daß es für uns nicht schicklich sey, neben der Verkündigung des Evangelii eigentliche Plantagen zu besizen, und dabey in die unvermeidliche Nothwendigkeit gesezt zu seyn, die Neger oft mit Strenge behandeln oder behandeln laßen zu müßen.']. The previous years of bad harvest due to the drought has meant that an advantageous sale was less likely, but now that the situation had been rectified with good crops, there was a chance that a good sale could be made. The recent events in the French islands (St Domingo) might also add to value. UA R.15.B.b.26.d, 121. Missions Department to Helpers' Conference in St Thomas, Herrnhut 19 October 1792.
[74] Wied to Verbeek, New-Herrnhut d. 20 July 1797: 'Nun da sie alle Güttigkeiten und gute Ermahnungen nicht geachtet, und sie es nach langem Warnen dahin gebracht, daß wir genöthigt sind, uns von ihnen loszumachen, möchten sie sich die Hare aus den Köpfen reisen über das Unerhörte, das wir damit an ihnen begehen, und zu gleicher Zeit freuen sie sich darüber, daß sie sich - wie uns verschiedene verständige Geschwister erzehlt haben –besprechen mit einander: Den Tag wen es geschehen wird, wollen sie auf der Plantage einen Tanz mit Combeé - eine heidnische art Trommel –anstellen; bisher hätten sie es heimlich thun müssen und zu andere gehen, aber dann wollen sie es öffentlich vor uns thun'. MDF 2282.1, n.

'Plantation Disposition'

While the plantation was bought with only one slave, by the name of Isaac, it was sold with more than sixty.[75] Some of these were members of the community,[76] some were not.[77] It is, however, indisputable that for the Moravian leadership, the plantation had since 1784 constituted a separate, economic sphere, which was distinct from the mission. It was an economic venture, nothing more and nothing less.

Out of the seventy-one slaves on Bethel, two couples and their children were transferred to New-Herrnhut before the sale, namely Gideon[78] and Maria Magdalena, David and Lucia and two children, Maria Phöbe and Christian David. These were, or became, part of the Oeconomie of New-Herrnhut.[79]

---

[75] An inventory, drawn up on 9 June 1797, shows that the sale included the land itself, 210 acres (6,000 by 1,400 feet), buildings (windmill, boiler-house including accessories, distillery, residential house), 74 enslaved men, women and children, 2 horses, 5 mules and 9 donkeys, as well as a wagon with accessories. UA MDF 2282.1.e.

[76] A superficial perusal of the diaries one and two years after the sale does reveal that Susanna, Gottlob and Jonathan from Rephun were all communicant members of the Moravian community who nevertheless were sold with the plantation. Furthermore, the missionaries baptized at least another unnamed baptized ill person at Rephun, who had called for the Moravians but had become very indifferent to them (UA R.15.B.b.9.e, 5 September 1799). A baptized boy, Christians Friedrich, died in Rephun on 15 October 1799 and was buried by a helper. 10 November 1799, missionary Haensel went to Rephun in response to a summoning by a woman baptized as a child, who wanted to be part of the congregation. On 3 January 1800, Haensel baptized a baby boy, Johannes Christian, who died immediately after. Likewise on 17 March 1800, Haensel baptized a sick child, Diana Amalia, on Rephun. Moravians only baptized children where one of the parents were members of the community, so these baptisms indicate that there still were slaves present on Rephun who were members.

[77] This is mainly based upon their names in the inventory, which of course is no foolproof method. Many slaves were given names upon arrival in St Thomas, some were given Roman names (Quintus, Cesar, Apollo), others names of places (Paris, London, Bristol, St Crux), while others (perhaps) retained their own name (Matamba, Coffee). Sarah Abel, George Tyson and Gísli Pálsson, 'From Enslavement to Emancipation: Naming Practices in the Danish West Indies', *Comparative Studies in Society and History* 61 (January 2019): 332–65. Thank you to John Balz for the reference. So, for example, in the Bethel list, there are two people with Roman names, which could perhaps indicate that they were not baptized, namely Fortuna, a male slave who was in Moravian ownership since at least 1784, as was the case with the female slave Apolonia. Colly and Takky are also 'slave names' that are not indicative of conversion. Benda or Binda and her son Dick were bought by Weidenbach (21 March 1797, UA R.15.B.a.31) and so were certainly not baptized yet.

[78] Gideon is very probably the son of Isaac and Rebecca, noted as the property of the missionaries in a list from 1764, where Gideon is listed as ten years old, UA MDF.1912, 3. He was baptized by the Moravians as a boy, and, on 24 November 1776, was accepted as a member of the Moravian community. Minutes from the Helpers' Conference, Danish West Indies UA R.15.B.b.20c, 1776, 24 November.

[79] They are listed in the New-Herrnhut inventory as being appraised with New-Herrnhut from 1797. In 1798 Gideon and Lucia were working in the fields, David as a watchman, Maria Magdalena was an invalid and died on 2 May 1798. There is a short summary of her life in the diary (UA R.15.B.b.9.e, 2 May 1798). In 1799, 1800, 1801, 1802, Gideon and Lucia were still in the fields and David still watchman. David died on 29 September 1802, and there is a brief description of him in the diary, along with six other enslaved members who died in that month (UA R.15.B.b.9.e, 29 September 1802). Christian David minded cattle from 1802 until his death in 1805, 15 July. This is mentioned briefly in the diary (UA R.15.B.b.9.e, 25 July 1805). Lucia and Gideon continue to work in the fields, until 1808, when Lucia is listed as working in the laundry. Maria Phoebe is listed as working in the fields, 1808.

Household after 1760

In 1776, following the wish of the synod the preceding year, the UAC decided to arrange a visitation to the Danish and British West Indies, and Brother Thrane was chosen by lot. The instructions he received give us a good sense of the communal household as basis of the mission. The letter from the UAC states that the common household is the basic principle of all the missions and that no one should conduct business for himself. What is earned during one's service in the mission belongs to the mission and not oneself. In return, one's basic needs are met. Thrane was admonished to hold fast to this plan and reinstate it where it has been relaxed or abolished, since this was the core of the missionary cause. The UAC noted that in St Thomas, St Croix and St John, Brothers Mack and Kremser have kept them in good order. By contrast, Barbados and Antigua had started to deviate, in that the brothers and sisters distribute among themselves everything that has been sent to them, even cash, and everyone works for themselves. In Jamaica, it has never been set up in the proper way, and the UAC hoped that it might be established there, following the pattern of the Danish West Indies. Thrane was requested to examine whether all the brothers and sisters were happy and satisfied in the communal household, and whether there was any oversight or cause for complaint. Questions on this matter included: Is the house kept too abundantly or too sparingly? And how are 'our Blacks' treated? What improvements would he like to see in the Oeconomie and the trades?[80]

These directives for Brother Thrane give us a vague idea of what a communal household was and what it was not. It meant that the income of the brothers and sisters was deposited centrally, from where expenses such as food and clothing were covered. This is also mentioned as an 'Old Founding Principle' (*Alte Gründsatze*) in Loretz's visitation report eight years later.[81] As Thrane's instructions indicate, the Danish West Indies were regarded as a good example of proper organization. We also see the organization in the following quote from a 1765 report written by the Moravian missionaries to the Danish colonial

---

[80] UA MDF 1918, 1: UAC to Thrane: Barby, 6 February 1776, 11 b and c. Thrane died before he could leave, and Mack, who was chosen in his place, also received a letter with similar, though less, comprehensive instructions. UA MDF 1918, 2. Mack's visitation travels only took him to the British West Indies, since he was settled in the Danish West Indies, as mentioned earlier.

[81] Although, it is also noted that in the past there had been brothers in the Danish West Indies who had driven private business for their own enrichment and caused offence. Loretz had reminded everyone that such a way of thinking and acting was not only a disgrace to a missionary himself but was contrary of the principles of the synod, and hence the Unity, and would not be tolerated by any missionary or missionary-helper. UA MDF 1920, 1 May 1784.

authorities, describing their work in the West Indies. The ten brothers, five women and two widows are on the three islands

> for no other purpose than to convert the Blacks, and each seeks to help where he/she can; even if they don't all preach and teach, they still seek to lend a helping hand to those brothers who are there to teach the slaves, so that they receive adequate upkeep, and that with the work of their hands provide assistance as much as possible.[82]

Here, we see emphasized that the household is organized so that there are some brothers who do not preach and teach, but instead work to provide sustenance for those who do – as in the early days. In Bethlehem this was practised on a very large scale through the General Economy. However, this sort of communal household was precisely what the Unity wanted to dissolve in Bethlehem after Zinzendorf's death, so it is curious to see it referred to here, as a matter-of-fact way of dividing labour. This begs the question whether it is the same thing. Given the disagreements between Bethlehem and the missionaries in the Danish West Indies concerning the balance between mission and economy, the original purpose and its necessary, but subordinated, supplement, it would seem that it is not the same thing, and the question then remains, what is the difference?

In a 1769 report back to Herrnhut written by Martin Mack, Matheus Kremser and Johann Christoph Auerbach, a description of the outer circumstances on St Thomas concludes with an explanation of the presence of 'our own Blacks', who are all there in order to 'help to support the Mission-Work, since we without them would be unable to continue our work among this people'.[83] Examples of this support include laundry, cooking and baking all year round, gathering firewood weekly and fetching water daily for their own cooking, gathering grass daily for the missionaries' horses and cattle and carrying the things of the brothers travelling to other islands. The rest of the time they spend working in sugar production, which is, the missionaries note, the greatest assistance to their survival.

---

[82] Declaration by the Danish West Indian missionaries on their work. 1765: 'Diese alle sind zu keiner andern Absicht in diesen Eylanden, als alleine zu Bekehrung der Neger, und jedes sucht zu helfen wo es kan; ob sie gleich nicht alle predigen oder lehren, so suchen sie denjenigen Brüdern, die zum Lehren der Sclaven da sind, Handreichung zu thun, damit sie ihren gehörigen Unterhalt kriegen, und das mit ihrer Hände Arbeit so viel möglich besorgen zu helffen'. UA R.15.B.a.23.
[83] From the Missionaries on St Thomas to the brothers of the General Synod, New-Herrnhut, 28 January 1769, point 9: 'Etwas von unsern eigenen Negern, die wir haben, zu melden: So sind sie alle deswegen da, das Missions-Werck unterstützen zu helfen, weil wir ohne dieselben die Arbeit unter diesem Volck nicht fortsetzen könnten.' UA MDF 1912.13.

From all of this and more of the same, the reporting of which would be too extensive, it is apparent that the Blacks that we have belong to the support of the mission, and without which such a big family could not survive here. It would be desirable for the missionary cause that we would like to have further 10-15 good and skilled Blacks, which would be a great relief both for us on St. Thomas and for the other isles.[84]

The New-Herrnhut family thus relied on slave-labour for its material upkeep, be it launderesses, cooks or surplus from the sugar plantation. In any case, this material upkeep is placed outside ('belongs to the support') of the mission, indicating that is not part of the family, but rather its necessary supplement. This difference between the community, household or family at New-Herrnhut and its externalized economic supplement is a microcosm of the larger organization of the Moravian missions.

All decisions were made in Herrnhut, far away from the horrors of slavery, and it is clear that the decisions were there made on the basis of economic considerations, with the slaves regarded as mere numbers, or livestock, as is the case with absentee owners.[85] However, the bookkeeping which Reichelt was to institute was delayed because of his death the same year and was not commenced properly until the arrival of Göttling, who was appointed to take his place.[86] From then on, we have annual accounts sent to Barby concerning the economic activities of each settlement, including inventories of the enslaved persons owned by the Moravians in Bethel, Neuherrnhut and so on. The folder in which the accounts are found also contain a summary by the chair of the Mission Deputation, Renatus Verbeek, on the status of each settlement based on the annual numbers. From Verbeek's comments, we see that the Mission Deputation have been comparing the lists of slaves and wondering whether a given missing slave was sold or had died. Verbeek complains that the inventory is not carried out after 'the Suriname form' which gives a more precise account of the fate of each slave.[87]

---

[84] From the Missionaries on St Thomas to the brothers of the General Synod, New-Herrnhut, 28 January 1769: 'Aus diesem allen und dergleichen mehr, welches alles zu anzuführen zu weitläuffig seyn würde, ist zu ersehen, daß die Neger, die wir haben, zur Unterstützung der Mission gehören, und ohne welche so eine große Familie hier nicht durchkommen kan, und wäre wohl zu wünschen für die Missions-Sache, daß wir noch bey 10 oder 15 gute und tüchtige Neger mehr haben möchten, welches sowohl für uns auf St. Thomas, als auch für die andern Eylande zu großer Erleichterung seyn würde.' UA MDF 1912.13.
[85] Rosenthal, *Accounting for Slavery*, 198.
[86] Thus Verbeek in MDF 2282.e notes that proper bookkeeping did not take place until 1 January 1786.
[87] 'vermuthlich (nach dem surinamischen Formular würde man das alles gewiß wißen)', MDF 2092.1790.7a. This is commenced in 1797 and is an accounting method begun by Hans Wied in Suriname. See Verbeek's comments in MDF 2092.1797.14a.

As these examples indicate, the economic sphere in St Thomas manifested itself in the slave-holding practices of the missionaries. The missionary community established between the missionaries and the slaves from all over the islands was a church community and with a structure and fellowship not (relatively) unlike what we will see in Greenland. The enslaved Moravians helped maintain the church building on their Sundays and congregated in non-working hours. There is mention of the Black brothers and sisters supporting the missionaries from their plantation food.[88] There were Black helpers who participated in the Helpers' Conference and reported concerning the various spiritual conditions on the different plantations. In this sense, it was a community. However, as we have seen, there was a portion of slaves owned by the Moravians who were *not* part of this community. They were the workforce generating the financial support for the Danish West Indian mission at large. This is a clear, distinct sphere of economy which is *externally* connected to the mission. And while Moravian slave-based sugar production in the West Indies came to an end in 1804 with the final sale of Bethel, slave-based production continued in the smithy until the 1830s, in both Friedensthal, St Croix, and Niesky, St Thomas, as demonstrated by Jan Hüsgen.

The establishment and development of the 'outer' sphere was a condition of life in St Thomas, but it also took on a life of its own. In his study of the later Moravian mission to the islands, the Danish church historian Harald Lawaetz notes that 'nothing can be said in defence of industry in the way it is driven in the Danish West Indies'. He continues, 'It had become like a certain tropical parasitical plant, which slowly but surely will strangle the tree upon which it grows, while it seemingly holding it up with its strong, pillar-like supports.'[89] A number of points may be added to this blunt assessment, which are not intended as a defence of industry but a better understanding of the broader circumstances.

First, the missionaries in St Thomas did not do this on their own. It was directed from the central leadership in Europe, who could make use of the surplus raised in the Danish West Indies to fund less profitable mission ventures, such as Greenland. Second, the Moravian missions in both Europe and overseas had always relied on wealth produced by exploited classes, namely the peasants on the estates of the nobles who sponsored the Unity in various ways. What was different in the West Indies was the shift to an active participation in the creation

---

[88] Georg Ohneberg to Johannes von Watteville. St Croix, 15 January 1758. UA R.15.B.a.12.119.
[89] Lawaetz, *Brødremenighedens Mission i Dansk-Vestindien*, 157. See also 144: 'The main issue for the brothers was becoming a side issue, and the side issue, the main issue. The mission becomes a business, and a profitable business at that, the letters become business letters, where the joy is expressed less over the sinners who convert, than the good thalers that flow in; at least this is what it looks like.' My translation of the Danish original.

of wealth to be consumed elsewhere. Finally, the West Indies constituted one of the sites of extreme development, with high levels of production, high risk and high gain, and was thus a visibly brutal example of primitive accumulation. As such it was capitalism in the making and here we see how the Moravians adapted to the local circumstances with the extremity of the adaptation aligned with the extremity of the context. In its basic nature, though, the production of an external, objective and deeply exploitative economic sphere supporting an otherwise moral, edifying, humanist cause is capitalism in a nutshell.

Conclusion

This chapter has analysed the economic development of the Moravian mission in St Thomas, where the separation of mission and economy as distinct spheres escalated after 1760. It had already been flagged as a problematic issue before 1760, namely in Cammerhof's letter, in which he expressed his concern with the precedence given to economic concerns over missionary matters. This letter already indicates a development well underway, namely that the economy was separated out and given equal if not more attention than the primary task, instead of the mission itself being the main concern. The separate economic sphere meant that there was a distinction between the slaves working for the Moravian mission and the enslaved Moravian congregations of the islands. The surplus from the plantation enterprise and slave-ownership provided the Danish West Indian mission with funds to support itself.

The repercussions of the changes in organization and management following Zinzendorf's death were felt more strongly in the Danish West Indies than they would be in Greenland, because the new economic principles were more significant in contexts of high economic activity and potential yield. In Greenland, as we will see shortly, the possibilities for economic activity beyond that of household management was impossible due to a very different colonial context.

New-Herrnhut in Greenland

6

Greenland and colonial authorities

Introduction

The mission to Greenland was the second mission commenced by the Moravians[1]. On 19 January 1733, three Moravian Brethren, Christian David and the cousins Matthäus and Christian Stach, set out from Copenhagen by ship. Their destination was Greenland. On the south-west coast of Greenland, a Danish trade settlement, Godthaab, had been established in 1728. This was also the centre of the Danish mission, established and led by the Lutheran minister Hans Egede. Thither went the three Moravian men, all part of the German-speaking Moravian (*mährisch*) immigration to the Oberlausitz more than a decade earlier. The three Moravians were given a somewhat frosty welcome and instead of being accommodated at Godthaab as promised in Copenhagen, they were left to find their own means of dwelling. They settled on a spot on the peninsula outside Godthaab, initially in a turf house, then in a wooden building, and finally, from 1747, in the impressive mission station of New-Herrnhut – which, with substantial modifications, still stands today.[2] 167 years and 5 mission

---

[1] There is not much material on the Moravians in Greenland, especially in regard to the eighteenth century. The most recent work is that of Thea Olsthoorn, 'Wir haben keine Ohren.' Kommunikationsprobleme und Missionsverständnisse bei der Verbreitung und Rezeption des Christentums in Grönland und Labrador im 18. Jahrhundert', *Pietismus und Neuzeit* 39 (2013): 47–85; Thea Olsthoorn, 'Das Herz auf der Zunge: Der Streit der Herrnhuter mit Hans Egede wegen der Lehre', *Unitas Fratrum* 79 (2021): 261–77. Older contributions include Israel, *Kulturwandel*; Inge Kleivan, 'Herrnhuterne eller Brødremenigheden i Grønland 1733-1900', *Tidsskriftet Grønland* 8 (1983): 221–35; Henrik Wilhjelm, 'Menneske (inuk) først og kristen så? : en vinkel på missionshistorien i Vestgrønland', *Dansk Teologisk Tidsskrift* 68 (2005): 1–20.; Wilhjelm, 'How a Man Accused of Being Wizard and Murderer Determined the Development of the Moravian Mission in Greenland', in *Sbornik VI. Konferenz Moravian v Roce 2012: Moravsti Bratri v Polarnich Oblastech* (Suchdol nad Odrou: Edice Moravian, 2015), 35–41. Studies on Greenland which include significant engagement with the Moravian presence include Kai Merten, *'Ich habe im Himmel keine Spur von dir Gesehen.' Religionsbegegnungen in Grönland Im 18. Jahrhundert.*, Nordic Studies in Religion and Culture (Münster: LIT Verlag, 2020); Finn Gad, *The History of Greenland 2 (1700-1782)* (London: C. Hurst, 1970), but both of these works rely heavily on Cranz for their presentation of the Moravians.

[2] For a history of the building, which has undergone numerous renovations, see Kathrine Kjærgaard and Thorkild Kjærgaard, *Ny Herrnhut i Nuuk 1733-2003: Missionstation, Rævefarm, Embedsbolig*,

Figure 6 New-Herrnhut in Greenland copper etching, 1770. TS.Mp.126.2. Reproduced with permission from Unity Archives, Herrnhut.

stations later,[3] the Moravians left Greenland in 1900, and their six congregations were subsumed into the Danish state church (Figure 6).[4]

When the Moravians arrived, there was no commercial society in Greenland; it was an enormous country with a sparse and widely distributed Indigenous population and a single colonial settlement. Due to the nature of the environment, the colonial development and the basic nature of the Moravian mission, the Moravians never managed to develop any kind of enterprise in Greenland. Thus, the mission was largely focused on 'inner' matters. With the ever-sharper separation of the 'inner' and 'outer' spheres in the Moravian Church as a whole, there was not only a transformation of the 'outer' as we found with the mission in the Danish West Indies but also a transformation of the 'inner'. This transformation was most notable in Greenland and is therefore the concern of this chapter. Thus, the material analysed in this chapter provides an

---

 Museum, Universitet (Nuuk: Ilisimatusarfik, 2005). The building used to house Ilisimatusarfik, the University of Greenland, which since has moved out to more spacious buildings.
[3] The six mission stations the Moravians left behind were New-Herrnhut (1733), Lichtenfels (1758), Lichtenau (1774), Friederichstal (1824), Umanak (1861) and Idlorpait (1864).
[4] Henrik Wilhjelm, 'Brødremissionens Overgivelse: Udviklingen i og omkring Brødremissionen i Grønland 1850-1900', *Tidsskriftet Grønland* 6 (2000): 203–44.

instructive counterpoint to my analysis of the Danish West Indies in the previous two chapters.

Relation to colonial authorities

While Greenland was claimed by the Danish-Norwegian crown in the early seventeenth century, the actual colonization of Greenland began in 1721 and took place through a number of separate settlements (*kolonier*) on the west coast. These were founded and funded by a string of 'privately' run trading companies with royal concessions.[5]

Danish colonial monopoly

The first trading company was initiated by Hans Egede and was created with the sole purpose of supporting the missionary effort.[6] Egede arrived in 1721, along with his family and a motley crew of sailors, merchants and workers for the settlement. Initially placed on an island off the mainland (Haabets ø – Island of Hope), the settlement was relocated to the mainland in 1728. This was Godthaab (Good Hope), which is today known as Nuuk, the capital of Greenland. The Danish colonial settlement at Godthaab (Nuuk) thus included both the mission and its economic underpinning, known as the 'Trade'. This was the situation when the Moravians arrived in Greenland in 1733.

After a number of trading companies had managed to establish the foundations for profitable trade in Greenland, the Danish state took over the Trade in 1774 and established *Den Kongelige Grønlandske Handel* (KGH). This outfit effectively governed Greenland until 1953, when Greenland was subsumed into the Danish Commonwealth (*Rigsfællesskabet*). From 1721 onwards, nineteen settlements were established up and down the west coast, mainly to keep English and Dutch merchants and whalers at bay.[7] Five of these settlements were later

---

[5] The four trading companies were *Bergenskompagniet* (1721–8); *Det kongelige grønlandske Dessein* (1728–31); Jacob Severin's company (1734–49); and *Almindelige handelskompagni* (1749–74).

[6] Egede was initially interested in the Norse settlers who had settled on the west coast of Greenland around the year 1000, established a bishopric in the year 1154 but not heard from since the second half of the fifteenth century. Egede's most heartfelt desire was to find these poor abandoned Catholics and bring them the 'good news' of the Reformation. Egede only ever found the ruined settlements and so turned his fervour to the Indigenous population of Greenland.

[7] Godthaab (Nuuk) 1728; Christianshaab (Qeqertasussuk) 1734; Jakobshavn (Ilulissat) 1741; Frederikshaab (Pamiut) 1742; Claushavn (Ilimanaq) 1752; Fiskenæsset (Qeqertarsuatsiaat) 1754; Sukkertoppen (Kangaamiut) 1755–81, from 1781 moved to the current site of Manitsoq; Rittenbenk (Saqqaq) 1755–81, moved to the current site in 1781; Egedesminde (Aasiaat) 1759–63, in 1763

abandoned.[8] The continuing settlements were functionally independent centres, controlled by merchants and missionaries employed by the trading companies and the Missionary Board in Copenhagen respectively.

The colonization of Greenland, then, did not take place through European settlers but through the appropriation and explosive increase of the production of the Kalaallit hunter population by European merchants.[9] A reservation policy to ensure the continuation of this colonial pattern became formalized in 1782 with the so-called *Instruction of 1782*. This included the establishment of two KGH inspectorates, one to the north in the settlement of Godhavn (present-day Qeqertarsuaq) and one to the south, in Godthaab (present-day Nuuk).[10] The idea behind this policy was to ensure that the Kalaallit remained within their semi-itinerant way of life (winter settlement and summer hunting trips) and not be urged to take on a European way of life or diet. In this way, they would continue to produce valuable items for trade, especially blubber from seal and whale. The inspectors constituted the highest colonial authority in Greenland, and the *Instruction*, issued from Denmark, was binding for all employees of the KGH, all the way from merchants, through those in charge of the whaling stations, to anyone employed in the Trade. The *Instruction* covered every conceivable item, from marriage regulation to ensuring Christian morality, from managing social relations between Europeans and Kalaallit to preventing and punishing crime. The layout of the colonial network in Greenland established in the *Instruction* was that the chief merchant at each settlement was now termed a 'settlement-manager', or *kolonibestyrer*, who was accountable to the inspectors and in charge of implementing the *Instruction* within his settlement and its outposts. One of the significant tasks was to ensure that the monopoly on trade with the Kalaallit was maintained. No one except KGH representatives was allowed to buy up the Kalaallit products that were the preserve of the Trade.[11]

While the Moravian Brethren may have had good relationships with a number of individual Danish-Norwegian merchants and missionaries, the default relationship with the colonial authorities was one of antagonism,

---

moved to the current site; Uummannaaq 1761; Holsteinsborg (Sisimiut) 1764; Upernavik 1772; Godhavn (Qeqertarsuak) 1773; and Julianehaab (Qaqortok) 1774.

[8] Haabets Ø (the first settlement of Egede 1721–8); Nipisat (1724–5 and 1729–31); Sydbay (1756–64); Nuusuuaq (1758–61); and Amerloq (1759–67).

[9] Hans Christian Gulløv, *Grønland. Den Arktiske Koloni*, Danmark og kolonierne (Copenhagen: Gads Forlag, 2017), 107 See also Jørgen Viemose, *Dansk kolonipolitik i Grønland* (Copenhagen: Demos, 1977).

[10] Gulløv, *Grønland. Den Arktiske Koloni*, 110. Finn Gad, *The History of Greenland 3: 1782-1808* (London: Hurst, 1982), 9–15.

[11] Gulløv, *Grønland. Den Arktiske Koloni*, 116; Gad, *The History of Greenland 3*, 20–9.

which manifested itself in different ways. In the earlier days, when the Danish-Norwegian trade was consolidating itself, the struggles focused on produce and transportation of supplies. Once the trade had firmly established its monopoly, the struggles concerned the distribution of the Kalaallit and the dwelling patterns of the Moravian congregations. And finally in the mid-nineteenth century, due to wars between Prussia and Denmark, nationalism and anti-German sentiment was added to the grievances.[12]

What exactly is meant by 'colonial authorities', then, changes through the decades and is particularly unclear in the years before 1774 and the consolidation of the Danish colonial state apparatus in Greenland. The ultimate authority was, of course, the king, and this was also the only authority the Moravians obeyed.[13] The two other bodies that constantly attempted to impose regulations and rules on the Moravians were the Missionary College in Copenhagen and the trading company. This was demonstrated in Moravian elder Andreas Grassmann's visitation diary, where he notes that they were summoned to the colony and presented with an edict from the Missionary College and head of the trading company, Jakob Severin.[14]

Nitschmann's letter to the Danish king, Christian VI

The Moravian resistance to these 'intermediate authorities' comes through in the submission sent by one of the chief government negotiators, David Nitschmann (Syndicus), to the Danish king, Christian VI (1730–46) in January 1742.[15] In his submission, Nitschmann points out that a few difficulties have arisen which makes it difficult to carry out their task of evangelization among the Kalaallit and thus would like to see remedied. First, Hans Egede, who by then was superintendent of the Missionary College in Copenhagen, had in an instruction

---

[12] The bilingual pamphlet Die Grönländische Frage/The Greenlandic Question from 1899 (UA R.15.J.a.24, 16) presents a number of responses to questions asked of the missionaries as to the possible termination of the mission in Greenland. Question 3, on page 8, asks, 'Is the desire to get rid of the German element at the bottom of the present official attitude?' The reply is that the desire to get rid of the Germans in Greenland was a long-standing one and had been proposed to the Danish Parliament in 1864, but had been thwarted by the intervention of the Danish Missionary Society. The year 1864 marks the last of the Danish-Prussian wars of the mid-nineteenth century, where Germany seized the duchies of Schleswig and Holstein which hitherto had been part of the Danish realm. The Danish Moravian settlement of Christiansfeld is in northern Schleswig, which became part of Denmark by the referendum in 1920.

[13] See the letter from Johannes von Watteville to the Unity Syndicate College dated 17 February 1769, where he refers to the trading company as a mere accessory to the king, chancellery and council. UA R.15.J.a17.5.

[14] Andreas Grassmann's visitation report, 29 and 30 June. UA R.15.J.a.16.3.

[15] David Nitschmann's submission to the king of Denmark, 24 January 1742. UA R.15.J.a.3.a.10.

forbidden the Moravians to carry out baptisms. Nitschmann asks that the king dispense with Egede's ban and grant the Moravian Church full freedom to teach, baptize and convert in the same manner as the king graciously has granted the Moravians this freedom on St Thomas in the Danish West Indies.

Second, the previously granted freedom to fish, shoot, and gather wood, and so on, has been rescinded and forbidden by the merchant Mr Severin – or rather limited to places and times where there was nothing to collect or catch.[16] Here Nitschmann reminds the king that the Moravians are completely reliant on the little opportunities the land offers to survive. Nitschmann insists that they do not do these things to trade but only for their subsistence. Therefore, on behalf of the Moravians, Nitschmann most humbly requests that they be granted the same essential freedom (*unentbehrliche Freyheit*) which they had during the first seven years, and which the people at Godthaab also have, without any limitations.

Third, every year, multiple difficulties arise concerning transportation, not only of the Moravian missionaries themselves but also of their supplies, and every year they are forced to bring the matter before the king and ask for his intervention.[17] Nitschmann asks that this matter be resolved once and for all through regulation so that they do not have to bother the king with such complaints again.

From the king's response, we see that he made enquiries with Hans Egede and merchant Jacob Severin who both denied these allegations. In relation to the first issue, this had already resolved itself, since the Moravian missionary Matthäus Stach had been recently ordained and could thus return to Greenland with royal permission to baptize and perform other 'ministerial acts'.[18] Severin rejected both charges and said that the intention with the instruction was not absolutely to deny the Moravians the right to shoot and fish, only that they were not to spoil the shooting and fishing at Godthaab or collect driftwood at times other

---

[16] Israel quotes an excerpt from the 1739 New-Herrnhut diary, which notes that the missionaries were summoned by the ministers and merchant of the settlement (Godthaab) and presented with instructions from Severin which forbade the Moravians to trade with the Kalaallit apart from what was needed for clothing that they were not to go hunting or fishing, and not to go out to collect driftwood in June, July and August, unless those from Godthaab also went out. Israel, *Kulturwandel*, 150, n. 793.

[17] A note, undated but from Severin's years, indicates the Moravians' frustrations with him, and his refusal to carry them and their supplies on his ships and considers whether it might be worth to apply for a trading licence of their own, so that they could ship their own supplies and not rely on an antagonistic merchant. This was never carried out. See UA R.15.J.a.11.1, 4. Remarks concerning Greenland, especially points 3, 12 and 14.

[18] Royal Decree, Copenhagen, 16 March 1742. UA R.15.J.a.3, 6. Up until this point, the Moravians did not have an ordained minister at New-Herrnhut but were reliant on the missionaries at the colony to perform baptism, which, as Henrik Wilhjelm notes, creates a problem in that Stach actually baptized Qujarnaq, the first convert, in 1739. See Wilhjelm, 'How a Man Accused of Being Wizard and Murderer Determined the Development of the Moravian Mission in Greenland', 37.

than the settlers at Godthaab, lest they would gather it all. This complaint was not resolved directly in the king's letter, but by taking Severin's justification of his instruction, a more specific limitation on his jurisdiction was now in writing and sealed by the king. The final issue, that of transportation, was resolved by suggesting that the Moravians who intended to go to Greenland notify Severin in a timely manner and follow his instructions. Here the Moravians received in writing what they must do to secure passage, and Severin was pushed to comply. Little wonder that David Nitschmann saw this as a victorious outcome in a subsequent letter to the missionaries in Greenland.[19] This example alerts us to the ongoing attempts to curtail Moravian practice in Greenland.

The problem of passage

Jacob Severin, it should be noted, was not against the Moravians per se. This is evident from his attempts to get the Moravians to work for him in the colonial settlements he was planning on establishing along the coastline.[20] This also indicates that he sees them primarily as tradesmen and labourers, not much different from the peasants on his estate from where he usually acquired his colonial workforce. The Moravians, however, resisted these offers and pressures.[21]

Another interesting point in this struggle is the fact that by his actions, Severin was pushing the Moravians into the arms of the Dutch, with whom the Moravians had very good connections.[22] Andreas Grassmann arrived with a Dutch ship and describes in his diary how the captain wanted to trade in certain locations and

---

[19] David Nitschmann to New-Herrnhut. Copenhagen, 27 March 1742: 'Ich habe es gewagt und bin beym König deßwegen mit einem Memorial eingekommen und das Lämmlein hat mir die Freude gemacht, daß es wohl ausgefallen ist, wie ihr geliebtes Geschwister durch die hierbey folgende Abschriften von der königlichen Resolution ersehen könnet.' ('I risked it and have therefore reached the king through a petition, and the Lambkin has given me the pleasure of a successful outcome, as you dear members will see in the enclosed copy of the royal resolution'). UA R.15.J.a.3. 20.
[20] See Grassmann's visitation report, 29 June, and also a letter by Stach to Praetorius, UA R.15.J.a.4.10. Matthäus Stach to Praetorius concerning Severin's suggestion, 2 May 1742.
[21] The Moravian Brethren had earlier, in 1733, accepted an offer to work as overseers on the Danish Lord Chamberlain Carl Adolf von Plessen's plantations in St Croix, where they assumed they would lay the ground for future missionary work. This ended up being a small disaster with enormous loss of lives and little spiritual outcome. I mentioned this briefly in the previous chapter. Plessen wanted Moravian men, because they would be good Christian people ('12 Christliche, fromme, vernünftige, wohlgesetzte Persohnen'), Pro Memoria des Ober-Kammerherrn von Plessen wegen Ansiedlung der Brüder auf St. Crux (UA R.15.B.a.3.3). Partially printed in Oldendorp, *Historie der caribischen Inseln*, 2/1: 70–1.
[22] Zinzendorf's close helper August Gottlieb Spangenberg had connections with the Suriname Society and a very good friend in Isaac Lelong. Louise Sebro, 'Mellem mange Verdner: Netværk, vækkelse og transnationale forbindelser i det Atlantiske rum i begyndelsen af 1700 Tallet', *Temp - Tidsskrift for Historie* 10/20 (2020): 139–59, here 151–5.

how around 100 Kalaallit came on board to trade their products.[23] The Dutch and English provided stiff competition for Severin, and the establishment of the various settlements up and down the coast was undertaken primarily to limit the access of the Dutch and the English to the Kalaallit. The danger of the Moravian-Dutch connections is noted in a 1750 letter from the king, Frederik V (1746–66), to the General Trading Company which held monopoly and charter to trade in Greenland (1750–74). The complaint was, yet again, that of transportation and cost, and the king then points out that if the brothers and their baggage and provisions could not be taken on board one ship, they would use their Dutch connections to obtain passage. While the ostensible purpose was to ship the brethren and their provisions to Greenland, the complaint was that this gave the Dutch shipper an excuse to trade with the Kalaallit, which cut into the profits of the General Trading Company.[24]

While the Moravians eventually procured their own ships to transport goods to the mission in Labrador,[25] the *octroy* in Greenland belonged exclusively to the Greenlandic trading companies (see note 5), and so the Moravians were continually reliant on other ships for freight. But the problem seems to have resolved itself in the 1770s,[26] where the issue of grievance changed from passage to that of settlement – to which we return shortly.

In spite of these issues, the Trade was not completely dismissive of the Moravians, especially during the time of head merchant, Lars Dalager, who held the post in Godthaab between 1754 and 1767. His close relationship with and appreciation of the industriousness of the Moravians brought him into conflict with the Danish mission, and after fisticuffs with the missionary Bjørn at the settlement, Dalager was removed from service in Greenland.[27] This ongoing conflict (in which the Moravians were very reluctant to get involved[28]) laid bare

---

[23] Grassmann's visitation report, 11–12 and 18 May. UA R.15.J.a.4.10.
[24] Rescript Friedrich V. an die octroyierte Handels-Compagnie in Kopenhagen, 13 February 1750: 'und wenn es nicht thulich gewesen, daß man hier ihre Provision und Geräthschaft mitnehmen können, weil sie sich nicht gemeldet, ehe die Schiffe zu geladen und seegelfertig gewesen, sollen sie sogar durch Brüder an andern Orten von Holland aus Schiffe befrachtet haben, welche unterm Schein, ihnen Lebens-mittel und andere Sachen zuzuführen, würcklich gedienet Handlung mit den Grönländern zum Nachtheil und Schaden der Octroy zu treiben.' UA R.15.J.a.12, 1.
[25] See list of Moravian ships in Hutton, *A History of Moravian Missions*, 801–2.
[26] See the pile of receipts, containing the name of the ship, captain, items shipped and place of delivery from 1770 through to 1880 in UA R.15.J.b.4.
[27] H. Ostermann, *Lars Dalager* in *Dansk Biografisk Leksikon* på lex.dk. Accessed 30 July 2022 at https://biografiskleksikon.lex.dk/Lars_Dalager. Finn Gad, *Grønlands Historie II* (Kbh.: Nyt Nordisk Forlag, 1969). 450–1.
[28] Letter from Inner Council to the missionaries in New-Herrnhut and Lichtenfels, 24 February 1763: it is asked that may the Saviour give them the wisdom to treat 'Hr Dallager' right. 'He has served the cause of the Savior a lot, for which the Savior will reward him, but he is to be treated with much caution' ('Insonderheit gebe euch der Heiland Weisheit, den Herrn Dallager recht zu behandeln.

the success of the Moravian mission and its production capacities,[29] as well as the depleted status of the mission at the colony itself. This led to the Missionary College in Copenhagen initiating a plan to reshape the mission in Godthaab, and in 1767 asked the Moravians to document its privileges and rights to evangelize in Greenland.[30] The particular events and correspondence in this matter are not clear, but the outcome was determined by events in Denmark, where the Hallensian doctor Johann Friedrich Struensee became de facto regent between December 1770 and January 1772. One of the many changes that took place during his brief government was the approval of the Moravians to operate freely in the Danish realm.[31] This new concession gave the Unity a very firm footing over against the Danish mission in Greenland and the Missionary College in Copenhagen.[32]

The question of settlement

In spite of individual merchants appreciation for the Moravian mission, the Moravian settlements and the concentration of Kalaallit had been a bugbear to the Danish-Norwegian trade and its desire to have the population spread out

---

Er hat der Sache des Heilands viel gedient, davor ihn der Heiland lohnen wolle, aber er ist mit vieler Vorsicht zu tractiren'). UA R.15.J.b.I.26a, 34. See also the diary 1765, 14 February, where a note had been sent to Dalager in reference to a 'strong visit from the settlement's Greenlanders', which was discussed at a meeting. In response to this, Missionary Bjørn had sent them a long letter the following day, to which they responded: 'what we wrote to Mister Dalager was to protect our Greenlanders, not to engage in polemics with Herr Bjørn. Adieu' ('daß, was wir an Monsieur Dalager geschrieben, ist geschehen um unsre Grönländer zu conserviren, nicht aber uns mit Herr Biorn in Streitschriften einzulaßen. Adieu.'). UA R.15.J.b.I.2.a, 14–15 February 1765. I have not been able to ascertain what happened during this visit. See UA R.15.J.a.3.b-c for correspondence with the Missionary College in Copenhagen regarding accusations levelled at the Moravians by Missionary Bjørn and their response.

[29] In the annual letter from the Inner Council, they note: 'We know that you have managed much in this respect [i.e. keeping the Kalaallit industrious] and therefore that our congregations also have a good name with the Company; keep to this, and even more so, that it remains so and constantly improves' (('Wir wissen, daß von euch darinnen sehr viel praestirt worden und unsere Gemeinen deshalben auch bey der Compagnie einen guten Namen haben; haltet daher ja drüber daß es in diesem Gange bleibe und immer besser werde.'). Letter from Inner Council to the missionaries in New-Herrnhut and Lichtenfels, 24 February 1763. UA R.15.J.b.I.26a, 34.

[30] This is known as 'Privilegiestriden', the conflict over privileges. See Gad, Grønlands Historie II, 464–5. See the extant correspondence in UA R.15.J.a.17.

[31] The edicts banning travel to and from Herrnhut were rescinded, Moravians were granted full and exclusive oversight over their own congregations and missions in Denmark, the duchies, and the colonies by their own bishop and a Moravian settlement, Christiansfeld, was established in Denmark. Gad, Grønlands Historie II, 465. The new edict is printed (in Danish) in Louis Bobé, Diplomatarium Groenlandicum 1492-1814. Aktstykker og Breve til Oplysning om Grønlands Besejling, Kolonisation og Missionering, vol. 55/3, Meddelser Om Grønland (København: C.A. Reitzels Forlag, 1936), 339–40.

[32] Struensee was overthrown in January 1772 and the Mission Deputation in Barby did contemplate whether this would have repercussions for the new concession. See the Minutes of the Mission Deputation, 25 February 1772, UA R.15. A.65.53.

rather than concentrated.[33] In his 1775 report to the Unity,[34] Christoph Micheal Königseer, leader of the mission in Greenland, noted that there was a serious matter on the horizon, namely that of 'distributing the Greenlanders in small clusters throughout the country for the best of trade'. Königseer questions the extent to which it is damaging for the Trade to have the Moravian congregation living together during winter, 'because if the balance is drawn from what the colonists scattered here and there acquire, and what our brothers who live together acquire, the sum of the blubber of our brothers always exceeds that of the colonists'. Nevertheless, it seems that there has been put forth a proposal to disperse the congregations, and Königseer points out that this would be a very worrying development, since the Moravian mission does not have the infrastructure to organize themselves like the Danish missionaries, 'who have a part of their congregation in one place, and a part in another, and supplies them with a catechist, who is there for them, and teaches them, and the priest visits them once or a couple of times a year'. This is not a model the Moravians are able to follow.[35]

In the previous year, 1774, the Danish state had taken over the trade and established the Royal Greenlandic Trade (*Den Kongelige Grønlandske Handel*, KGH), and were interested in spreading out the Kalaallit population away from the centres – as Königseer had reported. The head merchant, Raun, had been conferring with the Danish mission as to this purpose and had also in 1775 approached the Moravian missionaries in Lichtenfels. Here he had received the answer that the missionaries were not their own masters and thus could not possibly comply with this request without receiving the order from the leadership in 'Teutschland'.[36] This response generated an escalation of events that took the Unity by surprise.

---

[33] Heinz Israel has documented the various settlements of the Kalaallit and their populations. Israel *Kulturwandel*, 60-66 and the appendices 1-3 (179–88).
[34] Annual reports from Greenland, UA R.15.J.b1, 1775.
[35] Nevertheless, once this threat became reality, this was the pattern they would follow. At Karosuk, for example, there was a helper named Daniel. Diary, New-Herrnhut, Greenland UA R.15.J.b.I.3.a, 18 December 1784.
[36] The document containing this explanation of events is from 10 May 1777 and is contained within a copy of another letter, namely UAC to Königseer, 24 March 1777 (UA R.15.J.b.26.a.110). The precise wording is: 'so wäre es ihnen doch für die Zeit nicht möglich weil diejenigen, die die evangelischen Brüdermissionen hierzulande besorgen, nicht so völlig ihre eigene Herren wären, daß sie eine beträchtliche Veränderung fürnehmen könte ohne Anfrage und dazu nöthige Ordre von ihrer Haupt-direction in Teutschland' (it would not be possible for them for the time being because those who are missionaries from the evangelical Brethren-mission here, are not so much their own masters that they could undertake a considerable change without request and the necessary order from their main direction in Germany).

Since the Trade was no longer in the hands of semi-private trading companies and middling merchants, but now under the direct management of the state, this response was seen as a refusal to comply with the order of the king and thus a refusal of the sovereignty of the majesty. Koeber, whom we discussed in previous chapters, was put to the test in exercising all his diplomatic skills to resolve the situation. He explained that this was not the intended meaning of the response, but that it merely meant that the missionaries wanted to ensure whether the significant expenses involved could be covered by the Unity. Koeber also delicately reminds Lorenz Praetorius, councillor to the king and the highest-ranking Moravian in Copenhagen, that the Moravians are working in Greenland at their own expense. After explaining the practical and financial nature of the communications between the leadership in Saxony and the missions in Greenland, Koeber goes on to say that it could never be questioned whether the Moravian missionaries in Greenland want to be subject to the orders of the highest king because this is 'self-evident according to the teaching of Jesus and his apostles, which is the sole norm in the teaching and life of the United Brethren'.[37] Consequently, no one can be a member of the Moravian Brethren, much less a servant thereof, who does not recognize this essential Christian duty and does not want to fulfil it with all his heart. Koeber emphasizes that the missionaries are subjects of the king and submit themselves to the highest royal commands in the strictest obedience, not only out of necessity but out of conscience.

> If, according to the King's Majesty as sovereign of Greenland, for the good of the state and with the greatest interest of the trade, it is commanded that the baptized Greenlanders should be distributed to their previous hunting grounds, then the missionaries are bound as the most loyal subjects, to help put this highest will into action with all possible faithfulness and diligence.[38]

In equilibrist and subservient prose, Koeber ensures that the Moravians (United Brethren) are in fact loyal subjects to the Danish king not only because they have to but because their conscience demands it. This can never be called into question.[39] Koeber emphasizes that if the king has decided that this plan of

---

[37] Memorandum from Friedrich Koeber to Preatorius, Barby, 12 May 1777. UA R.15.J.a.17, 7.
[38] Memorandum from Friedrich Koeber to Preatorius, Barby, 12 May 1777 'Wenn solchem nach des Königs Majestät als Souverain von Grönland zum Besten des Staats und höchst dero Handlungs-Intresse befehlen, daß die getauften Grönländer auf ihre vorherigen Erwerbungs-Pläze vertheilet werden sollen, so sind die Mißionarien als treugehorsamste Unterthanen verbunden, diese allerhöchste Willensmeynung mit aller nur möglichen Treue und Sorgfalt pflichtschuldigst ins Werck sezen zu helfen.' UA R.15.J.a.17, 7. 7.
[39] The nature of this obedience and loyalty to the king as an essential Christian duty and the sole norm of the Moravians most likely refers to Paul's letter to the Romans, chapter 13, a letter which has served many authorities well. Romans 13:1-7 states that every person should be subject to the governing

dispersing the baptized Kalaallit to their former hunting grounds is of interest to the state and trade, then the Moravians will put in all efforts to help realize this plan. The suspicion of disobedience to the absolute monarch was thus averted.

After 1777 the Moravian Kalaallit were spread out on a range of different outposts.[40] As the minutes from the house-meeting demonstrates, the missionaries planned and executed visits to the outposts, primarily Kangeq, Kokörn, Kellingarsuk.[41]

Further restrictions

Another change that took the Moravian missionaries by surprise was the aforementioned *Instruction of 1782*. In 1783, the diary notes that Brothers Beck and Möhne went to the settlement to sort out a matter with the inspector at Godthaab, because one of the Kalaallit converts, Thomas, had gone out sealhunting, and the missionaries had given him a shotgun to see if he could obtain something for their sustenance. This was, according to the merchant at Godthaab, against the *Instruction*. The diary notes that 'we already have [the Instruction] in Danish, but don't understand [it] adequately'. They received a reprimand and were informed they would be served with a fine and summoned for an interrogation.[42] This occurred on 10 February 1783, when Beck and Möhne were summoned early in the morning. They were instructed to bring Thomas with them. In the presence of the governor, the deputy factor and the assistant, Thomas was presented with fifteen questions which he answered boldly, was given a piece of tobacco and two rusks, and sent on his way. The missionaries were charged with a fine of 4 Danish Rigsdaler. On 14 March, the inspector paid them a visit and presented the *Instruction* in Danish and German, which they were to copy. On 17 March in their evening study hour, they then familiarized themselves with this document.

---

authorities, because this authority is ultimately from God. Hence, any resistance to this authority is a resistance to God. This letter is one of the central documents in Lutheran Protestantism and the particular passage a crucial one in cementing the power of the absolute monarch in Denmark. Christina Petterson, 'En Konge i sin Faders Sted – bibel og konge i den danske enevælde', in *Bibelske Genskrivninger*, ed. Jesper Høgenhaven and Mogens Müller, Forum for Bibelsk Eksegese, vol. 17 (København: Museum Tusculanum, 2012), 413–34. Romans 13 does present challenges for Lutheran Christians and fascist state authority, for example Hitler. See, for example, James W. Voelz, 'A Self-Conscious Reader-Response Interpretation of Romans 13:1–7', in *The Personal Voice in Biblical Interpretation*, ed. Ingrid Rosa Kitzberger (London: Routledge, 1998).

[40] Israel, *Kulturwandel*, 179.
[41] See, for example, Minutes from house-meeting, 15 November and 6 December 1779, 24 April 1780. UA R.15.J.b.I.18. See also the report on the group at Kangeq, which is included in the diary from 1784, UA R.15.J.b.I.3.a, 9 November 1784.
[42] Diary, New-Herrnhut, Greenland, 5 February 1783. UA R.15.J.b.I.3.a

What happened here was that while they had presumably done as they had always done, the circumstances had changed. Lending a gun to Thomas was against the *Instruction of 1782*, Item 3, paragraph 6, where it is stated:

> With regard to shooting, everyone shall observe that it is not allowed to hand out guns, powder or lead to the Greenlanders either at or outside the facilities of the Royal Greenland Trading Department with the purpose of shooting foxes or other game, in such a manner, as is said to have been rife in the past, that the person who makes this loan to the Greenlanders stands to benefit from it. Anyone violating this is to be fined 2 to 10 Ridgsdaler or more, depending on the circumstances.[43]

The interrogation in front of senior civil servants at the colonial settlement also testifies to the intensification of power, expansion of jurisdiction and the implementation of the right to adjudicate over the behaviour of Kalaallit (and Moravians) outside the boundaries of the settlement. This is also apparent in August 1783, when the deputy factor and the assistant arrived at New-Herrnhut and seized the items that the missionaries used to trade with Kalaallit for their own sustenance, proclaiming them to be 'articles of trade',[44] and included tobacco, (gun) powder, arrow-iron, knives, fish-hooks, thimbles, needles, flint and women's knives (sg. *ulo*, pl. *uluit*).[45] In a letter to the Mission Deputation from 1783, the missionaries explain that the value of said articles would be given them as credit in the store, so that they could buy things there.[46] Simply put, the KGH had enforced a complete monopoly of the Trade and any direct barter between the Kalaallit and the Moravians was forbidden, and henceforth replaced by direct value in the form of credit.[47]

---

[43] The English translation of the *Instruction* is taken from Inge Seiding, '"Married to the Daughters of the Country": Intermarriage and Intimacy in Northwest Greenland ca. 1750 to 1850', unpublished PhD thesis, Ilisimatusarfik – University of Greenland, December 2012, appendix, 7.

[44] Israel, *Kulturwandel*, 84 and 152, note 805. Declaring something as article of trade was claiming it as the property of the KGH, as per the *Instruction*, item 4, §4: 'No one, whoever it is, whether he be in the service of the Royal Greenland Trading Department or of the mission, and whether he be married or unmarried, may buy from the Greenlanders or procure for himself through illicit trade (far less send home or sell to own or foreign ships under any sort of pretext) blubber, train oil, baleens, the skin of bears, reindeer, seals or foxes, unicorn horn [narwhal tusks], walrus tusks, eiderdown or any other article that is the property of the Royal Greenland Trading Department.' Seiding, '"Married to the Daughters of the Country"', appendix, 6.

[45] Letter from New-Herrnhut to Mission Deputation, 16 July 1783. UA R.15.J.b.I.24. Womens' knives is the particular tool used by women, for example to scrape sealskin, but also to cut open and part whale and seal.

[46] The general taxation document according to which value was determined is in UA MDF 1890, along with the receipt of seized goods from Lichtenfels.

[47] Money was not introduced in Greenland until Finn Gad, *Grønlands Historie III. 1782-1808* (København: Nyt Nordisk Forlag, 1786), 480–9.

Sustaining Moravian activities

This stranglehold of the colonial powers on the economic development of Greenland posed a challenge to the Moravians in that the available resources were often scarce. For many years, the question was always how to sustain themselves,[48] but closely following upon this was the question of how to pay for some of the provisions they received from Europe.[49] Already from an early stage, the missionaries were urged to look for ways in which they could sustain themselves through the work of their own hands, but the missionaries repeatedly explained how difficult this was in Greenland. In an assessment of the ways to support themselves in Greenland and the limitations concerning labour, it is stated that the only viable path of work is in trade, which would work only if they had the rights to a piece of land on which they would have the right to trade.[50] As we saw earlier, in their ongoing attempts to monopolize the trade the colonial powers kept expanding the number of items that counted as 'articles of trade'. All of these were to be collected only by the merchants at the Danish settlements in Christianshaab and Godthaab, who went on expeditions to buy up blubber, baleens and skins along the coast, and then sent them to Denmark by ship.[51] Thus, any large-scale trading by the Moravians was made impossible by the colonial powers.

In 1751, Johannes von Watteville arrived on a visitation of the Greenlandic mission and upon his departure left a farewell letter to the missionaries, where he admonishes the members to be frugal, and understands that the Danish trade regulations prohibit the missionaries from sending products to Europe

---

[48] In the early days, the missionaries relied on food gifts, such as reindeer and seal, from the Danish missionaries and the Kalaallit, supplies and occasional gifts from benefactors in Europe and whatever they could make as day-labourers, such as working as carpenters at the Danish colonies. See Christina Petterson, 'From Communal Economy to Economic Community: Changes in Moravian Entrepreneurial Activities in the Eighteenth Century', *Journal for the History of Reformed Pietism* 3, no. 1 (2018): 25–48 for more detail.

[49] Already in 1733, spinning was mentioned, and an account page from 1742 shows that the finished product was accounted in Herrnhut as an income, thus functioning as payment. UA.R.15. R.15.J.b.I. 32, 5. It is noted that in 1742 they had produced 13 pounds of flax and 37 pounds of tow. In Petterson, I mistakenly assumed that it was sold back to Herrnhut, but I am now convinced it was sent back as payment for supplies.

[50] Document on work and nourishment, 15 November 1741. UA.R.15.J.a.11.1,1. This is mentioned again in a letter from New-Herrnhut to the Missions Department, 16 July 1783. UA R.15.J.b.I.24.b.

[51] See Diary, New-Herrnhut, Greenland, 20 April 1745, where Joachim from the colony tells the missionaries about his *Handels-tocht*, his trading expedition. *Tocht* could be a Germanification of the Danish *togt*. 25 November 1747, we hear of Andreas' trip to buy up blubber, only because he had been gone for four weeks, and Paul, the merchant from the colony, asked the brothers whether any of their Kalaallit could go searching for him in their kayaks. UA R.15.J.b.I.01.b.

as payment for their provisions. Watteville emphasizes that it is absolutely necessary to obey royal orders and not engage in illicit trading. He continues, 'now that I have seen the circumstances myself, I do not know what you could possibly send us, other than if you get a little more [eider]down than your house needs. In the meantime, be assured that as long as we have bread in Europe, we will also not fail to send you what you need.'[52]

This shows us that while the missionaries did receive some provisions from Europe, it was expected that they pay for it, so as not to be an unnecessary burden on the small funds collected to support the missions (the *Diaconie*). However, as Watteville now has seen and understood, the monopoly of the trade makes this difficult, because the Moravians were not allowed to trade with the Kalaallit in monopolized goods. This left only eiderdown as a possible commodity, which they themselves needed for warmth in their household.

The question of scarce resources and reimbursement was a frequently recurring topic, and in the annual letter from the Inner Council in 1763, we see that no topic is small enough for attention. The council emphasizes that the Mission Deputation will take care of necessary expenses, but that they also in this case expect the missionaries to 'act according to Jesus' heart and try to spare the *Heidendiakonie* all unnecessary expenses'.[53] They offer three suggestions as to saving on undue expenses. The first is that the maids employed by the missionaries should work as maids for the whole house instead of serving each family (except in the case of a missionary woman with an infant). The second concerns whether the expense of keeping chickens rather outweigh the benefits. Of added concern is that the chickens' running around 'and all the other circumstances occurring there would not be edifying, even outrageous, for the Greenlandic children'. Third, the experimentation with sheep seems to be successful and should be pursued. The council approves the creation of meadows and employment of Kalaallit Sisters at 3-4 Reichsthaler to mind the sheep. 'Also, do not forget to make good use of the wool. Even if you initially only process it into stockings for your house (maybe some Greenlanders can learn spinning and knitting) this will also spare the *Heiden-Diaconie* an expense.' This testifies

---

[52] Johannes von Watteville's farewell letter after his visitation, 3 August 1752: '8. [...] Nachdem ich mir nun die Umstände selber angesehen habe, so weiß ich nicht, was ihr uns etwa wieder schicken köntet, als wenn ihr etwas mehr Duun krieget als eure Haus nöthig hat. Indeß seyd versichert, daß solange wir in Europa Brot haben, wir auch nicht unterlaßen wollen, euch das Nöthige zu schicken.' UA R.15.J.a.9.21.
[53] Letter from Inner Council to the missionaries in New-Herrnhut and Lichtenfels, 24 February 1763: 'daß ihr auch in dem Theil werdet nach Jesu Herzen handeln, und der Heiden-Diaconie alle unnöthige Ausgaben zu ersparen suchen'. UA R.15.J.b.I.26a, 34.

to the level of detailed management in Herrnhut and the missionaries were thus trusted to put an effort into saving the Diaconie every possible penny and to be as careful and thrifty as possible. Nevertheless, the UAC did not cease to explore options for an income that would make the Greenlandic mission self-sufficient. To this end, Sternberg was presented in 1771 with a number of questions to clarify some of the intricate rules for trade:

> We would like to have more clarification on a matter relating to the trade in eiderdown, fox skins, and the like. Can a Danish skipper buy something from the brothers at his own expense? Has the company given him certain freedom to publicly unload for himself in Copenhagen? Or, must everything be sold to the merchant? What price do the Danes allow or give to the European brothers for the goods they procure with their bows and arrows? And what is the situation with lending arrows and projectiles to the Greenlanders? Does the company allow the brothers to do so? On what condition is it allowed? Or was it done under unauthorized pretexts? Now, assuming that the Oeconomie has such products; may it send them to Copenhagen for sale? May everyone do this when he has shot the foxes and collected the eiderdown? May he say, I had them shot with my arrow or my powder and lead and so on? We know that they can send their sheepskins and wool at their own expense. What concerns articles of trade, however, it is so difficult to understand the actual matter from everything one hears. At most it seems that a brother can sell and send out what he has acquired with his gun and hands.[54]

This bewilderment at the numerous and constantly changing rules and regulations is understandable, but the UAC does not seem to have been granted much clarity on the issue. Furthermore, once the trade shifted to the hands of the Royal Greenlandic Trade in 1774, utmost care had to be taken to balance

---

[54] UAC to Martin Gottfried Sternberg, 30 March 1771: 'Eine Materie betreffend den Handel mit Eiderdawn, Fuchsfellen, und dergleichen möchten wir gern mehr in Klarem haben. Darf ein dänischer Schiffer vor seine Rechnung den Brüdern was abkaufen? Ist ihm von der Compagnie ein gewißes, so er öffentlich für sich ausschiffen darf in Copenhagen, freygegeben? Oder muß alles an den Kaufmann verkauft werden? Was für einen Preis erlauben oder geben die Dänen den europäischen Brüdern für die Waare, die sie mit ihrem Pfeil und Bogen erwerben? Wie ist es aber eigentlich beschaffen mit dem Pfeil und Geschoß Borgen an die Grönländer? Ist das unsern Brüdern von der Compagnie vergönnt? Auf was Bedingung ists ihnen vergönnt? Oder geschiehet es unter unerlaubten Prætexten? Gesetzt nun, die Oeconomie hat dergleichen Producte; darf sie solche zum Verkauf nach Copenhagen schicken? Darf es ein jeder thun, wenn er die Füchse geschoßen, die Eiderdawn Federn gesammelt hat? Darf er sagen, "Die habe ich mit meinem Pfeil oder mit meinem Pulver und Bley schießen laßen" usw? Daß sie ihre Schaaf-Felle und Wolle vor ihre Rechnung heruasschicken können, daß wißen wir. Handelguth aber, davon ist so schwehr das Eigentlichen aus allem, was man hört, zu verstehen. Höchstens will uns vorkommen, kan ein Bruder das verkauffen und herausschicken, was er mit seiner Flinte und Händen erworben hat.' UA R.15.J.a.18.a.7.

evenly between paying Kalaallit for their services while avoiding suspicion of illicit trade, as indicated in the instructions to the missionaries who were sent out on a reconnaissance trip to find a site for the third Moravian settlement. Here, Königseer admonishes:

> If they [the Kalaallit] do something for you, pay them in an appropriate way. Especially, dear brothers and sisters, please take care that the trading company does not cast suspicion on you, that you are engaged in an illicit trade with them [Kalaallit]. You know the royal regulation, and you also know that the UAC directs you according thereto.[55]

As mentioned earlier, the *Instruction* of *1782* had repercussions for the Moravians in relation to their practices and barter with the Kalaallit. After the *Instruction*, eiderdown now joined the list of banned items. The missionaries complain about the increased restrictions in a letter to the leadership in Europe[56] and note how they are hardly allowed to acquire items for their sustenance through Kalaallit, which is a problem because they themselves cannot reach the places where this acquisition is possible.[57] Eider birds cannot be shot, because they fall into the water and the missionaries need Kalaallit in kayaks to pick up the birds. This is no longer permissible, because 'good Greenlanders' are to go hunting, and 'bad Greenlanders' cannot be sent out, because they might drown. Furthermore, they are not allowed to procure fur or blubber directly from the Kalaallit, but have to purchase this via the account at the Danish settlement, which means that there is a problem with clothing, since furs and pelts are required. Blubber was an issue – especially in the large choir houses – because it was used for heating and light. Finally, the limitations of the *Instruction* meant that exchange interactions were completely abstracted, with the Danish-Norwegian colonial powers as the mediator.

Barter, the exchange of one item with another, was the exchange mode between Kalaallit and the Moravians. A note from 1783 shows what items were used for payment in the process of direct exchange: 7 ½ ells of tobacco,

---

[55] Annual reports from Greenland, 30 May 1774, pkt 15. UA.R.15.J.b1, 1774: '[...] und wenn sie euch was thun, bezahlt sie auf eine billige Weise. Besonders, liebe Geschwister, bitte ich, nehmt euch in Acht, daß die Handlungs Compagnie nicht einen Verdacht auf euch wirft, als ob ihr einen unerlaubten Handel mit ihnen triebet. Ihr wißt die Königlichen Verordnungen, ihr wißt auch der UAC ihren Sinn. Darnach richtet euch.'

[56] Letter from Elders' Conference, New-Herrnhut to the Mission Deputation, 16 July 1783. UA R.15.J.b.I.24a.

[57] They did manage eventually, because on 18–19 November 1784, they went birdhunting and managed to shoot more than thirty. Diary, New-Herrnhut, Greenland, 18–19 November 1784. UA R.15.J.b.I.3.a.

Figure 7 This note from 1783 shows the items used for payment in the process of barter: for turf work: 15 ells of tobacco and 1 knife; for the fish, 1 roll, 14 ells, for the mail kayaks: 7 ½ ells of tobacco, 13 arrows, 5 knives and 9 loths of gunpowder; for [eider?] down and eggs: 6 ells and 4 inches of tobacco and 3 arrows; for seal meat for our housemaids: 1 roll and 3 ells of tobacco, 2 knives and 6 arrows; expenditure for grass: 7 ells, 7 inches; expenditure for wood, 4 [1] ells of tobacco, 4 arrows. The Napparsok load with 4 women's boats, along with their payment 1 roll of tobacco, 5 knives; as a present for the boatsman and the helmsman for bringing along our provisions, for foxes: 8 ells, 4 inches tobacco, 2 knives, 2 arrows. MDF 1890, 16 June 1780. Reproduced with permission from the Unity Archives, Herrnhut.

13 arrows, 5 knives and 9 loths of gunpowder for the mail kayaks; 6 ells and 4 inches of tobacco and 3 arrows for [eider?] down and eggs; 1 roll and 3 ells of tobacco, 2 knives and 6 arrows for seal meat for their housemaid (Figure 7).[58]

---

[58] Note on expenses. UA MDF 1890, 16 June 1780.

'Tobacco is money in Greenland' (*tabak hier daß Geld ist*),[59] more specifically Dutch tobacco (*hollandischer tabak*). And the Moravians used, as mentioned earlier, tobacco and other small items, such as arrowheads and knives, to pay for services and produce, both within their communities and outside. Despite the fact that barter as such assumes an understanding of value,[60] it nevertheless meant a direct interaction of exchange and as such, social interaction. When this activity was forbidden by the trading company, which redirected all exchange through their store and a credit system, this meant that their determination of value became fixed and that the store became the mediator of exchange between the Moravians and the Kalaallit – even those who were part of the Moravian community. This was an agreement between KGH and the Moravians, who in exchange for free transportation agreed to relinquish their bartering practice and commence trading with Kalaallit through the Trade and its store.[61] However, there seems to be an indication that these rules were either relaxed or the Moravians found a way to surreptitiously barter, because in the 1814 diary there is mention of small-scale barter of a couple of eider birds and murrelets for some tobacco.[62]

The command to disperse and the *Instruction of 1782* had far-reaching consequences for the Moravians' room to move as well as their relation to the Kalaallit. The gradual tightening of the colonial trade made inroads into the communal fellowship in New-Herrnhut. Their close-knit community was dispersed, and the social interaction of exchange was fully abstracted and placed at the settlement of Godthaab.

I have provided a reasonable amount of detail concerning the social and economic context in which the Moravian mission functioned in Greenland.

---

[59] Jakob Beck to the Mission Deputation, 16 September 1782. UA MDF.1890. Israel also has a number of examples, Israel *Kulturwandel*, 89–90, as well as an appendix listing the tobacco expenditures of 1797. Appendix 7, 194–8.

[60] See, for example, the minutes from the house and business meeting, 18 April 1781, where missionary Meyer assessed the relative value between malt and lead to determine that the Moravians would get the correct amount of lead for the malt they lent to the merchant at the colony. UA R.15.J.b.I.18. The notion of barter was proposed by Adam Smith to have been the natural proclivity of humanity and a trait which led him to argue for the natural tendency in humanity for a market economy. However, as argued by David Graeber, Smith's 'Natives' who engaged in this supposed ubiquitous activity were actually fictitious, and barter, rather than being an ancient practice, is a modern one, based on the assumption of value and thus of money. David Graeber, *Debt: The First 5,000 Years* (Brooklyn: Melville House, 2011), chapter 2, esp. 37–8.

[61] Gad, *Grønlands Historie III. 1782-1808*, 42. Diary, New-Herrnhut, Greenland, notes that on 28 September 1784, the missionaries go to the settlement to pick up some things from the store. On 25 October, the merchant arrived at New-Herrnhut to buy up the blubber from the Greenlanders there, and of the 7 5/16 barrels he procured, the missionaries bought two of them from him. He also came down on 20 November. UA R.15.J.b.I.3.a.

[62] See Diary, New-Herrnhut, Greenland, 14 February and 24 March. UA R.15.J.b.I.04.a.

Apart from the intrinsic interest of this archival material, it shows very clearly that there was – due to the stranglehold of Danish colonial control – simply no room at all to develop an 'outer' sphere, an 'outer' Oeconomie. It was not even possible to do so for the sake of supporting the mission, let alone developing one that was remotely comparable to the Danish West Indies. By now, we can see that the social and economic conditions of the Greenland mission were completely different. It should not be a surprise that they focused on developing the 'inner' sphere.

7

Developing the 'inner sphere'

As discussed in Chapter 4, the 1764 Marienborn Synod had highlighted the Kalaallit mission as a stellar example of settlements based on the segregation of sexes, common childcare and a members-only settlement policy. In a subsequent discussion on the fruitfulness of evangelization in settled congregations, Greenland was also mentioned as a positive example: 'In Greenland there can be no doubt as to the settlement, it can and must be so, and since the Greenlanders in settling remain in their way of life, and excel therein, it encourages the spread of the gospel.'[1]

The question regarding whether the Kalaallit remained in their way of life by settling around the Moravian missions was discussed in the 1960s by Heinz Israel in his short but dense study on the cultural change of the Kalaallit in the eighteenth century.[2] He concluded that while the settlement itself certainly was a change in the Greenlandic way of life, the choir system did offer a counterbalance to the corroding influence of colonialism and its exploitative practices. This chapter, while building upon Israel's analysis, is less focused on the changes in Kalaallit social structures and cultural practices, and rather looks to understanding the close interaction between the missionaries and the Kalaallit in the settlement, and the role of the European leadership in the management of the mission. We begin with the magnificent mission station at New-Herrnhut (*Neuherrnhut*, in Kalaallisut *Noorliit*) which was inaugurated on 16 October 1747 (see Figure 6). Built with wood gifted and shipped from Europe and assembled by Christian David, the building testified not only to the

---

[1] Minutes from the Marienborn Synod, session XII: 'In Grönland kann man über das Zusammen ziehen kein Dubium machen, da kann und muß es seyn, und da die Grönländer beym Zusammenziehen bey ihrer Lebens-Art bleiben, und darinnen excelliren, so beförderts die Ausbreitung des Evangeli.' UA R.2.B.44.1.c.1.
[2] Israel, *Kulturwandel*.

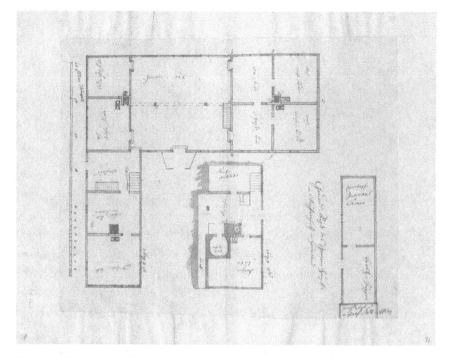

Figure 8 Floor plan of the mission station from 1750. UA TS 22.2, 'Grundriss des Gemeinhauses in Neu-Herrnhut in Grönland'. Reproduced with permission from the Unity Archives, Herrnhut.

success of the Moravians in Greenland but also to their connections and friends in Europe, especially in the Netherlands.[3]

The structure at New-Herrnhut was not a free-standing church. The very large building had an assembly room flanked by school rooms, residential units, kitchens, storehouses and so forth. This multi-purpose architectural style was a common feature of the Moravian *Saal*. Thus, the assembly hall of the first period in Moravian history (1724–60) was never a building unto itself but a part of the *Gemeinhaus*, 'the community house'.[4]

Figure 8 is a floor plan of the mission station from 1750.[5] The left wing of the L-shaped building is a two-storey structure, where the ground floor (placed in the middle, with shading) contains the kitchen area and stove. On the first floor

---

[3] At a presentation on slavery (by Jan Hüsgen) at the Völkerkundemuseum (Ethnological museum) in Herrnhut, a Surinamese visitor made a remark on the paucity of wood in the Netherlands and the import of wood from Suriname. It would thus be interesting to follow the wood in New-Herrnhut to see whether it in fact came from Suriname and not, as hitherto assumed, from the Netherlands.
[4] Wolf Marx, *Die Saalkirche der deutschen Brüdergemeine im 18. Jahrhundert* (Leipzig: Dieterichsche Verlagsbuchhandlung, 1931), 9.
[5] "'Grundriss des Gemeinhauses in Neuherrnhut in Grönland'", UA TS 22.2.

we find, beginning from the bottom, the room of the single brothers, the school room for the boys, an antechamber with a stairwell down to the kitchens. The main length of the building contains the assembly hall in the middle flanked by the married couple's parlour and the room for the single sisters on the left side, and, on the right side, three rooms for the married couples and a dining room. The free-standing structure to the right is divided into a European storage room, a wood shed, and the small room at the end is a goat stable and a workshop.

This integrated nature of worship and everyday life is a very significant point because it indicates an important aspect of Moravian Christianity, namely its emphasis on community. As mentioned in Chapter 1, Moravian theology manifests itself in actions and engagement within its congregations, in the structure of its community, as well as the relationship of the believer with the Saviour (the *Heiland*, the Lamb). As this building demonstrates, one's relationship to the Lamb was not confined to a certain space at a certain time but continued throughout the day, in the company of one's brothers and sisters. This is why the building as such contains more than a room for worship; it is a building of community. In the diary entry describing the day of the inauguration, Johann Beck emphasizes the function of the building as a place to 'cover us from snow, rain, and where to speak with one another from our hearts and the bloody wounds of the Lamb, and we asked the Lamb for a house where we could hold gatherings'.[6] This building model tells us much about how the Moravian missionary approach functioned in practice and its immense attraction for the Indigenous population of Greenland. It was a lived community and as such offered an alternative not only to the social structures of the Indigenous communities but also to the individualizing and abstracting Danish-Norwegian mission.

The settlement around New-Herrnhut was seasonal and followed the pattern of the Kalaallit hunting year. The Kalaallit members settled around New-Herrnhut in turf houses for the winter in early October[7] and broke up for the capelin gathering in early May.[8] During summer, the Kalaallit members lived in tents and travelled up and down the coast, occasionally dropping in at New-Herrnhut, and receiving visits from the missionaries. Contact was thus

---

[6] Diary, New-Herrnhut, Greenland, 16 October 1747: 'uns vor Schnee, Regen, und Kälte zu verbergen um uns miteinander zu besprechen von unsern Hertzen und des Lämmleins blutigen Wunden, und wir haben das Lamm gebeten um ein Haus, wo wir könten Versamlungen halten.' UA R.15.J.b.I.1b.

[7] Diary, New-Herrnhut, Greenland, 14–15 October 1747, 9 October 1748. UA R.15.J.b.I.1b.

[8] Diary, New-Herrnhut, Greenland, 23 and 29 May 1746, 13 May 1747; 5 May and 8 June 1748. UA R.15.J.b.I.01.b.

maintained over summer, but the winter-months were the time for regular communal activities and edification.

Community organization: Developing the 'inner' sphere

By community organization, I mean the internal structuring of the community and the relations to the Indigenous members. As indicated in the first chapters, the Moravian Brethren were a tightly structured organization. This was not present from day one but was a mode of organization that developed over decades. In particular, the introduction of the choir structure generated a range of organizational features, which enhanced the liturgical day. In Greenland the organization was, as indicated earlier, a compromise between the Kalaallit settlement patterns and the Moravian structures.

Choirs

As mentioned in Chapter 1, the choirs and choir houses were a very characteristic feature of Moravian settlements in Europe.[9] And while choirs as liturgical and pastoral organization were possible in most missions, choir houses and their communal dwelling were not. In slave congregations, for example, it was not possible, given that the slave quarters were on different plantations and included both converted and unconverted slaves. Consequently, as in St Thomas, the

---

[9] Heinz Israel notes that it would take fifteen years from the institutionalization of this choir system in Herrnhut to reach Greenland. Israel, *Kulturwandel*, 42–3. This assertion contains the popular assumption that the choir system began fifteen years earlier, that is, in 1730, when 'the young women united together into a "choir", the choir of the single sisters' (p. 41). Following Otto Uttendörfer's study into the economic life of Herrnhut (Uttendörfer, *Wirtschaftsgeist Herrnhuts*, 189), Israel states that up until now (1744), the choir structure had 'not exercised any cataclysmic effect on the social relations of Herrnhut' (p. 41) The problem with this narrative is that it rests upon a number of misconceptions. First, the 'Banden' and 'Gesellschaften' (groups and associations) of early Herrnhut (1727–40) were a highly different mode of organization than the choirs, as Gottfried Schmidt has shown in his analysis. Gottfried Schmidt, 'Die Banden oder Gesellschaften im alten Herrnhut', *Zeitschrift für Brüdergeschichte* III (1909): 145–207. One is voluntary and fluid (i.e. *Banden*) and the other is hierarchical and rigid (Choirs) (p. 204). Schmidt argues that 1736 was a turning point in the role of the Banden and that the use of the term declines from here, which is connected to the banishment of Zinzendorf from Saxony (p. 192). Israel cites Schmidt for the point on Zinzendorf's banishment. But where Schmidt is saying that the banishment meant a decline in the use of the Banden, Israel interprets it to mean that it meant the beginning of the use of the more common term 'choir'. Israel, *Kulturwandel*, 40. Nevertheless, as I have shown in my archival work at the Herrnhut diaries, the use of choir in any 'common' sense does not happen before 1742, and any consolidation in terms of overarching structure, symbolic value and commemorative days is not before 1744. I argue this in a larger monograph on Herrnhut and the choirs based on archival sources from 1740 to 1760. Petterson, *The Moravian Brethren in a Time of Transition*.

Developing the 'Inner Sphere' 155

model akin to that followed in the Moravian societies was more prevalent.[10] However, in Greenland the choir house became a fixed feature of winter settlements from 1749, when the single sister Judith Issek, one of a group of five Kalaallit who travelled to Europe in 1747, returned to New-Herrnhut. During her stay in Herrnhut, Judith had lived in the house of the single sisters and been part of the choir. After her return to Greenland in 1749, she wanted to introduce these concepts to the Kalaallit congregation and, on her initiative, the first choir house was built for the single sisters. The brothers' house was built in 1753 and, several years later, the widows' house (and then also older girls and older boys houses).[11]

The choir structure of the Moravians in Greenland has suffered under the misconception that it was a failure.[12] This assumes that just because the choir structure was eventually discontinued, it was a failure, but this overlooks the specific function and ideological consequences of the choir system, not only in the time of operation but also afterwards. The choir houses were given up in 1783 after thirty-four years,[13] after which the choir system as the organizational feature of the community continued until the general dissolution of the choir structure in the course of the nineteenth century.[14] Thus, the choir structure, and its social organization, was a central part of Moravian practice in Greenland for a century or so, where less than half was in actual settlements. And, as we will see, they did have long-term effects on Moravian missionary mentality and practice.

The pattern of living overlapped to *some* extent with traditional Kalaallit ways, in that it was regular for extended families and larger groups to live together, in order to share maintenance of equipment, hunt and the subsequent sharing,

---

[10] This is also the case in Suriname.
[11] Israel, *Kulturwandel*, 43–4.
[12] E. L. Jensen, K. Raahauge and H. C. Gulløv, *Kulturmøder ved Kap Farvel: De østgrønlandske indvandrere og den tyske Brødremission i det 19. Århundrede* (Museum Tusculanum Press, 2012), 90; Kleivan, 'Herrnhuterne eller Brødremenigheden i Grønland 1733-1900'; Wilhjelm, 'Menneske (inuk) først og kristen så?: en vinkel på missionshistorien i Vestgrønland', 3. Both Wilhjelm and Kleivan note, in passing, that the Moravians attempted to implement European-style choir houses in Greenland, but that these houses were quickly abandoned because of their massive disruption to the traditional way of life in Greenland (Kleivan) and problems relating to trade and sexual behaviour (Wihjelm). In another article on the surrender of the Moravian mission in Greenland in 1900, Wilhjelm more accurately notes that this practice was discontinued after 'some decades': Wilhjelm, *Brødremissionens overgivelse*, 207.
[13] Israel mentions that the Unity board early had reservations regarding the choir houses. The Kalaallit winterhouses, which provided the model for the Kalaallit choir house, were built to make the most of body heat. They were thus not big, and the Kalaallit slept closely together. It was estimated that six to eight barrels of blubber was needed to heat the large brothers' house, and in the end, the brothers and boys moved out of the choir house and into the family houses instead. Israel, *Kulturwandel*, 46–7.
[14] Israel, *Kulturwandel*, 47.

consuming and storage of game during winter.[15] The choirs, then, replaced the traditional community structures in hunting, gathering and fishing, and as such could be seen as an extension of the subsistence shared economy of the traditional Kalaallit. They also followed the seasonal pattern of the Kalaallit.[16] As in Europe, the choir houses in Greenland served as units of production, albeit production as understood on Kalaallit terms and bearing the character of subsistence survival. This is not only evident in the seasonal dwelling pattern but also in the hunting patterns. There are many examples of the Kalaallit brothers going out on seal hunts[17] and the Kalaallit brothers and sisters going out for ammassat (capelin) gathering every year.[18] The settlement of New-Herrnhut had a Kalaallit storage house for provisions in winter.

What did vary from traditional Kalaallit practice was that the houses were bigger than was the custom in Greenland, the winter settlements around the mission stations more populous, and the segregation of sexes – this latter issue being one that directly affected the Kalaallit hunting culture.

The question of the choir houses was raised in 1781, when Michael Königseer was in Europe, and reported on several matters to the UAC.[19] He stated that it was worth contemplating whether to keep or discard the houses and that the Kalaallit were disposed to the latter. He further noted that the purpose of the choir houses had not been reached and that the missionaries had come to realize that since the dispersion of the Kalaallit brothers and sisters, the single brothers and sisters would be better living in the family houses. Königseer read out an assessment by Jakob Beck:

> In the choir houses there is a lack of the necessary supervision; since the unmarried men could not subsist without the help of the women, they would have to turn to the unmarried sisters or widows' house, which gives rise to some disorders; in the latter especially, there is a gathering of all the unmarried choirs; the young unmarried men lack the necessary lessons in seal trapping in the

---

[15] Robert Petersen, 'Some Considerations Concerning the Greenlandic Longhouse', *Folk* 16–17 (1974): 171–88.
[16] In my article, Petterson, 'From Communal Economy to Economic Community', I incorrectly assume that the Kalaallit choir houses are permanent.
[17] Kalaallit on seal hunt. See Diary, New-Herrnhut. Entries from 1745: 9 March. From 1746: 25 March, 25 and 27 June, 1 July, 3, 4, 8 and 10 October. From 1747: 22 September, the Kalaallit were in the sound to hunt seal for winter. From 1748, 26 August, a number of brothers went to the sound and were catching seal for winter, and came back 4 October with a couple of hundred seals. UA R.15.J.b.I.01.b.
[18] Ammassat gathering: See Diary, New-Herrnhut. Entries from 1746: 23 and 29 May 1746. From 1747, 13 May. From 1748, 5 May and 8 June. UA R.15.J.b.I.01.b.
[19] Minutes UAC, 23 November 1781.

choir house, and they become poor providers; and the unmarried sisters are also not properly used to work, etc.[20]

Here we see the problem with gender segregation, in that it interferes with the Kalaallit way of life and division of labour.[21] It was the women's task to flense the seal, carve up the meat, prepare the skins, the organs and the intestines (used for thread). The Kalaallit single brothers then, as the quote indicates, would turn to the women in the congregation, thus violating the gender segregation. This segregation also had an effect on women's labour in that the women were also not trained to work within this particular relation. The missionaries had employed Kalaallit women to work for them, cooking and making and repairing clothes, which was paid for in tobacco. But in terms of Greenlandic subsistence, choir houses were not ideal. The effects of this showed up in the younger generations, who then did not benefit from being taught by the older married men in hunting and thus providing for the community.

While nothing was resolved in this issue in 1781, it was taken up again in the UAC 1783, on 27 February, where Jakob Beck's writ was reread, and another by missionary Meyer, who preferred to dissolve only the Single Brothers' House which was, he noted, absolutely necessary but to keep the choir houses of the widows and single sisters. Königseer and Beck wanted to get rid of the choir houses completely, mainly because of the lack of supervision, which led to disorder and 'bad things' (*schlechte Sachen*), more so than in family houses. For these and other reasons, it was decided to give up choir houses entirely in all three Greenlandic congregations. This decision (*not* made by lot) was copied and sent to Greenland.[22]

In the New-Herrnhut congregation, the missionaries received the news and made preparations accordingly. In the minutes of the Elders' conference on 8 September 1783, it is noted that it is very necessary that the single brothers, the older boys and boys are taken care of separately, and that they need to be spoken to separately in the parlour. It is also necessary to maintain the evening blessing. Several months later, in the minutes from the Elders' conference of 30 December 1783, it is noted that Königseer held speakings with the single

---

[20] Minutes UAC, 23 November 1781: 'In den Chorhäusern fehle es an der nöthigen Aufsicht; da die ledigen Mannsleute ohne Hülfe der Weibsleute nicht bestehen könten, so müßten sie sich ins ledigen Schwestern- oder Witwenhaus wenden, welches zu manchen Unordnungen Anlaß gebe; in Letzterem sey sonderlich eine Zusammenkunft aus sämtlichen ledigen Chören. Den jungen ledigen Mannsleuten fehle es im Chorhause am nöthigen Unterricht im Seehundfange, und sie werden schlecht Erwerber; so würden auch die ledigen Schwestern im Chorhause nicht recht zur Arbeit gewöhnt'.
[21] Also noted by Israel, *Kulturwandel*, 97.
[22] From the Minutes of the UAC to New-Herrnhut. 27 February 1783. UA R.15.J.b.I.26, 136.

brothers and older boys, and noted that now that they did not live together any longer, but were distributed in the family houses, 'the spirit of temptation (*Geist der Verführung*) which so long had reigned in their choir house, and which had been impossible to quell, had vanished'. This observation sought to affirm that dissolving the choir house was the right decision.[23] It also demonstrates that the choir *order* was maintained, despite the new living arrangements. On 6 October 1783, it is noted that the choir assemblies are upheld despite the dissolution of the choir houses, and a plan was made up for the choir assemblies, where each choir had a weekly quarter-hour (*Viertelstunde*) and an evening blessing. The diary from 1784 also indicates that settling down for winter is the same as usual, except for the choir houses.[24]

The choir houses are by and large seen as imposing a European settlement pattern in the Kalaallit world.[25] They did, however, contribute to creating a close-knit community, with a high level of communal activities. By the time they were abolished, it was more of a practical measure and did not have an impact on the organization of the settlement. The communal fellowship was thus left intact.

Households

As mentioned earlier, Kalaallit society had households consisting of extended families and larger groups which lived together, shared maintenance of equipment, hunted together and so forth. They were settled in turf houses during winter and were itinerant in tents in the summer period. This practice continued with some modifications for the converted congregations pre-1777. There are many examples of the Kalaallit brothers going out on seal hunts, and the Kalaallit brothers and sisters going out for ammassat (capelin) gathering every year, marking the beginning of the summer and the break-up of winter camps.[26]

The European household, on the other hand, remained settled throughout the year. From the very early days the European household did not run smoothly. Already in the first household, there was tension between the brothers.[27] In his farewell letter from 1752 to the missionaries after his visitation, Johannes von

---

[23] Conference Minutes, New-Herrnhut, 30 December 1783. UA R.15.J.b.I.9.
[24] See Diary, New-Herrnhut, Greenland, 12 November 1784, on the establishment of the *Gesellschaften* and the children beginning school. UA R.15.J.b.I.3.a.
[25] Müller, *200 Jahre Brüdermission I*, 134; Kleivan, 'Herrnhuterne eller Brødremenigheden i Grønland'.
[26] For diary entries, see footnotes 17-18.
[27] As manifested in the secret diary of Christian Stach 10 October 1734–7 August 1735, where he complains extensively about an unnamed brother (UA R.15.J.a.2.b).

Watteville devoted a separate section of the letter to the internal disputes within the missionaries' household.

He encourages them to keep a common household as a 'family of the Lamb', rather than in two to three separate 'economies' (Oeconomien). He also addresses what seems to be a matter of petty ownership by noting that what is sent to the missionaries from the Diacony is not sent to one person but to everyone: 'it therefore belongs to the whole of the economy and everyone gets what he needs from it.'[28] As for what is acquired from the land, or given as present, it is necessary, so as to prevent discord, that it is considered as a gift to the commune (*Commun*), and so no one has the right to regard it as his own. To manage the household and its provisions, a couple is appointed. Finally, Johannes suggests that they make good use of the *Gemein-Nachrichten* that he has brought along.[29] A look in subsequent diaries confirms that this advice is taken to heart in that they spent the evenings reading to each other from the community news. This is not an insignificant fact in the separation and consolidation of separated European and Kalaallit households: while the Europeans read 'European news', the Kalaallit were presented with 'Native news' on the community days.

Discord is still the case in the correspondence from the leadership in Herrnhut from 1763, after the establishment of the Mission Deputation: in the letter sent by the Inner Council to Greenland, they recommend that the German (*deutsche*) members have a weekly thorough 'talking through', so that old discords do not stay fixed in people's minds.[30]

The matter is raised again in relation to Martin Gottfried Sternberg's visitation in 1771.[31] This was the first visitation to Greenland after Zinzendorf's death. As he himself notes, it was a very long time since the previous visitation of Johannes von Watteville in 1752. Sternberg noted the appalling state of the missionaries at New-Herrnhut: no one spoke to each other, everyone sat in their own rooms and did not attend any gatherings if they were not in charge. Sternberg then realizes that the annual letters written by the Unity leadership to the missionaries, as well as the synod decision, 'were peacefully lying in the cupboard and dust' and had

---

[28] Johannes von Watteville's farewell letter after his visitation: 'und es gehöret also ins Ganze der Oeconomie und jedes bekommt davon, was er braucht.' R.15.J.a.9.21.
[29] Johannes von Watteville's farewell letter after his visitation: 'Abends macht ihr euch im eurem Hause die vielen Gemein-Nachrichten zu Nuze, die wir euch mitgebracht haben.' R.15.J.a.9.21.
[30] Inner Council to the missionaries in New-Herrnhut and Lichtenfels, 24 February 1763, points 9 and 10. UA R.15.J.b.I.26, 34.
[31] Some of the sources are printed in Karl Müller, *Der Weg des Matthäus Stach. Ein Lebensbild des ersten Grönland-Missionars der Brüdergemeine. Aus alten Briefen und Tagebuchblättern zusammengestellt von Karl Müller* (Berlin: Furche-Verlag, 1926).

not been read since the day of their initial arrival and had not been thought of after a reply had been sent.

Sternberg set to work. He held a number of meetings with the Europeans and arranged a communion assembly in which thirty-four Brothers and sixty-seven Sisters partook. On 23 July, all the European brothers and sisters were called together in the newly organized house-meeting, which Sternberg had been under orders to establish. Its intention was that the European brothers and sisters should meet frequently and together consider, plan and distribute the industrious activities according to everyone's strength and particular ability. Apart from a concern with collective activity, the purpose was also not to make it too difficult for the person in charge (*Diakonus*), but rather to facilitate his task to care for the household. The *Diakonus*, on the other hand, was regarded as being at the service and discretion of the house-meeting, which should remind him of his responsibility and direct everything to the point that the house is ordered according to Brethren values and that it proceeds in a moderate order, and that the arguments over house, food, hunting and work will cease, never to return. Not only, Sternberg admonishes, is such behaviour irreconcilable with the character of a child of God and the relation to the Saviour, but also spreads to other areas, and the damage caused by such destructive behaviour cannot be rectified. These meetings should be held often and should not – as before – be omitted in the annual letters.

This organizational drive was not something that came out of the blue but was a resurrection of a structure which had been implemented decades earlier.

Early organization

The implementation of the changing structures and their theological foundations in the mission fields were mediated first and foremost through correspondence between the leadership in Europe and the mission station(s),[32] but also, as per Sternberg's example, through visitations. Visitations – as we have through examples in previous chapters – entailed a visit by a senior member to the mission to inspect, oversee and advise the missionaries on procedure, and to communicate decisions from home. The first visitation in Moravian mission history was Spangenberg's visitation to the mission in St Thomas in 1736.

---

[32] For example, Johannes von Watteville's letters to the missionaries as a group each year in spring includes extensive comments on their diaries, their practice, their organization and so forth. See Johannes von Watteville 6 March 1750; 25 March 1751; 22 February 1753; 6 March 1754; 8 March 1755; 8 April 1756; 7 March 1757; 16 March 1758; 19 March 1759 all in UA R.15.J.b.I.26.a.

The first visitation to Greenland took place in 1740, by Andreas Grassmann, followed by Rosina Nitschmann (1745), Johannes von Watteville (1752), Martin Gottfried Sternberg (1771) and Ernst Reichel (1859). Of these five visits, only the latter two are formally described as visitations in the archives. However, the trips by Grassmann, R. Nitschmann and Watteville are good examples of early visitations and the ad hoc process that characterized the early missions. Thus, Grassmann's travel diary is more a replica of the regular diaries, with descriptions of wood-gathering, fishing and so on. There are few mentions of speaking with the individual missionaries and discussions on the future of the mission, which is the only indication of it being a supervisory visit.[33]

Rosina Nitschmann's visit was also not designated a visitation.[34] However, she was given instructions by Zinzendorf before leaving and had a range of tasks to complete while there. Rosina Nitschmann (1704–53) was known as *Mutter*,[35] a term that indicates a position of female leadership, the office of an Eldress.[36] While the diary concerning her visit is brief,[37] it is mentioned that she conducted 'speakings'[38] with all of the missionaries, after which the lot approved a Eucharist to be held. Also, during her visit they held a conference on the situation in New-

---

[33] See, for example, Andreas Grassmann: Visitation to Greenland, 22 May, 7 and 11 June. UA R.15.J.a.16.3.
[34] In the diary from 1783, where the achievements of the first fifty years are mentioned, Rosina Nitschmann's visit is not mentioned in the list of visitations. UA R.15.J.b.I.3.a, 19 January 1783. This is also implied in the English version of her Lebenslauf from the archives in Bethlehem (MemBeth 0027). Her Lebenslauf from the archives in Herrnhut (UA. NB.I.R.4.291.c.2.30) is a summary of Zinzendorf's words about her, where he says that he does not want to mention her travels to Greenland, Denmark, Sweden, Lithuania and twice to Pennsylvania, and thus does not mention the capacity in which she travelled.
[35] According to Paul Peucker, Anna Maria Lawatsch held the office from mid-1744 till January 1746, where Anna Nitschmann took it over. Peucker, *Herrnhuter Wörterbuch*, 41. According to the diary, then, Rosina Nitschmann's office would be within the period of Lawatsch's, unless it is a different office, such as the leader of the Married Choir.
[36] One way in which this capacity shows up in her duty regarding marriage. A document containing a series of question and answers (UA R.15.J.a.11.2) shows that her task was to initiate (*einrichten*) the already married brothers and sisters into the new understanding of marriage which had developed in the past years in Herrnhut. For more detail on this, see Petterson, 'Moravians in Greenland: Barren Shores and Fruitful Missions'.
[37] Diary New-Herrnhut, July–August 1745. R.15.J.b.I.01.b. Her instructions in relation to the visitation are given by Zinzendorf in a letter UA R.15.J.a.9.17.
[38] 'Speakings' were one to one conversations with each and every member, where the choir-helper examined whether there was any reason for this or that member to not take part in the Eucharist. See Katherine M. Faull, *Speaking to Body and Soul: Instructions for the Moravian Choir Helpers, 1785-1786*, Pietist, Moravian, and Anabaptist Studies (University Park: Pennsylvania State University Press, 2017). See also Christina Petterson and Katherine M. Faull, 'Speaking About Marriage: Notes from the 1744 Married Choir Conferences', *Journal of Moravian History* 17, no. 1 (2017), for an example of notes taken after such a round of speakings with the married couples in Herrnhut in 1744.

Herrnhut, appointed leaders within the congregation and, before she departed, they had their first choir-eucharist.[39]

In 1745, the congregation was growing. Kalaallit were coming from Kangeq and the surrounding area, but also, come spring, from the south. There was thus heightened activity in community organization: there are frequent *Grönländerstunden* (literally Greenlander-hours) held with Kalaallit, there are meetings with the Kalaallit members, who are organized into pastoral care groups (*Banden*) and are spoken with, men and women apart. There are also meetings with prospective converts, and finally, there are meetings with people from the colony. Of note in the last category is the Danish missionary Drackhart, who was very partial to the Moravian missionaries and who would later that year join the Moravians and, many years later, travel to Labrador as a Moravian.[40] There is a definite change of pace and organization in the diary after Rosina Nitschmann's arrival on 19 July 1745. Before then, we have heard of *Cor-stunde* and *Cor-viertelstunde*,[41] the members' conference, where they spoke with all the members individually and cast lot as to who was to be baptized.[42]

It is, however, in the following months that we can see the effects of her visit and the organizational leaps it occasioned. After Nitschmann left on 1 September 1745, the missionaries brought their house in order, with the brothers moving into one room and the sisters into the other.[43] Several weeks later they held their first conference and decided forthwith to hold a fourfold conference weekly, namely, the elders' conference (leadership), the workers' conference (all missionaries), the heathen-workers' conference (meetings with the Kalaallit workers) and the house-conference (domestic matters). There was of course an overlap in terms of who was a member of what group, and so the name of the meeting indicated rather what was to be discussed.[44] Not until decades later, after Sternberg's visitation, do we have more organized meeting minutes. On 2 October 1745, they held the first Kalaallit workers' conference, where they decided on choir-workers – which means from among the Kalaallit members. On 4 October they had the first elders' conference, and here we hear

---

[39] The document of questions and answers also has a question on this, namely whether choir-eucharists should be celebrated in the congregation or merely the congregational Eucharist. The answer is only in the married choir. At this stage, the married choir consisted of Moravian missionaries.
[40] See Olsthoorn, "'Wir haben keine Ohren'" for more on Drachart and his work in Labrador.
[41] Diary New-Herrnhut 14 and 28 February 1745. R.15.J.b.I.01.b.
[42] Diary New-Herrnhut 16–17 February 1745. R.15.J.b.I.01.b.
[43] All references here are from the diary from 1745, UA R.15.J.b.I.01.b.
[44] UA R.15.J.b.I.7 are meeting minutes from conferences held between 1749 and 1761 and consists mainly of names of prospective candidates for baptism and communion with the lot decision. The meetings are named after whether it is baptism (*Tauf-Conferenz*) or communion (*Abendmahlsconferenz*) which is to be decided. See figure 1 on page 31.

that those present spoke sharply with one another, but no further details are given. On 13 October, the workers' conference made plans for the school for Kalaallit children. Five girls and three boys were to learn how to read, and one boy and two girls were to learn how to read German.[45] On 22 October, they had 'heathen-conference', a category not included in the weekly plan, and, on 29 October, another Kalaallit workers' conference. These were meetings with the Kalaallit helpers, where they helped to assess the candidates and the progression of their spiritual condition. At this meeting, it was decided by lot to baptize all three candidates, which took place on the following day, when they held the first Kalaallit community day (*Gemeintag*) of the year. This rather full list of meetings and activities indicates a beginning organization in various spheres. In general, the diaries from these years indicate the various liturgical gatherings, private edification, community organization and hunting. Thus, with the visitation from Rosina Nitschmann, the organization began to take firmer shape. In the subsequent years, the settlement itself also underwent a transformation with the erection of the missionary station building and the establishment of a Single Sisters' House, as mentioned in the previous section.

This organization was replicated in the new settlement, Lichtenfels. In a letter to the missionaries announcing the realization of this long-awaited project, Watteville writes that

> They must establish themselves on your community foundation just like in New-Herrnhut: conferences, community- and choir-events, communion, community-day, associations and everything that you have, even when you are few. Every beginning is difficult, but it will be a hundred times easier than the beginning in New-Herrnhut; and the blessing of the community will accompany our brothers and sisters.[46]

This organization had deteriorated in the years following Zinzendorf's death and was what Sternberg resurrected during his visitation, trying to ensure, so to speak, a tight ship.

---

[45] This was organized the following years in October after the Kalaallit settled in for winter. See Diary, New-Herrnhut, Greenland, 13 October 1745, 15 October 1746, 22 October 1748, UA R.15.J.b.I.01.b.

[46] Johannes von Watteville to the missionaries in Greenland, 16 March 1758. 'Sie müßen sich gleich dort just so wie in Neu-Herrnhuth auf euern gantzen Gemein-Fuß einrichten, Conferenzen, Gemein- und Chor-Gelegenheiten, Abendmahl, Gemeintag, Gesellschafften und alles wie bey euch haben, wenn ihrer auch gleich wenig sind. Aller Anfang ist schwer, doch wirds 100 mahl leichter gehen als der Anfang in Neu-Herrnhuth; und der Seegen der Gemeine wird unsere Geschwister begleiten.' UA R.15.J.b.I.26.a.24.

Implications and transformations in a colonial context

As mentioned in Chapter 1, Mettele argues that life on the mission stations was to follow life in Herrnhut and its community and liturgical forms, but that there was 'no indication of *Gemeintag* celebrations on the mission stations.'[47] As Watteville's letter indicates, there *was* a *Gemeintag* in New-Herrnhut – albeit only in the settled period between October and May.[48] On these community days, new members were baptized and admitted into the local community, where letters and liturgical texts had been translated and were read out to the congregation. There was also communication from Herrnhut to the Kalaallit community and back, letters and notes from the Kalaallit brothers and sisters to Zinzendorf and his son Christian Renatus, and letters from Rosina Nitschmann and Johannes von Watteville to New-Herrnhut.

Interestingly, and this certainly relates to Mettele's point on the incorporation of non-white peoples in the Moravian Unity, we see that in Greenland on the community day – *Gemeintag* – the material read is increasingly material concerning other missions, and more importantly, the people being converted. In the period from 1760 to 1765, *Gemeintagen* were held every month in the settled period: always on 6 January (Epiphany), which was celebrated as the 'heathen-day',[49] three to four times in spring[50] and two to three times in winter.[51] On these days material was translated and read aloud from 'the Indian diary' and the diaries of the 'black congregations', letters from Berbice, Saramacca and Saron in Suriname, letters from Jamaica, letters from Nain in Labrador and diaries from Pachgatgoch (Wampanoag mission station, 1742–70) and the Danish West Indian missions in St Thomas, St Croix and St John, as well as from Antigua. It is thus less a community-as-such-day and more a 'Native-convert' day.[52] While the emphasis is on community, the community is increasingly twofold, European and Native. In Greenland this development took place at

---

[47] Mettele, *Weltbürgertum oder Gottesreich*, 107.
[48] Just to give some examples from a five-year period: in 1745, it was held on 30 October and 27 November. In 1746, on 6 January (Ephiphany, celebrated in New-Herrnhut 1746 as the 'Heathen-feast', that is, the day of revelation to the gentiles), 13 May, 21 December. In 1747, it was held on 25 January, 24 February, 5 April, 18 November. In 1748 it was held on 19 January, 17 February, 16 March. In 1749, it was held on Epiphany, 6 January, 9 February, 15 March, 12 April. All from Diary, New-Herrnhut, Greenland. UA R.15.J.b.I.01.b.
[49] Diary, New-Herrnhut, Greenland, 6 January 1760, 6 January 1761. UA R.15.J.b.I.01.c. Diary, New-Herrnhut, 6 January 1762-1765. UA J.b.I.02.a.
[50] Diary, New-Herrnhut, 30 March 1760, 1 March 1761 UA R.15.J.b.I.01.c. Diary, New-Herrnhut, 28 March 1762, 27 March 1763, 6 May 1764, and -1765 UA J.b.I.02.a.
[51] Diary, New-Herrnhut, 9 November 1760; UA R.15.J.b.I.01.c. Diary, New-Herrnhut, 8 November 1761, 7 November 1762, 6 November 1763, 4 November 1764, and -1765. UA R.15.J.b.I.02.a.
[52] One exception is the 27 March 1763, where the material is a speech given by Johannes von Watteville in Niesky. UA R.15.J.b.I.02.a.

some time in the 1750s: in the material from the late 1740s, there is mention of letters and translations of liturgical texts, whereas the diaries of 1760s include stories from other missions.[53]

This distinction is, in fact, a logical outcome of the choir system. As mentioned earlier, the choir system was a way of dividing up the community into several subordinated categories, namely gender, marital status and age. Further and as mentioned, the choirs were kinship groups and liturgical fellowships, as well as pastoral groups and economic entities.[54] Here we see the effect of the pastoral logic of the choir, which was to target the individual believer in his or her specific situation and level of faith. Basically speaking, choirs were hierarchical and focused on mediating the relation of the individual to the Saviour and the individual to his or her community. The structure itself was in constant development and underwent a series of changes in terms of offices within the choirs, principles and instructions from the 1740s to the mid-nineteenth century. This in itself makes any definite statement about choirs somewhat tricky. However, before 1760, a given choir in Europe, say, the Single Sisters' choir in Herrnhut, had two leaders, one for spiritual aspects (*Chorpflegerin*) and one for the material aspects (*Chorvorsteherin*) – as discussed in Chapter 3. Furthermore, the choirs had helpers, or workers, who helped monitor the spiritual and physical well-being of the choir members. The members were divided into subgroups called classes, which were arranged according to spiritual compatibility, and thus subject to reorganization, mainly every three months. The hierarchical leadership structure of the choir mirrored the hierarchical leadership structure of the settlement. This particular structure of leadership and governance replaced the former more egalitarian organization into so-called *Banden* (groups), *Gesellschaften* (societies) and classes, although the terminology, especially of *Gesellschaften*, remained long after.[55] Once this structure was transposed to the missions, it clearly had

---

[53] In the nineteenth century colonial authorities established a newspaper, *Atuagagdliutit*, which was published in Greenlandic. As Hanne Thomsen argued, this was one of several attempts on behalf of the colonial authorities to forge an 'imagined community'. Hanne Thomsen, 'Ægte grønlændere og nye grønlændere — om forskellige opfattelser af grønlandskhed', *Den Jyske Historiker* 81 (1998): 21–56, here 27–8. In this newspaper, Kalaallit could read descriptions of Aboriginal Australians, Natives of Patagonia and Tierra del Fuego, Pacific Islanders and Canadian Inuit in the most derogatory and colonialist language, over against descriptions of Kalaallit as peaceful Christian seal-hunters. See also Petterson, *The Missionary, the Catechist and the Hunter*, 138–50, for a fuller discussion. This notion of 'imagined community' is much more in line with Benedict Anderson's understanding of 'imagined community' as a nationalist and inward-looking understanding of society and less of the kind offered by the Moravians. I would like to thank Kirstine Eiby Møller for alerting me to the parallels between the two.

[54] Petterson, *The Moravian Brethren in a Time of Transition*.

[55] The go-to study for the early organization of Herrnhut and its pastoral organization is Wollstadt, *Geordnetes Dienen*. I have analysed the transition to the choir structure and its ideological implications in Petterson, *The Moravian Brethren in a Time of Transition*.

implications not necessarily imagined, namely the racialized consequences of (a) the Native converts' spiritual development; (b) the racialized consequences of the leadership structure and (c) the racialized consequences of the division of the community into Europeans and, in Greenland, Kalaallit. At the same time, this segregating choir structure also had an enabling feature in that it promoted Indigenous leadership. By the 1760s, the Kalaallit workers in the communities had been in charge of their own daily gatherings for two decades. In a way akin to the active participation and leadership roles of women in the movement during Zinzendorf's time,[56] it was assumed that Kalaallit themselves participated in the liturgical organization and administration of their fellowships.

In the correspondence from the Inner Council to the missionaries in Greenland from 1763, there are several indications of a desire to increase control with the Kalaallit congregation.

> We consider it necessary that you not only hold a German conference in each community before communion and the community days, but also take a few hours every week to confer with one another about the course of your Greenlandic brothers and sisters, the particular evidence of grace, and their occasional blessed expressions etc. in short, tell everything good and bad, and agree thereupon.[57]

The individual assessments of and speakings with the Kalaallit members before communion and before the Community day, where it is assessed whether or not to proceed to baptism, is here supplemented with yet another assessment task. Here the missionaries are directed to hold a weekly meeting to assess the spiritual situation of the Kalaallit members.

In Europe, these assessments would also take place, although at different administrative levels. Thus, the procedure towards acceptance into the community would be initiated by the leadership and put towards the lot. The speakings for Communion were dealt with by the leaders of the choirs, who

---

[56] The amount of literature on this is enormous, but see Becker-Cantarino, 'Zur Bedeutung der Oeconomia'; Homburg, 'Glaube – Arbeit – Geschlecht'; Pia Schmid, 'Frömmigkeitspraxis und Selbstreflexion. Lebensläufe von Frauen der Herrnhuter Brüdergemeinde aus dem 18. Jahrhundert', in *Der Bildungsgang des Subjekts. Bildungstheoretische Analysen*, ed. Sonja Häder (Weinheim und Basel: Beltz Verlag, 2004); Katherine M. Faull, *Moravian Women's Memoirs: Their Related Lives, 1750-1820* (New York: Syracuse University Press, 1997).

[57] Inner Council to the Brothers and Sisters in New-Herrnhut and Lichtenfels, 24 February 1763, '12 ‚Wir halten für nöthig, daß ihr in jeder Gemeine nicht nur vor den Abendmahlen und Gemeintagen eine deutsche Conferenz haltet, sondern setzet auch alle Wochen ein paar Stunden dazu aus, da ihr über den Gang eurer grönlandische Geschwister mit einander conferiret, und die besondern Beweise der Gnade und hier und da vor gekommenen seligen Aeuserungen derselben etc., kurz alles Gute und Schlechte, erzehlet, und darüber Abrede nehmet'. UA R.15.J.b.I.26.a, 34.

were responsible for this task. The choir workers, who had responsibility for monitoring the spiritual welfare of the members, would also hold regular meetings to assess the members. In Greenland, however, these tasks were all carried out by the missionaries, adding a racial difference to the structures of the community. Even a European who was not active in the spiritual but rather the material aspects of the mission, such as managing the household, was still committed to the community as a whole, and thus his assessment would also carry weight.

Another request is that while it is 'truly wonderful' that the Kalaallit workers hold *Gesellschaften*, the Inner Council urge the missionaries to consider whether it would not be both good and necessary if a brother or sister visit these meetings to see how they proceed.[58] There is no indication that this happened, but the diaries from 1760 and onwards give a small summary of the address of the Kalaallit helper to the congregation. Whether this is to demonstrate their presence and the proper content of the address is not to say. It could also be a suggestion from David Cranz, who in the preface to his *History of Greenland*, lamented that the diaries did not include more material from the Kalaallit members and their participation.[59] In sum, while there was certainly a difference between the European and non-European brothers and sisters in Greenland at many levels, there was nevertheless a very close community and the sense of a shared grander purpose as well as everyday survival. While the choirs and communal organization are one way of understanding the relationship between the mission congregation in Greenland and the larger Unity, another path is to consider its commemoration days and how this was connected to the larger Moravian history.

Days of celebration

The Moravians are big on commemorative days. In eighteenth-century European congregations, annual celebrations included (and still includes) 13 August (the commemoration of the birth of the community in 1727) and 13 November (the celebration of the Saviour taking the position of chief elder in the community in 1741). In Herrnhut, 17 June is an important day because this was the day the

---

[58] Inner Council to the Brothers and Sisters in New-Herrnhut and Lichtenfels, 24 February 1763, 32. Es ist recht schöne, daß die Grönl. Arbeiter die Geschellschaften halten; aber überleget doch obs nicht gut und nöthig sey, daß dann und wann ein Bruder oder Schwester von euch sie besuchet, und nach siehet, wie es in denselben geht. UA R.15.J.b.I.26.a, 34.

[59] Cranz, *The History of Greenland*. xii. cited in Olsthoorn, 'Wir Haben Keine Ohren', 51.

first tree to build the town was felled, back in 1722. Added to this were various annual choir days, where the individual choirs have their special celebration and then there was the day of all choirs, on 25 March each year.[60]

We may therefore ascertain how the missions were integrated into the larger community by considering how they were connected to the larger history and attendant historical reflection of the Moravian Brethren. In Chapter 1, I referred to the fiftieth anniversary of the mission to Greenland on 19 January. This was celebrated with great splendour, with a very long letter written by Spangenberg to the Greenlandic congregation. Another commemoration was the inauguration of the mission house on 16 October.[61] The following is a list of days that were marked in a special way in the Moravian congregation in Greenland at least until 1784.[62]

- 6 January: Epiphany. Revelation of Christ to the Gentiles. This was celebrated as a big *Gemeintag, Heidenfest*
- 19 January: the departure from Copenhagen and the beginning of the mission to Greenland. Sometimes the corresponding arrival on 20 May was noted, but this is the big day
- Late January/early February: Community day (*Gemeintag*)
- 2 February: Choir day for Widows and Widowers
- Late February/early March: Community day (*Gemeintag*)
- 25 March: Choir day for Older Girls and Single Sisters (Single Sisters sometimes on 4 May)
- Late March/early April: Community day
- Easter
- Late April/early May: Community day
- Pentecost.

Here we have the summer-period, which lasts from mid-May to mid-October

- 7 September: Married couples' day
- 16 October: the inauguration of the Saal. The mission station was inaugurated in 1747 and this is marked every following year.

[60] See Petterson, *The Moravian Brethren in a Time of Transition*, 81–8, for a genealogy of this celebration.
[61] 1760, 1761, 1762, 1783.
[62] There are other days, specifically tied to Herrnhut's history which are marked, but it looks like this is only commemorated by the missionaries rather than the community as a whole. This includes the death day of Zinzendorf (9 May) and the birth of the community in Herrnhut (13 August). The 13 August could be because it is in the middle of the itinerant summer period, where not many people were at New-Herrnhut.

- 18 October: The birthday of Johannes von Watteville. Johannes von Watteville was a special person in Greenland, where he was known as Johannes Assersok, the loving one, since his visitation in 1751. He was also the primary correspondent with the missionaries from 1750 to 1765. His birthday was celebrated with much flourish, but this petered out over the years.
- Early November: *Gemeintag*
- 13 November *Festtag*: The appointment of Christ as Chief Elder. This is a very important day in the Moravian calendar. It marks the decision by the Saviour (whose will, as we have seen, is understood to be expressed through the lot) that he wished to take on the leadership of the community. The celebration in the communities included amnesty for those members who were under punishment for various misdemeanours such as disobedience or sexual indiscretions. The day on which the lot was drawn, 16 September (1741), is sometimes also marked.
- December: Community day
- Christmas
- 28 December: The birthday of Henriette Benigna Justine von Watteville. Benigna was the oldest daughter of Zinzendorf and was married to Johannes von Watteville in 1746. She did not accompany Johannes to Greenland, but nevertheless was commemorated on her birthday until the mid-1760s.

This is quite a list already, and this is added to the daily and weekly events noted earlier, which meant that every week was full of big and small assemblies and meetings. Twice a week there was a morning assembly for the Kalaallit, where a national helper, that is, a Kalaaleq, would speak to the assembly, and every evening one of the choirs would have their evening blessing. Mid-week, there would also be a general assembly led by one of the missionaries and then of course the Sunday service. Once a month, communion was held, which also required preparation in the individual speakings that preceded partaking of communion. And then, there were the meetings every two weeks within the missionary group to ensure that the group ran smoothly. Added to this was the need to procure food: tend the garden and the sheep, bake, hunt and fish. In particular, hunting and fishing were tasks undertaken by the missionaries with their Kalaallit brothers. There are numerous examples in the diaries of the missionaries going fishing or out on land-hunts for reindeer and birds.[63] The very

---

[63] Mentions of missionaries on hunting expeditions: Diary, New-Herrnhut, Greenland. Entries from 1745: 25 May, 12 June (two barrels of eider-eggs) 25 June, 17 August. Entries from 1746: 9 May, 3

close quarters and living conditions within which they lived made community inevitable, even if these did take shape along a European/Kalaallit axis.

Conclusion: The 'inner' sphere of the Greenland mission

The Moravian mission in Greenland was an extensive, expensive and impressive endeavour. As we have seen in this chapter, it was not possible for the missionaries to earn their keep through tradesmanship and there was no stable financial contribution on which to draw in the early years. The lack of industry available for the missionaries meant that their sole focus was on their missionary duty. Due to the ever-tightening control of the Danish colonial regime, it was simply impossible for the mission to engage in any form of trade. In other words, the 'outer' sphere or Oeconomie could not be developed; the result was a singular concern with the 'inner' sphere. While some subsistence survival activities could be undertaken in the earlier years, such as hunting and fishing with the Kalaallit brothers, the mission relied on intermittent supplies and funds from Europe. That said, external funding eventually became stabilized through the significant centralization and systematization of economic and missionary organization in the 1760s. The earlier ad hoc approach was gradually replaced by tighter organization, support and control. Paradoxically, because the significant profits from slave plantations of the Danish West Indian missions – where the 'outer' sphere took on a whole new life – were appropriated by the Unity's central body and redistributed, the Greenland mission was able to survive and flourish. In this way, it became a model of the 'inner' sphere.

The eighteenth century was the time in which 'economy' generally was becoming a distinct field, separated from the household and managed in a particular way.[64] In Greenland, the household, albeit the mission station as a household, never expanded beyond its own meaning. By this, I mean that economy never became a separated sphere from the inner life of the settlement as we saw happen in the Danish West Indies and Bethlehem. This does not mean that the mission in Greenland went untouched by economic developments, in that the mission to the Kalaallit received economic assistance from profits gained from slavery.

September, 3 November. Entries from 1747: 14 April, 7 August. Entries from 1748: 20 July (four reindeer), 11 August (salmon fishing, very successful), 26 August, missionaries return with six reindeer. UA R.15.J.b.I.01.b.

[64] Michel Foucault deals extensively with this as a theoretical issue rather than as a historical process. Foucault, *Security, Territory, Population*.

Conclusion

Moravians and capitalism

Introduction

As I have been arguing in the course of this book, Moravian missionary practice and organization changed in the 1760s and became more closely tied to an economic practice connected to capitalist ideals, and this had an impact on how they organized their missions. This was especially evident in the externalization of the economic sphere and the ensuing reification of humans in the West Indies. The Moravians' experiments with sugar plantations and slavery and other ways of economic organization should not, however, be understood as simply adapting to or resisting early capitalism; instead, they were actors within and developers of early capitalism. Such a viewpoint, while completely obvious, is nevertheless impeded by Max Weber's framing of the question, which is already determined by the logic of capitalism and its objectified categories of 'economy' and 'religion'. This is a topic we need to address in this chapter.

Connected to this, and in a way that will become apparent, are the three crucial Moravian elements mentioned in Chapter 1: individual, community and history. These aspects are important because they are at odds with the liberal ideology so prevalent in the Western Enlightenment, in whose image our modern academic disciplines are shaped. Thus, there is a danger of flattening out some of the particularities of Moravian-ness, if one is not attentive to these elements, which in turn will reinforce liberal ideology.

Religion and capitalism

As mentioned in the introduction, the Moravian Brethren are an excellent case for studying the relationship between Christianity and capitalism, because of their global presence and their entrepreneurial activity, and, as we have seen throughout the book, their archives.

However, one of the problems often encountered in research on religion is the reluctance to regard religion as a significant force on anything outside the private sphere. Despite the valiant efforts by individual scholars from a range of disciplines such as history and sociology,[1] religion's impact on society and history has *generally* been disregarded or at best relegated to a discrete chapter. The situation in the field of early economic history is no better, where theories and histories of early modern economics do not engage with religion in any depth (e.g. Isenmann 2014; Gray 2000).[2] This means that theories of early economic formations are presented so as to exclude religion from the outset. Pietism, in spite of a slow but growing regard for its overall importance for early modernity,[3] is not regarded as contributing to the economic practices and thinking of the time.[4] This is – perhaps – due to the theological reasoning behind Pietism's engagement in economy, business and industry, *Wirtschaft*. The theological drive and religious purpose of these smaller groups mean that they are not raised to the more abstract theories of rational economic development.

These separate spheres of religion and economy were in slow development since the early Enlightenment, but there can be no doubt that Max Weber's *The Protestant Ethic and the Spirit of Capitalism* has set the parameters for the lines of questioning for anyone approaching the relation between religion and economy.[5]

---

[1] For history, see Katherine Carté Engel, 'Religion and the Economy. New Methods for an Old Problem', *Early American Studies* 8 (2010): 482–512, Heinz Schilling, *Religion, Political Culture, and the Emergence of Early Modern Society: Essays in German and Dutch History*, Studies in Medieval and Reformation Thought 50 (Leiden: Brill, 1992); Heinz Schilling, *Konfessionalisierung und Staatsinteressen: Internationale Beziehungen 1559-1660*, Handbuch der Geschichte der Internationalen Beziehungen, Bd 2 (Paderborn: Ferdinand Schöningh, 2007); Heinz Schilling, *Martin Luther: Rebel in an Age of Upheaval*, trans. Rona Johnston Gordon (Oxford: Oxford University Press, 2017); Hartmut Lehmann, *Transformationen der Religion in der Neuzeit: Beispiele aus der Geschichte des Protestantismus* (Göttingen: Göttingen : Vandenhoeck & Ruprecht, 2007). For sociology, see Gorski, *The Disciplinary Revolution*.

[2] Gray in particular is astonishing, given that the study deals in depth with the *Haustafel* literature of the seventeenth and eighteenth centuries.

[3] Carl Hinrichs, *Preußentum und Pietismus: Der Pietismus in Brandenburg-Preußen als Religiös-Soziale Reformbewegung* (Göttingen: Vandenhoeck & Ruprecht, 1971); Martin Brecht et al., *Geschichte des Pietismus / im Auftrag der Historischen Kommission zur Erforschung des Pietismus* (Göttingen: Vandenhoeck & Ruprecht., 1993); Hartmut Lehmann, *Pietismus und weltliche Ordnung in Württemberg vom 17. bis zum 20. Jahrhundert* (Stuttgart: Kohlhammer, 1969); Hartmut Lehmann, *Geschichte des Pietismus. 4, Glaubenswelt und Lebenswelten / Im Auftrag der Historischen Kommission zur Erforschung des Pietismus*, ed. Martin Brecht and Hartmut Lehmann (Göttingen: Vandenhoeck & Ruprecht, 2004); Jonathan Strom, Hartmut Lehmann and James Van Horn Melton, *Pietism in Germany and North America 1680-1820* (Farnham: Ashgate, 2009); Richard L. Gawthrop, *Pietism and the Making of Eighteenth-Century Prussia* (Cambridge: Cambridge University Press, 2006).

[4] A notable exception to this is Gerhard Bondi's analysis of Hallensian Pietism as a contributor to German economic thought. Gerhard Bondi, 'Der Beitrag des Hallischen Pietismus zur Entwicklung des ökonomischen Denkens in Deutschland', *Jahrbuch für Wirtschaftsgeschichte* 5/2-3 (1964): 24–48. I would like to thank Kristian Mejrup for this reference.

[5] One cannot escape Weber when working with economy and religion, and yet, it is difficult to see how one can make use of such a bizarre study, which claims to be historical (p. 12: a few remarks are necessary, first on the peculiarities of the phenomenon of which we are seeking an historical

The reason for this entrapment can best be explained with recourse to Fredric Jameson, the Marxist literary critic with a soft spot for Weber. In his intertextual analysis of Weber, he notes:

> In reality, Weber's most influential legacy to the anti-Marxist arsenal lay not in some idealistic reaction against a materialism he himself clearly shared with Marx but rather in the strategic substitution, in his own research and theorization, of the political for the economic realm as the principal object of study, and thus, implicitly, as the ultimately determining reality of history. Thus, Weber made of political history – the growth of bureaucracies, the influence of the charismatic individual and his function in political institutions – an autonomous field of study which may then be examined in relative isolation from questions of economic development.[6]

If Jameson is correct, the reason we cannot address questions of economy using Weber is because he has shifted the focus of analysis to that of the political which is then treated in isolation from the economic. And so, instead of discussing the socio-economic disruptions of capitalism, and the economic practices of various communities, Weber focuses on what in a Marxist framework is called the superstructural elements, namely political, religious and cultural change as that which propels history. This is perhaps not that surprising when we remember that Weber is a sociologist and as such operates within the structures determined by a liberal framework,[7] but it is important to keep this limitation in mind when framing our line of questioning.

In this study of the Protestant ethos and the cumulative spirit of capitalism,[8] Weber collapsed Francke's Halle and Herrnhut together under the star of Zinzendorf, and claimed that this was all too emotional and inward-focused to have had any impact on economic rationality. However, while Weber dismisses the participation of Pietism in early modern economy, his ostensible reasons for doing so are not the same as those who relegate religion to the private sphere. Weber was precisely interested in the theological drive and its impact on

---

explanation, see also pp. 13–14) but rests on ideal types which 'at best but seldom be found in history' (p. 56, see also footnote 68 on page 194), and claims to avoid psychological language (footnote 114 on p. 208), and yet refers to psychological sanctions (p. 55, p. 80, p. 121, etc.) and effects (p. 80, p. 115), on more than one occasion, and also psychological stimulus (p. 62), basis (p. 78), course (p. 97) and force (n. 30, p. 181). I would like to thank Kristian Mejrup for multiple discussions on Weber and Pietism.

[6] Fredric Jameson, 'The Vanishing Mediator: Narrative Structure in Max Weber', *New German Critique* 1 (1973): 52–89, here 53–4.
[7] Wallerstein, *The Modern World-System 4. Centrist Liberalism Triumphant, 1789-1914*, 251–8.
[8] Max Weber, *Die protestantische Ethik und der Geist des Kapitalismus* (Tübingen: Mohr, 1934). My references are to Max Weber, *The Protestant Ethic and the Spirit of Capitalism*, Routledge Classics (London and New York: Routledge, 2001).

capitalism. But for Weber, as mentioned, the ethos of Pietism was not ascetic and rational enough to have a significant impact on the thrifty spirit of capitalism:

> [I]nsofar as the rational and ascetic element of Pietism outweighed the emotional, the ideas essential to our thesis maintained their place. These were: (1) that the methodical development of one's own state of grace to a higher and higher degree of certainty and perfection in terms of the law was a sign of grace; and (2) that 'God's Providence works through those in such a state of perfection,' i.e. in that He gives them His signs if they wait patiently and deliberate methodically.[9]

This quotation demonstrates the problem: Weber operates at the level of theological ideas, not on the level of what we might call economic thinking and planning. Weber wants to show how the theological doctrines *as* theological doctrines had (or did not have) an effect on the capitalist spirit. Furthermore, the spirit of capitalism is a peculiar disembodied and even noble asceticism, an 'ethically coloured maxim for the conduct of life':[10]

> Unlimited greed for gain is not in the least identical with capitalism, and is still less its spirit. Capitalism *may* even be identical with the restraint, or at least a rational tempering, of this irrational impulse. But capitalism is identical with the pursuit of profit, and forever *renewed* profit, by means of continuous, rational, capitalistic enterprise.[11]

Despite Weber's insistence that his aim was not 'to substitute for a one-sided materialistic an equally one-sided spiritualistic causal interpretation of culture and of history',[12] it should be noted that his 'spirit of capitalism' is somewhat metaphysical, and that the affinities he presents between Protestantism and capitalism are in the realm of spirit. Weber himself believed that he was showing the effects of religious ideas on material culture,[13] but we hear very little of actual industry and entrepreneurial activity. In fact, Weber states that 'the mercantilistic regulations of the State might develop industries, but not, or certainly not alone, the spirit of capitalism; where they assumed a despotic, authoritarian character, they to a large extent directly hindered it.'[14]

Weber was thus not interested in the practices on the ground, but only in the drive, ethos or spirit, or whatever we might call this urge for the rational acquisition of profit. And so, for anyone trying to ascertain the relation between

---

[9] Weber, *The Protestant Ethic and the Spirit of Capitalism*, 84.
[10] Weber, *The Protestant Ethic and the Spirit of Capitalism*, 17.
[11] Weber, *The Protestant Ethic and the Spirit of Capitalism*, xxxi–xxxii.
[12] Weber, *The Protestant Ethic and the Spirit of Capitalism*, 125.
[13] Weber, *The Protestant Ethic and the Spirit of Capitalism*, 261, note 188.
[14] Weber, *The Protestant Ethic and the Spirit of Capitalism*, 99.

economic thinking and practice in Pietism, Weber is not helpful. In fact, by arguing for the influence of the Protestant ethos on the spirit of capitalism or the affinity between the two, Weber regards religion as an *external* factor with agency. This places religion in an outside position, or in other words, compartmentalizes it. And whoever follows him down the rabbit-hole, by either refuting or embracing him,[15] accepts the parameters and follow the line of questioning defined by Weber and the separation of the religious and economic spheres.[16]

So, because Weber's understanding of capitalism is an obsession with money and profit, capitalism's social disruptions, its ideological import and its effect on social relations hold little or no significance. Weber, then, does not regard capitalism as what the Marxists call a 'mode of production' which includes economy, society and ideology, but rather as a distinct category which concerns only money. By contrast, Sombart has advocated a more dialectical approach:

> It is fully justified to uncover the influence that a certain religious conviction – Puritanism – has exerted on the formation of capitalist entrepreneurship; just as justified (and necessary), however, is the other effort to investigate: 1. whether, apart from Puritanism (before it), certain courses of capitalist entrepreneurship have not already been formed from other causes (for instance, of unmediated origin), 2. to what extent Puritanism itself is in turn historically conditioned (and has, for instance, one – or all – of its roots in an already developed capitalist economy). Max Weber is the latest person to consider this addition to his work unnecessary.[17]

In this proposal, Sombart follows Marx, who had also spotted the relationship between Protestant movements and capitalism:

> For a society based upon the production of commodities, in which the producers in general enter into social relations with one another by treating their products as commodities and values, whereby they reduce their individual private labour to the standard of homogeneous human labour — for such a society, Christianity

---

[15] Peter Vogt, 'Let Our Commerce Be Holy unto Thee! Economic Practice in the Eighteenth Century Moravian Church', in *Pietismus und Ökonomie (1650-1750)*, ed. Wolfgang Breul, Benjamin Marschke and Alexander Schunka, Arbeiten zur Geschichte des Pietismus 65 (Göttingen: Vandenhoeck & Ruprecht, 2021), 269–300.

[16] In a less charitable vein, Werner Sombart states that 'only the myopic "historian" of our time is capable of the fallacy that Max Weber's investigations "disprove" all "immediate" origins of the capitalist entrepreneur and all "economic" causation (or conditionality) of religious (and any other spiritual) phenomena'. Werner Sombart, 'Der Kapitalistische Unternehmer', in *Werner Sombart: Die Modernität des Kapitalismus. Herausgegeben von Klaus Lichtblau*, 2nd edn, Klassiker der Sozialwissenschaften (Wiesbaden: Springer VS, 2019), 241–300, here 296.

[17] Sombart, 'Der Kapitalistische Unternehmer', 296.

with its *cultus* of abstract man, more especially in its bourgeois developments, Protestantism, Deism, &c, is the most fitting form of religion.[18]

This quote from *Capital* is not the type of vulgar Marxism that is Weber's concealed adversary in his study. What differs is what it qualifies as economy, in that the quote from Marx has a much broader understanding of economy, as socio-economics, than Weber, who sees it as merely profits and money.

Bürgergeist

It should now be clear to us that Weber's representation of the relationship between Protestantism and capitalism is woefully inadequate, as well as fundamentally counterproductive for historical analysis. In fact, some of the most challenging and innovative research into economy and Moravians has been carried out precisely by not letting oneself be trapped by Weber.[19] This is the approach I have followed here in this book. For this last section, I want to stay with Werner Sombart, mentioned earlier. While Sombart, in the end, gave up on his dialectical point of the historically conditioned nature of evangelicalism, I still find him useful to address this issue, because of his careful attention to the intricacies of the historical developments of early modern capitalism and its cultural effects.

As I have demonstrated, the Moravians were not immune to the socio-economic changes of the eighteenth century. Erbe's charge of the creeping *Bürgergeist* in the post-Zinzendorf era is an indication of this.[20] The term is derived from the work of Sombart, on whom Erbe relied for his analysis of Bethlehem. It is a less charged term than those of liberalism, non-liberalism and conservatism,[21] which I used in Chapter 1 to describe the distinct Moravian ideas of individual, community and history. Furthermore, it is an

---

[18] Marx, *Capital*, 90.
[19] The work of Katherine Carté Engel (*Religion and Profit*), Homburg 'Glaube – Arbeit – Geschlecht' and 'Gläubige und Gläubiger'), and Thomas Dorfner ('Commercium nach dem Sinn Jesu') and 'Von "Bösen Sektierern" zu "Fleißigen Fabrikanten": Zum Wahrnehmungswandel der Herrnhuter Brüdergemeine im Kontext Kameralistischer Peuplierungspolitik (ca. 1750-1800)', *Zeitschrift für Historische Forschung* 45/2 (2018): 283–313. See also Ester Sahle's work on the Quakers. Esther Sahle, *Quakers in the British Atlantic World, c.1660-1800*, People, Markets, Goods: Economies and Societies in History, vol. 18 (Woodbridge: Boydell Press, 2021).
[20] Erbe, *Bethlehem, Pa*, 133.
[21] Even more so in our times. My use of these terms is thus *not* to be understood in terms of the US positions of Democrats and Republicans.

apt term, because it captures the changes underway before they congealed into the categories of conservatism and liberalism after the French Revolution, as identified by Wallerstein. Before the French Revolution, then, there was a variety of ideological innovations as a result of the changing world and the emergence of capitalism, which only after the revolution would take shape as distinct political ideologies.[22] It is of course this pre-Revolutionary period which has been the interest in the present book and where we are trying to pinpoint how to understand the Moravians in all of this.

That Sombart also sees a difference between conservatism and liberalism is evident in his distinction between the old-style bourgeois and the modern entrepreneur, a difference which he notes lasts until the end of the eighteenth century. As mentioned in chapter 1, Sombart defines the old-style bourgeois as one, who, in all his thinking and planning, was still determined by the well-being of living humans. Those who served capitalism were, until the end of the eighteenth century operating within the requirements of life, and this was so for the grand estate holder, the overseas merchant, the banker, the speculator, the manufacturer and the wool merchant: 'for all of them business remained only a means to the ends of life; for all of them their own life interests and those of the other people for whom they work decided the direction and extent of their activity'.[23] While the reasons were multiple, such as sustenance, traditionalism or ethical concerns, 'there is always something that inhibits the free development of the drive for acquisition, the spirit of enterprise and economic rationalism'.[24]

Bürgergeist, by contrast, marks the spirit of capitalism, and Sombart traces its beginnings to the Italian merchant cities of the fifteenth century. In *Der Bourgeois*, Sombart distils two groups of sentiments from the works of the quintessential Renaissance man, Leon Battista Alberti: those that relate to the internal organization of the economy, which he dubs 'the sacred economy'; and those that regulate the economic relations to the outside world, which is named 'business ethics'.[25] Here, I am interested only in the first group, which clarifies what defines good business/economy, namely the rationalization of management. This entails establishing a proper balance between income and expenditure –

---

[22] See Losurdo, *Liberalism*, chapter 1, where he discusses the various positions of pro- and anti-freedom, slavery and monarchy, and the difficulty of determining the various positions in the seventeenth and early eighteenth centuries.
[23] Sombart, *Der Bourgeois*, 196.
[24] Sombart, *Der Bourgeois*, 211.
[25] Sombart, *Der Bourgeois*, 137.

and is, thus, an art of house-holding (*Haushaltungskunst*) and consequently a discarding of all the principles of a seigneurial way of life. That is to say, an economy of expenditure (seigneurial) had to be changed into an economy of income. The second characteristic of a good economy is the emphasis on saving as a virtue rather than as a necessity, namely the economization of business management. What all of this required, however, was computational ability, namely the aptitude and skill to dissolve the world into numbers and reassemble these numbers into a system of income and expenditure.[26] In *Der Moderne Kapitalismus*, Sombart expands on this point, defining the capitalist enterprise as an organization of wealth, which is characterized by the independence of the business and is enabled by jurisprudence, business technique and commercial intercourse. The role of jurisprudence was to transfer onto companies or businesses a series of rights, recognitions and agencies. By themselves, these have no significance without the overall structural changes, which in turn were enabled by the interaction and traffic between these independent agents – here we also see the significance of the contract-form, which Sombart sees as fundamental to capitalist organization.[27] The second feature that enabled the independence of the business enterprise was the technique of bookkeeping, a technique to which Sombart attributed enormous significance but which has since been attacked, mainly by neoclassical economists.[28] Sombart's argument is that since its beginnings in the Italian cities in the thirteenth century, bookkeeping went through a number of developments so that it was fully developed already in the early capitalist period.[29]

Sounding *almost* Foucauldian,[30] Sombart posits that

> Double-entry bookkeeping rests on the consistently implemented basic idea of recording all phenomena only as quantities, the basic idea, therefore, of quantification, which has brought to light all the wonders of natural knowledge, and which here, probably for the first time in human history, has in full clarity been made the backbone of a system.[31]

---

[26] Sombart, *Der Bourgeois*, 164.
[27] Sombart, *Der Bourgeois*, 104–10. For the form of the contract, see 29–33.
[28] See several critical essays on Sombart in B. S. Yamey, *Essays on the History of Accounting* (New York: Arno Press, 1978). John Ryan gives a good background to the discussion in 'Historical Note: Did Double-entry Bookkeeping Contribute to Economic Development, Specifically the Introduction of Capitalism?' *Australasian Accounting, Business and Finance Journal* 8, no. 3 (2014): 85–97.
[29] Sombart, *Der Bourgeois*, 110–17.
[30] Michel Foucault, *Order of Things. An Archaeology of Human Sciences* (Random House, 1973), 56–8.
[31] Sombart, *Der Bourgeois*, 119.

Again, as mentioned in chapter 1, Sombart points to double-entry bookkeeping as separating profit from 'all natural purposes of subsistence'.[32] This enabled the idea of acquisition, as well as the organization of wealth and, not least, the independent business. This newly enabled independence is granted by separating the enterprise from the entrepreneur and arranging it according to purely objectified characteristics, which would be recognizable by an outsider. This abstraction renders the the enterprise recognizable *as* an independent enterprise without regard to a person or owner.

In light of this treatment of Sombart, we may now return to Erbe's point concerning the battle over the socio-economic organization of Bethlehem: it was Johann Friedrich Koeber who was an embodiment of the *Bürgergeist* of the time (around 1760) and that such an emerging *Geist* was also to be found in the Unity as a whole.[33]

Johann Friedrich Koeber (1717–86) was born in Altenburg. After finishing his legal studies in Leipzig, he became private secretary for Friedrich Caspar von Gersdorf, in whose service he worked for six years. Koeber's memoir, which was not written by himself, notes that these years served 'to ground his heart much deeper in the grace of Jesus as well as to train him in the businesses, from which the we (i.e. the Moravian Church) gained use and blessing for so many years'.[34] The restructures he undertook in the management of the Unity resonate with Sombart's emphases. Not only was Koeber a computational genius, he also ensured that double bookkeeping was introduced. Koeber was part of the movement to call for inventories from the settlements and for changing Bethlehem into a regular, independent settlement type within the Moravian Unity. Within the same leadership group, von Marschall's task was to confirm Bethlehem as a legal entity in Pennsylvania. The restructures in the West Indies in the 1780s were also part of creating more independent settlements with independent economies, with meticulous plantation accounts and inventories.

And yet, there were other features of the restructure that did not slip so seamlessly into this *Bürgergeist* or early capitalist logic. Although all of these communities were administratively distinct, they were nonetheless part of a Unity and so were not fully independent in economic terms. If they did not themselves rely on means from the Mission Diakony (such as St Thomas), they were obliged to pay tribute to the Mission Diacony, money which was then used

---

[32] Sombart, *Der Bourgeois*, 119.
[33] Erbe, *Bethlehem, Pa*, 133.
[34] Memoir of Johann Friedrich Koeber. GN 1786, VIIIa, appendix to week 32. The memoir is also printed in *Nachrichten aus der Brüdergemeine* (1847): 284–95, and (1864): 650–61.

to support the less profitable missions (such as those in Greenland). The economy of the Unity was thus centralized and heavily planned. As such it mirrored the relationship between the individual member and his or her congregation. The congregations and their members were also carefully planned and engineered, with members selected and approved by lot before moving around randomly.[35] We saw how the lot was used to select the new choir leaders for the restructure of Bethlehem in Chapter 2. Jeppe Brøndum, the bookkeeper in St Thomas, was also chosen by lot and after some persuasion took up this calling. This dialectic between individual and community is thus a central feature of the Unity at a general and at a particular level. This brings us to the final section.

Moravian particularities

In Chapter 1, I mentioned that eighteenth-century Moravian ideology contained what I called a non-liberal strain: the emphasis on the common humanity of its members, on community and on history. How are these connected with the emergence of capitalism? While I noted earlier that there were features that did not fit Sombart's *Bürgergeist*, we may still gain some help from his observation that the old-style bourgeois were still embedded in a world view where business was the means to a purpose, a purpose that directed every activity.[36] This indicates that there were leftovers from the old world, which now operate in the new.

In *The Moravian Brethren in a Time of Transition*, I argued that it should not come as a surprise that there are competing ideas in times of social change, and it is important to recognize that the social formations and relations in eighteenth-century German states were different from the liberal ideology that infuses and determines the ruling ideas of the Western world. In that earlier work, I deployed Fredric Jameson's concept of 'cultural revolution', which he defined as the moment when competing modes of production and their antagonisms have

---

[35] When Christiansfeld in the Dutchy of Schleswig was founded in 1773, the lot was used to approve this or that brother or sister who had volunteered their service in building up the congregation. See Christina Petterson, 'Christiansfelds "levende stene"'. Levnedsløb og kredsløb', in *En by på kongens mark. Grundlæggelsen af Christiansfeld 1773*, ed. Jørgen Bøytler, Michael Nobel Hviid and Christina Petterson (Århus: Aarhus University Press, 2023), 113–40.

[36] Sombart, *Der Bourgeois*, 196. Peter Vogt concludes that the Moravians 'embraced the sphere of economic activity but modified it according to their religious beliefs and values' arriving at the category of 'moral capitalism', a term used by Katherine Carté Engel to describe the Strangers Store in Bethlehem. Vogt, 'Let our Commerce be Holy unto Thee!', 300. Katherine Carté Engel, 'The Strangers' Store: Moral Capitalism in Moravian Bethlehem, 1753-1775', *Early American Studies: An Interdisciplinary Journal* 1, no. 1 (Spring 2003): 90–126.

moved to the centre of political and social life.[37] I made use of this framework to read through archival material as participating in the struggle between the old world and its new incarnation.[38]

Unsurprisingly, we see a similar situation here. While the Moravians in Europe experienced one set of challenges in relation to the changing times, the Moravian missionaries on the colonial frontier of the eighteenth century experienced others. The Unity as a whole was not immune to the changes. And as we have seen in the previous chapters, the Moravian Unity went through numerous changes, for example, in organization and management, in relation to money and in relation to slavery.

However, in their perception of individual and community and in their understanding of themselves as interconnected with generations past and communities hitherto, they did not change. And this was in spite of a range of challenges from without and within. For example, the Moravian sense of community came under severe pressure in Greenland. This was not only due to the trading company's dispersion of the Moravian Kalaallit and the complete domination of trading in produce but also due to internal pressures and discord, which was especially focused on acquisition and the perception of rights to things held in storage. The communal household did not fare well – and yet, the Unity held on to the Greenland mission until the synod in 1899. In St Thomas, where my focus was more on the 'outer', the congregation also faced the challenge of the members being spread out on numerous plantations, but this was resolved by using helpers, or enslaved Moravian men and women on the different plantations who were to supervise. The size and extent of the Moravian Church in the Caribbean today demonstrates that the 'inner' sphere was strong and unbroken, even as the congregations today wrestle with the legacies of slavery and dispossession.

In terms of the common humanity of the believers, the tone in both Greenland and St Thomas of the eighteenth century was in general one of inclusion and affection. Granted there were problems with the Kalaallit and enslaved brothers and sisters; disciplinary measures were taken and frustrations expressed, but the relation was maintained and treasured. However, and this cannot be emphasized enough, *this was solely within the community*. In Greenland, the non-Christian Kalaallit were most often referred to as 'the wild' (die Wilden), with heathen ways, a source of danger and temptation for 'our Greenlanders'. And in St Thomas, as

[37] Jameson *The Political Unconscious: Narrative as a Socially Symbolic Act* (Ithaca: Cornell University Press, 1981), 81.
[38] Petterson, *The Moravian Brethren in a Time of Transition*, 266.

we have seen, there was a distinction between the enslaved Moravians of the congregation and the slaves owned by the mission, who were treated in more or less the same manner as on other plantations, and in Herrnhut administered and valued along the same lines as by absentee slave-owners.

Finally, history. I submit that I have not sufficiently demonstrated the importance of history in the Moravian community. I find it difficult because our language and our theoretical concepts make it difficult to express. But if we think of it as akin to the aristocratic emphasis on lineage, tradition and institution, I think we have come close. The individual Moravian is but one incarnation or embodiment of the history and spirit of Moravian activity. It is a history from within, a connection to the entirety of Moravian history and activity. And perhaps history is not the best term, given its connection with fragmented time, because the Moravian relates to a totality of its own, not defined by scriptural interpretation or a history of dogmatics but by its practice, which is why it is so difficult to define. For an outsider, it is only available in its traces.

Speaking in purely secular terms, these three elements are part of the feudal heritage of the Moravians. Feudalism, in particular the world view of the aristocracy, or the *ancien regime*, had notions of community, individual and history that were at odds with an emerging liberal ideology. This showed up most clearly in Greenland, where the Moravian ideology could continue in a 'pure' form because of the specific economic conditions, which enabled a fairly singular focus on the inner sphere. As I have argued in this book, however, this particular development in Greenland was completely reliant on profits made in other, more violent and extremely exploitative contexts. As Gisela Mettele argued,[39] the Moravians are fascinating to study because of their global nature, but we must go all the way to understand this global nature and its entanglement with capitalism. We have to push beyond the focus on individual missions and congregations, draw in the centralized management in Germany and acknowledge the fundamental contribution of Quintus' labour in the sugar plantations of St Thomas to the conversion of Kalaallit in New-Herrnhut.

De te fabula narratur.

---

[39] Mettele, *Weltbürgertum oder Gottesreich*, 9–17.

Archival references

Unity Archives, Herrnhut (UA)

Herrnhut

Minutes

Central Council (*Ratskonferenz*) 1760–1761,	R.3.B.4.c.1
Inner Council (*Enge Konferenz*) 1762–1764,	R.6.A.b.47.d
Directorial Board 1759–1762,	UVC.P.6.2
Mission Deputation 1765–1769,	R.15.A.65.52
Mission Deputation 1770–1772,	R.15.A.65.53
Mission Department 1897,	R.15.A.65.49
Unity Elders Conference (UAC) IV/1781,	R.3.P.1781-4

Correspondence

Fr von Watteville to Zinzendorf, 21 June 1754 (Addendum to minutes),	R.2.A.34.3
C.A. von Plessen to Zinzendorf, 1 February 1735,	R.20.C.3.d, 136

Synod

Marienborn Synod Protocol, vol 1,	R.2.B.44.1.c.1
Marienborn Synod Protocol, vol 2,	R.2.B.44.1.c.2

Miscellaneous

Possessions of the Mission Diacony in East, West, South and North,	MDF 1027
Instruction for the Deputation for the Mission Diacony 1762,	R.15.4A.7a

Bethlehem

Reports

Memorandum on the Conference on the Pennsylvanian Oeconomies Herrnhut, 2 December 1760,	R.14.A.41.b.6
Hans Herman von Damnitz, Concerning the Pennsylvanian Issues Herrnhut, 8 February 1761,	UVC.X.143.a.b UVC.I.41, 135 (copy)
Friedrich von Marschall's Report on the Oeconomicum, February 1761,	UVC.X.141

Correspondence

Johannes von Watteville to Spangenberg. Herrnhut 15 July 1760,	R.14.A.20.7.31
Spangenberg to Johannes von Watteville. Bethlehem, 11 November 1760,	R.14.A.20.7.33
Koeber et al. to Spangenberg. Herrnhut, 31 March 1761,	R.14.A.41.b, 3
Spangenberg to Johannes von Watteville. Bethlehem, 9 May 1762,	R.14.A.20, 36

St Thomas

Diaries

Diary, New-Herrnhut, St Thomas 1796–1811,	R.15.B.b.09.e

Minutes

House Conference, St Thomas 1779–1882,	R.15.B.b.20.a
Helpers' Conference, Danish West Indies 1763–1780,	R.15.B.b.20.c
Helpers' Conference, Danish West Indies 1784–1800,	R.15.B.b.20.e

Visitations

Nathanael Seidel, New-Herrnhut, St Thomas (1759),	R.15.B.a.12, 127
Letters to Thrane and Mack regarding visitation (1776–1778),	MDF.1918
Johann Loretz, St Thomas and St Croix (1784),	MDF.1920

Correspondence

Christian David to the Brothers and Sisters in Herrnhut, 4 April 1733,	MDF 1874.1.3
Christian David to Thimotheus Fiedler. Herrnhut, 17 November 1736,	R.15.B.a.10, 30.
Spangenberg to Isaac Lelong. Skippack, 9 June 1738,	R.15.B.a.10, 80.
Spangenberg to Zinzendorf. Bethlehem, 27 November 1754,	R.15.B.a.12, 112.
Georg Ohneberg to Johannes von Watteville. St Croix, 15 January 1758,	R.15.B.a.12, 119.
Spangenberg to Georg Weber. Bethlehem, 23 January 1758,	R.15.B.b.25, 15.
Jens Korn to Christian Hillmar Saalwächter. St Thomas, 20 July 1759,	MDF.1911, 21.
Jens Korn to Christian Hillmar Saalwächter. St Thomas, 24 March 1762,	MDF.1911, 25.
Jeppe Brøndum to Jonas Paul Wiess. St Thomas, 20 March 1764,	MDF 1911, 37.
Johann Peter Schwimmer to Mission Deputation. St Thomas, 6 November 1766,	MDF 1911, 66.
Missionaries, St Thomas to the Brothers of the General Synod. St Thomas, 28 January 1769,	MDF 1912, 13
Johann Loretz to Johannes von Watteville. St Thomas, 23 April 1784,	R.15.B.a.21.a, 109.
Mission Department to Helpers Conference in St Thomas. Herrnhut, 19 October 1792,	R.15.B.b.26.d, 121.
Johann Loretz to Governor Malleville, 24 October 1792,	R.15.B.b.26.d, 123
Governor Malleville to Herrnhut. St Thomas, 22 May 1793,	R.15.B.b.26.d, 136.
Matthias Wied to Johannes Verbeek. Neuherrnhut d, 20 July 1797,	MDF 2282.1, n.

Miscellaneous

Annual accounts from Danish West Indies 1784–1810,	MDF 2092
St Thomas – Sale of the Plantation Raschun [i.e. Rephun] 1797–1804,	MDF 2282.1.

Acta Publica concerning the Mission on St Thomas, St Croix und St Jan Vol. I,   R.15.B.a.3
10: The best and surest means regarding the form in which a sugar plantation
must be started and how it should be worked on, as well as what is needed and
required for its establishment
31. Report by Friedrich Martins (copied by G. Weber), how the Brothers came
to own plantations with slaves, along with some remarks on the economic state
of the mission. 10 July 1738

Letters and remarks to the diaries of St Thomas, Croix, and John. 1733–1766,	R.15.B.a.14
Letter of purchase of Binda and Dick. 21 March 1797,	R.15.B.a.31.3.b, 2.
Declaration by the Danish West Indian missionaries on their work. 1765,	R.15.B.a.23.01

Greenland

Diaries

Diary, New-Herrnhut, Greenland January. 1745–11 August 1752,	R.15.J.b.I.01.b
Diary, New-Herrnhut, Greenland 12 August 1752–20 November 1761,	R.15.J.b.I.01.c
Diary, New-Herrnhut, Greenland 11 August 1761–31 July 1770,	R.15.J.b.I.02.a
Diary, New-Herrnhut, Greenland 1 March 1779–31 December 1784,	R.15.J.b.I.03.a
Diary, New-Herrnhut, Greenland 1 August 1796–29 May 1821,	R.15.J.b.I.04.a
Secret diary of Christian Stach 10 October 1734–7 August 1735,	R.15.J.a.02.b

Minutes

Conference, New-Herrnhut 1749–1773,	R.15.J.b.I.7, 1-4.
Conference, New-Herrnhut 1779–1783,	R.15.J.b.I.09
House and business conference 1779–1783,	R.15.J.b.I.18

Visitations

Andreas Grassmann: Visitation to Greenland (1740),	R.15.J.a.16.3
Johannes von Watteville's farewell letter after his visitation (1752),	R.15.J.a.9.21
Martin Gottfried Sternberg's visitation to Greenland (1771),	R.15 J.a.18.a

Correspondence

David Nitschmann to New-Herrnhut. Copenhagen, 27 March 1742,	R.15.J.a.3. 20
Matthäus Stach to Lorenz Praetorius. Dronninglund, 2 May 1742,	R.15.J.a.4, 10
Zinzendorf to Rosina Nitschmann, 12 March 1745,	R.15.J.a.9, 17.
Rescript from King Frederic V. to the Trading Company, 13 February 1750,	R.15.J.a.12, 1.
Johannes von Watteville to the missionaries in Greenland, 16 March 1758,	R.15.J.b.I.26.a, 24
Inner Council to the missionaries in New-Herrnhut and Lichtenfels, 24 February 1763,	R.15.J.b.I.26.a, 34
Johannes von Watteville to the Unity Syndicat College. Zeist, 17 February 1769,	R.15.J.a.17, 5.
UAC to the missionaries in Greenland. Barby, 16 March 1772,	R.15.J.b.26a, 86.
UAC to Christoph Michael Königseer. 24 March 1777,	R.15.J.b.26.a, 110

Memorandum from Friedrich Koeber to Lorenz Praetorius, Barby, 12 May 1777, R.15.J.a.17, 7
Jakob Beck to Mission Deputation. New-Herrnhut, 16 September 1782, MDF.1890
Elders' Conference to the Mission Deputation. New-Herrnhut, 16 July 1783, .15.J.b.I.24.b

Miscellaneous

Conference Matters 1741–1746, R.15.J.a.11
1, 1: Document on work and nourishment, 15 November 1741.
1, 4: Remarks concerning Greenland (undated)
2, 6: Missionary questions and Zinzendorf's (?) answers.
David Nitschmann's submission to the King of Denmark, 24 January 1742, R.15.J.a.3.a, 10
Royal Decree, Copenhagen, 16 March 1742, R.15.J.a.3.a, 13
Inventories and accountbooks, New-Herrnhut (1733–1899), here 1742, R.15.J.b.I.32, 5
Negotiations in Copenhagen regarding the mission in Greenland (1768–1777), R.15.J.a.17
The beginning of the Greenland Mission 1722–1771, MDF 1874
Annual reports from Greenland 1766–1788 (1774 and 1775), R.15.J.b.01
From the Minutes of the U.A.C to New-Herrnhut. 27 February 1783, R.15.J.b.I.26, 136
The Greenlandic Question from 1899, R.15.J.a.24, 16
Sketch of the Community house in New-Herrnhut, Greenland, TS 22.2

Memoirs/Lebensläufe

Johann Friedrich Koeber GN 1786, VIIIa, 32.
Gottlieb Oertel R.22.109.09.
Rosina Nitschmann NB.I.R.4.291.c.2.30

Bethlehem (MAB)

MissWI: The West Indian Papers

This collection is fully digitized.

Visitations

Johannes von Watteville's visitation in St Thomas, St Croix and St John, (1749), MissWi 173, 4
Diaries of Nathanael Seidel's visit to the West Indies (1753), MissWI 175
1. Conference notes, 2 June–22 July 1753.
2. Notes regarding Moravian assets and debts in St Thomas and St Croix.
3. Descriptions of the various African tribes.
4. Original draft of Nathanael Seidel's report of his visit to St Thomas, St Croix and St John
5. Copy of Nathanael Seidel's report of his visit to St Thomas, St Croix and St John.
Visitation reports of Christian Heinrich Rauch (1755), MissWI 154, 3

Correspondence

Friedrich Cammerhof to Georg Weber et al. Bethlehem, 14 July 1747,	MissWI 129, 3
Johannes von Watteville to F. Cammerhof. St Thomas, 27 April 1749,	MissWi 129.15
Johannes von Watteville to Jens Korn. Zeist, 6 September 1761,	MissWi 129, 24

Lists

Black men and women and children which are our property. July 1755,	MissWI 180, 7
Catalog of members on St Thomas, St Croix and St John,	MissWi 179, 2

BethCong

Bethlehem leadership to Directorial Board. 13 January 1759,	BethCong 425
Suggestions for separating the Oeconomie. 31 October 1760,	BethCong 610, 1
Directorial Board to Spangenberg et al. Herrnhut, 31 March 1761,	BethCong 637, 4.
Johannes von Watteville to Spangenberg. Lindsey House, 11 June 1761,	BethCong 637,2.

Miscellaneous

Rosina Nitschmann, English memoir.	MemBeth 0027
Diary of the Single Sisters	BethSS.2
Diary of the Single Brothers	BethSB.2
Johann Arbo's Memorandum book	BethSB.7

Letters

Mission Deputation to Johann Arbo. Herrnhut, 24 January 1770,	MAB PHC.140
Heinrich XXXI Reuss (Ignatius) to Nathanael Seidel. Zeist, 28 September 1762	PP SNath 6

Unprocessed

Results of the synod held in Bethlehem between 3/14th September and 8/19th September 1747, (AmSyn)
Spangenberg Papers, Box II, 1a
Declarations of members entering the Oeconomie

Danish National Archives (Rigsarkivet)

The archive's Danish West Indian collection is fully digitised.
Rigsarkivet 697: St Thomas Byfoged. 1755-1827 Testamentprotokoller for Notarius Publicus 1781–1796, pp. 151–3.

Bibliography

Abel, Sarah, George Tyson and Gísli Pálsson. 'From Enslavement to Emancipation: Naming Practices in the Danish West Indies'. *Comparative Studies in Society and History* 61, no. 1 (2019): 332–65. https://doi.org/10.1017/S0010417519000070.

Agamben, Giorgio. *The Kingdom and the Glory. For a Theological Genealogy of Economy and Government (Homo Sacer II, 2)*. Translated by Lorenzo Chiesa with Matteo Mandarini. Stanford: Stanford University Press, 2011.

Ahlbäck, Anders. 'The Overly Candid Missionary Historian. C. G. A. Oldendorp's Theological Ambivalence over Slavery in the Danish West Indies'. In *Ports of Globalisation, Places of Creolisation. Nordic Possessions in the Atlantic World during the Era of the Slave Trade*, edited by Holger Weiss, 191–217. Leiden: Brill, 2016.

Anderson, Benedict. *Imagined Communities: Reflections on the Origin and Spread of Nationalism*. Revised and extended edition. London: Verso, 2006.

Atwood, Craig D. 'Sleeping in the Arms of Christ: Sanctifying Sexuality in the Eighteenth-Century Moravian Church'. *Journal of the History of Sexuality* 8, no. 1 (1997): 25–51.

Atwood, Craig D. *The Theology of the Czech Brethren from Hus to Comenius*. University Park: Penn State University Press, 2009.

Atwood, Craig D. 'Understanding Zinzendorf's Blood and Wounds Theology'. *Journal of Moravian History* 1 (2006): 31–47.

Balibar, Etienne. 'Citizen Subject'. In *Who Comes after the Subject?* edited by Eduardo Cadava, Peter Connor and Jean-Luc Nancy, 33–57. London: Routledge, 1991.

Baumgart, Peter. *Zinzendorf als wegbereiter historischen Denkens*. Lübeck/Hamburg: Matthiesen Verlag, 1960.

Baumgold, Deborah. *Contract Theory in Historical Context: Essays on Grotius, Hobbes, and Locke*. Brill: Leiden, 2010.

Beck, Hartmut. *Brüder in vielen Völkern: 250 Jahre Mission der Brüdergemeine*. Erlanger Taschenbücher, Bd 58. Erlangen: Verlag der Ev.-Luth. Mission, 1981.

Becker-Cantarino, Barbara. 'Zur Bedeutung der *Oeconomia* im Engagement adliger Frauen im Pietismus: Erdmuthe Dorothea von Zinzendorf'. In *Pietismus und Adel: Genderhistorische Analysen*, edited by Ruth Albrecht, Ulrike Gleixner, Corinna Kirschstein, Eva Kormann and Pia Schmid, 155–77. Halle: Verlag der Franckesche Stiftungen, 2018.

Beiser, Frederick C. *After Hegel: German Philosophy 1840–1900*. Princeton: Princeton University Press, 2014.

Bobé, Louis. *Diplomatarium Groenlandicum 1492-1814. Aktstykker og Breve til Oplysning om Grønlands Besejling, Kolonisation og Missionering*. 55/3. Meddelser om Grønland. København: C.A. Reitzels Forlag, 1936.

Bondi, Gerhard. 'Der Beitrag des Hallischen Pietismus zur Entwicklung des ökonomischen Denkens in Deutschland'. *Jahrbuch für Wirtschaftsgeschichte* 5, no. 2-3 (1964): 24-48.

Boucher, David and Paul Kelly. *The Social Contract from Hobbes to Rawls*. London: Routledge, 2003.

Braudel, Fernand. *Civilization and Capitalism, 15th-18th Century*. 1st U.S. 3 vols. New York: Harper & Row, 1982.

Braudel, Fernand. *Civilization and Capitalism, 15th-18th Century Vol. 3: The Perspective of the World*. Translated by Sian Reynolds. New York: Harper & Row, 1982.

Brecht, Martin, Klaus Deppermann, Ulrich Gäbler and Hartmut Lehmann. *Geschichte des Pietismus: Im Auftrag der historischen Kommission zur Erforschung des Pietismus*. Göttingen: Vandenhoeck & Ruprecht, 1993.

Bredsdorff, Thomas. *Den brogede oplysning. Om følelsernes fornuft og fornuftens følelse i 1700 tallets nordiske literatur*. København: Gyldendal, 2003.

Breul, Wolfgang. *Pietismus Handbuch*. Tübingen: Mohr Siebeck, 2021.

Breul, Wolfgang. 'Theological Tenets and Motives of Mission: August Hermann Francke, Nikolaus Ludwig von Zinzendorf'. In *Migration and Religion Christian Transatlantic Missions, Islamic Migration to Germany*, edited by Barbara Becker-Cantarino, 41-60. Leiden: Brill, 2012.

Brinkmann, Carl. 'Die Aristokratie im kapitalistischen Zeitalter'. In *Grundriss der Sozialökonomik IX Das soziale System des Kapitalismus. 1.Teil : Die Gesellschaftliche Schichtung im Kapitalismus*, edited by G. Albrecht, G. Briefs and C. Brinkmann, 23-34. Tübingen: J. C. B. Mohr, 1926.

Carøe, Kristian. *Den Danske Lægestand. Doktorer og Licentiater 1479-1788*. København: Gyldendalske Boghandel Nordisk Forlag, 2021.

Catron, John. 'Slavery, Ethnic Identity, and Christianity in Eighteenth-Century Moravian Antigua'. *Journal of Moravian History* 14, no. 2 (2014): 153-78.

Christensen, Sigrid Nielsby. '"We Held a Quite Blessed Communion, the Lamb Was Unusually Close to Me": Individual and Community in the Moravian Society in Eighteenth-Century Copenhagen'. In *Crossroads of Heritage and Religion Legacy and Sustainability of World Heritage Site Moravian Christiansfeld*, edited by Tine Damsholt, Marie Riegels Melchior, Christina Petterson and Tine Reeh, 41-58. New York: Berghahn Books, 2022.

Ciccariello-Maher, George. *Decolonizing Dialectics*. Durham: Duke University Press, 2017.

Comaroff, Jean and John L. Comaroff. *Of Revelation and Revolution I: Christianity, Colonialism, and Consciousness in South Africa*. Chicago: University of Chicago Press, 1991.

Comaroff, Jean and John L. Comaroff. *Of Revelation and Revolution II: The Dialectics of Modernity on a South African Frontier*. Chicago: University of Chicago Press, 1997.

Conrad, Sebastian. *What is Global History?* Princeton: Princeton University Press, 2016.
Conze, Werner. 'Stand, Klasse VII: Zwischen Reformation and Revolution (16-18 Jahrhundert)'. In *Geschichtliche Grundbegriffe: Historisches Lexicon zur Politisch-Sozialen Sprache in Deutschland (Studienausgabe)*, edited by Otto Brunner, Werner Conze and Reinhart Koselleck, vol. 6, 200-17. Stuttgart: Klett-Cotta, 2005.
Cranz, David. *Historie von Grönland: Enthaltend die Beschreibung des Landes und der Einwohner [et]c. Insbesondere die Geschichte der dortigen Mission der Evangelischen Brüder zu Neu-Herrnhut und Lichtenfels; Mit Acht Kupfertafeln und einem Register.* Barby and Leipzig: Heinrich Detlef Ebers, 1765.
Cranz, David. *The History of Greenland: Containing a Description of the Country, and Its Inhabitants and Particularly, a Relation of the Mission, Carried on for above These Thirty Years by the Unitas Fratrum, at New Herrnhuth and Lichtenfels, in that Country.* Translated by John Gambold, 2 vols. London: Printed for the Brethren's Society for the Furtherance of the Gospel among the Heathen and sold by J. Dodsley etc., 1767.
Cronshagen, Jessica. '"A Loyal Heart to Go and the Governor." Missions and Colonial Policy in the Surinamese Saramaccan Mission (c. 1750-1813)'. *Journal of Moravian History* 19, no. 1 (2019): 1-24.
Cronshagen, Jessica. 'Contrasting Roles of Female Moravian Missionaries in Surinam Negotiating Transatlantic Normalization and Colonial Everyday Practices (Eighteenth Century)'. In *Das Meer. Maritime Welten in der Frühen Neuzeit/The Sea. Maritime Worlds in the Early Modern Period*, edited by Peter Burschel and Sünne Juterczenka, 323-34. Köln: Böhlau, 2020.
Cronshagen, Jessica. 'Herrnhuter Diaspora, Erinnerungskultur und Identitätsbildung "in Abwesenheit". Briefnetzwerke zwischen Europa und Surinam'. In *Religion und Erinnerung. Konfessionelle Mobilisierung und Konflikte im Europa der frühen Neuzeit*, edited by Dagmar Freist and Matthias Weber, 201-9. Münche: Oldenbourg, 2015.
Cronshagen, Jessica. 'Owning the Body, Wooing the Soul: How Forced Labor Was Justified in the Moravian Correspondence Network in Eighteenth Century Surinam'. In *Connecting Worlds and People: Early Modern Diasporas*, edited by Dagmar Freist and Susanne Lachenicht, 81-103. London: Routledge, 2016.
Degn, Christian. *Die Schimmelmanns im Atlantischen Dreieckshandel: Gewinn und Gewissen*. Neumünster: K. Wachholtz, 1974.
Dohm, Burkhard. *Poetische Alchimie: Öffnung zur Sinnlichkeit in der Hohelied- und Bibeldichtung von der Protestantischen Barockmystik bis zum Pietismus*. Berlin: De Gruyter, 2000.
Dorfner, Thomas. '"Commercium nach dem Sinn Jesu". Überlegungen zum Marktverhalten der Herrnhuter Brüdergemeine am Beispiel des Labradorhandels (1770-1815)'. *Jahrbuch Für Wirtschaftsgeschichte* 61, no. 1 (2020): 39-66.
Dorfner, Thomas. 'Von "bösen Sektierern" zu "fleißigen Fabrikanten": Zum Wahrnehmungswandel der Herrnhuter Brüdergemeine im Kontext kameralistischer

Bibliography

Peuplierungspolitik (ca. 1750–1800)'. *Zeitschrift für historische Forschung* 45, no. 2 (2018): 283–313.

Dupré, Louis. *The Enlightenment and the Intellectual Foundations of Modern Culture.* New Haven: Yale University Press, 2004.

Egede, Poul and Mads Lidegaard. *Efterretninger om Grønland Uddragne af en Journal holden fra 1721 til 1788.* Det Grønlandske Selskabs Skrifter, XXIX. København: Det Grønlandske Selskab, 1988.

Engel, Katherine Carté. *Religion and Profit: Moravians in Early America.* Philadelphia: University of Pennsylvania Press, 2009.

Engel, Katherine Carté. 'Religion and the Economy. New Methods for an Old Problem'. *Early American Studies* 8, no. 3 (2010): 482–512.

Engel, Katherine Carté. 'The Evolution of the Bethlehem Pilgergemeine'. In *Pietism in Germany and North America 1680–1820,* edited by Hartmut Lehmann and James Van Horn Melton, 163–81. London: Routledge, 2009.

Engel, Katherine Carté. 'The Strangers' Store: Moral Capitalism in Moravian Bethlehem, 1753–1775'. *Early American Studies* 1, no. 1 (2003): 90–126.

Engelhardt, Juliane. 'Pietismus und Krise. Der Hallesche und der Radikale Pietismus im Dänischen Gesamtstaat'. *Historische Zeitschrift* 307, no. 2 (2018): 341–69.

Erbe, Hellmuth. *Bethlehem, Pa. Eine kommunistische Herrnhuter Kolonie des 18 Jahrhunderts.* Stuttgart: Ausland und Heimat Verlags-Aktiengesellschaft, 1929.

Ertman, Thomas. *Birth of the Leviathan: Building States and Regimes in Medieval and Early Modern Europe.* Cambridge: Cambridge University Press, 1997.

Faull, Katherine M. 'Faith and Imagination: Nikolaus Ludwig von Zinzendorf's Anti-Enlightenment Philosophy of Self'. In *Anthropology and the German Enlightenment: Perspectives on Humanity,* edited by Katherine M. Faull, 23–56. Lewisburg: Bucknell University Press, 1995.

Faull, Katherine M. 'From Friedenshütten to Wyoming: Johannes Ettwein's Map of the Upper Susquehanna (1768) and an Account of His Journey'. *Journal of Moravian History* 11 (2011): 82–96.

Faull, Katherine M. 'Masculinity in the Eighteenth-Century Moravian Mission Field: Contact and Negotiation'. *Journal of Moravian History* 13, no. 1 (2013): 27–53.

Faull, Katherine M. 'Temporal Men and the Eternal Bridegroom: Moravian Masculinity in the Eighteenth Century'. In *Masculinity, Senses, Spirit,* edited by Katherine M. Faull, 55–79. Lewisburg: Bucknell University Press, 2011.

Faull, Katherine M. *The Shamokin Diaries 1745–1755: The Moravian Mission to the Iroquois.* University Park: Pennsylvania State University Press, forthcoming.

Faull, Katherine M. and Christina Petterson. 'Bodies in "Heathen" Places: Regulating Marriage without a State'. *Journal of Religious History* 43, no. 2 (2019): 180–94.

Federici, Silvia. *Caliban and the Witch: Women, the Body and Primitive Accumulation.* New York: Autonomedia, 2004.

Feest, Christian F. 'Moravians and the Development of the Genre of Ethnography'. In *Ethnographies and Exchanges: Native Americans, Moravians and Catholics in*

Early North America, edited by A. G. Roeber, 19–30. University Park: Penn State University Press, 2008.

Fogleman, Aaron Spencer. *Two Troubled Souls: An Eighteenth-Century Couple's Spiritual Journey in the Atlantic World*. Chapel Hill: University of North Carolina Press, 2013.

Foucault, Michel. *The Order of Things: An Archaeology of the Human Sciences*. New York: Random House, 1973.

Foucault, Michel. *Security, Territory, Population.:Lectures at the Collège de France, 1977-78*. Translated by Graham Burchell. London: Palgrave Macmillan, 2007.

Fukuyama, Francis. 'The End of History?' *The National Interest* 16, Summer (1989): 3–18.

Füllberg-Stolberg, Claus. 'The Moravian Mission and the Emancipation of Slaves in the Caribbean'. In *The End of Slavery in Africa and the Americas*, edited by Ulrike Schmieder, Katja Füllberg-Stolberg and Michael Zeuske, 81–102. Münster: LIT Verlag, 2011.

Furley, Oliver W. 'Moravian Missionaries and Slaves in the West Indies'. *Caribbean Studies* 5, no. 2 (1965): 3–16.

Gad, Finn. *Grønlands Historie II*. København: Nyt Nordisk Forlag, 1969.

Gad, Finn. *Grønlands Historie III. 1782-1808*. København: Nyt Nordisk Forlag, 1786.

Gad, Finn. *The History of Greenland 2 (1700-1782)*. London: C. Hurst, 1970.

Gad, Finn. *The History of Greenland 3 (1782-1808)*. London: C. Hurst, 1982.

Gawthrop, Richard L. *Pietism and the Making of Eighteenth-Century Prussia*. Cambridge: Cambridge University Press, 2006.

Gerbner, Katharine. *Christian Slavery: Conversion and Race in the Protestant Atlantic World*. Early American Studies. Philadelphia: University of Pennsylvania Press, 2018.

Gerbner, Katharine. '"They Call Me Obea": German Moravian Missionaries and Afro-Caribbean Religion in Jamaica, 1754–1760'. *Atlantic Studies* 12, no. 1 (2015): 160–78.

Goldberg, David Theo. *The Racial State*. London: Blackwell, 2002.

Gorski, Philip S. *The Disciplinary Revolution: Calvinism and the Rise of the State in Early Modern Europe*. Chicago: University of Chicago Press, 2003.

Graeber, David. *Debt: The First 5,000 Years*. Brooklyn: Melville House, 2011.

Gray, Marion W. *Productive Men, Reproductive Women: The Agrarian Household and the Emergence of Separate Spheres during the German Enlightenment*. New York: Berghahn Books, 2000.

Grotius, Hugo and Martine Julia Van Ittersum. *Commentary on the Law of Prize and Booty*. Indianapolis: Liberty Fund, 2006.

Grunewald, Thomas. *Politik für das Reich Gottes? Der Reichsgraf Christian Ernst zu Stolberg-Wernigerode zwischen Pietismus, adligem Selbstverständnis und europäischer Politik*. Hallesche Forschungen 58. Halle: Verlag der Franckeschen Stiftungen, 2020.

Gulløv, Hans Christian. *Grønland. Den arktiske Koloni*. Danmark og Kolonierne. København: Gads Forlag, 2017.

Habermas, Jürgen. *Strukturwandel der Öffentlichkeit: Untersuchungen zu einer Kategorie der bürgerlichen Gesellscahft*. Neuwied: H. Luchterhand, 1962.

Hall, Neville. 'Slave Laws of the Danish Virgin Islands in the Later Eighteenth Century'. *Annals of the New York Academy of Sciences* 292, no. 1 (1977): 174–86.

Heiberg, Knud. 'Kirkelige Brydninger i Aaret 1733'. *Kirkehistoriske Samlinger* 5, no. 1 (1909): 509–75.

Hinrichs, Carl. *Preußentum und Pietismus: Der Pietismus in Brandenburg-Preußen als religiös-soziale Reformbewegung.* Göttingen: Vandenhoeck & Ruprecht, 1971.

Homburg, Heidrun. 'Glaube – Arbeit – Geschlecht: Frauen in der Ökonomie der Herrnhuter Ortsgemeine von den 1720er Jahren bis zur Jahrhundertwende. Ein Werkstattbericht'. In *Gender im Pietismus. Netzwerke und Geschlechterkonstruktionen*, edited by Pia Schmid, 43–62. Franckeschen Stiftungen Halle: Harrassowitz Verlag, 2015.

Homburg, Heidrun. 'Gläubige und Gläubiger: Zum "Schuldwesen" der Brüder-Unität um die Mitte des 18. Jahrhunderts'. In *Pietismus und Ökonomie (1650–1750)*, edited by Wolfgang Breul, Benjamin Marschke and Alexander Schunka, 301–35. Arbeiten zur Geschichte des Pietismus 65. Göttingen: Vandenhoeck & Ruprecht, 2021.

Hull, Isabel V. *Sexuality, State, and Civil Society in Germany, 1700–1815.* Ithaca: Cornell University Press, 1996.

Hüsgen, Jan. *Mission und Sklaverei: Die Herrnhuter Brüdergemeine und die Sklavenemanzipation in britisch- und dänisch-Westindien.* Missiongeschichtliche Archiv 25. Stuttgart: Franz Steiner, 2016.

Hutton, James E. *A History of Moravian Missions.* London: Moravian Publication Office, 1922.

Israel, Heinz. *Kulturwandel Grönländischer Eskimo im 18. Jahrhundert.* Dresden: Abhandlungen und Berichte des Staatlichen Museums für Völkerkunde Dresden, 1969.

James, Roberta. *Rousseau's Knot: The Entanglement of Liberal Democracy and Racism.* Canberra: Aboriginal Studies Press, 1997.

Jameson, Fredric. *The Political Unconscious: Narrative as a Socially Symbolic Act.* Ithaca: Cornell University Press, 1981.

Jameson, Fredric. 'The Vanishing Mediator: Narrative Structure in Max Weber'. *New German Critique* 1 (1973): 52–89.

Jensen, E. L., K. Raahauge and H. C. Gulløv. *Kulturmøder ved Kap Farvel: De Østgrønlandske Indvandrere og den Tyske Brødremission i det 19. Århundrede.* København: Museum Tusculanum Press, 2012.

Jensz, Felicity. 'Publication and Reception of David Cranz's 1767 History of Greenland'. *The Library: Transactions of The Bibliographical Society* 13, no. 4 (2012): 457–72.

Jensz, Felicity and Christina Petterson. *Legacies of David Cranz's Historie von Grönland.* Christianities in the Trans-Atlantic World. London: Palgrave-Macmillan, 2021.

Kirton-Roberts, Winelle J. *Created in Their Image : Evangelical Protestantism in Antigua and Barbados, 1834–1914.* Bloomington: Authorhouse, 2015.

Kjærgaard, Kathrine and Thorkild Kjærgaard. *Ny Herrnhut i Nuuk 1733–2003: Missionstation, Rævefarm, Embedsbolig, Museum, Universitet.* Nuuk: Ilisimatusarfik, 2005.

Kleivan, Inge. 'Herrnhuterne eller Brødremenigheden i Grønland 1733-1900'. *Tidsskriftet Grønland* 8 (1983): 221-35.

Kojève, A. *Introduction to the Reading of Hegel*. Edited by R. Queneau. Ithaca: Cornell University Press, 1980.

Köstlbauer, Josef. "'I Have No Shortage of Moors": Mission, Representation, and the Elusive Semantics of Slavery in Eighteenth-Century Moravian Sources'. In *Beyond Exceptionalism: Traces of the Slave Trade and Slavery in Early Modern Germany, 1650-1850*, edited by Rebekka von Mallinckrodt, Josef Köstlbauer and Sarah Lentz, 109-36. Berlin: de Gruyter, 2021.

Kristof, Ildiko Sz. 'Greenland in Hungary: Inuit Culture and the Emergence of the Science of Anthropology in Late Eighteenth- to Early Nineteenth-Century Hungary'. In *Legacies of David Cranz's 'Historie von Grönland' (1765)*, edited by Felicity Jensz and Christina Petterson, 165-83. London: Palgrave Macmillan, 2021.

Kröger, Rüdiger. *Johann Leonhard Dober und der Beginn der Herrnhuter Mission*. Schriften aus dem Unitätsarchiv 1. Herrnhut: Comenius Buchhandlung, 2006.

Lawaetz, Harald. *Brødremenighedens Mission i Dansk-Vestindien 1769-1848 : Bidrag til en Charakteristik af Brødrekirken og dens Gerning og af den Farvede Races Stilling til Christendommen*. København: O.B. Wroblewski, 1902.

Leemann, Michael. '"Weiße" und "schwarze Schafe". Versklavung, Rassismus und Religion in Berichten zur Herrnhuter Mission in dänisch-Westindien'. In *Verglichene Körper. Normieren, Urteilen, Entrechten in der Vormoderne*, edited by Cornelia Aust and Claudia Jarzebowski, 137-60. Studien zur alltags- und Kulturgeschichte 35. Stuttgart: Franz Steiner Verlag, 2022.

Lehmann, Hartmut. *Geschichte des Pietismus. 4, Glaubenswelt und Lebenswelten / Im Auftrag der historischen Kommission zur Erforschung des Pietismus*. Göttingen: Vandenhoeck & Ruprecht, 2004.

Lehmann, Hartmut. *Pietismus und weltliche Ordnung in Württemberg vom 17. bis zum 20. Jahrhundert*. Stuttgart: Kohlhammer, 1969.

Lehmann, Hartmut. *Transformationen der Religion in der Neuzeit : Beispiele aus der Geschichte des Protestantismus*. Göttingen: Vandenhoeck & Ruprecht, 2007.

Levering, Joseph Mortimer. *A History of Bethlehem, Pennsylvania, 1741-1892, with Some Account of Its Founders and Their Early Activity in America*. Bethlehem: Times Publishing Company, 1903.

Litchfield, Carter, Hans-Joachim Finke, Stephen G. Young and Karen Zerbe Huetter. *The Bethlehem Oil Mill 1745-1934: German Technology in Early Pennsylvania*. Kemblesville: Olearius Editions, 1984.

Loskiel, George Henry. *Geschichte der Mission der Evangelischen Brüder unter den Indianern in Nordamerika*. Barby: P.G. Kummer, 1789.

Losurdo, Domenico. *Hegel and the Freedom of Moderns*. Durham: Duke University Press, 2004.

Losurdo, Domenico. *Liberalism: A Counter-History*. Translated by Gregory Elliott. London: Verso, 2011.

Lukács, Georg. *History and Class Consciousness: Studies in Marxist Dialectics*. London: Merlin, 1990.

Lundbye, Jørgen. *Herrnhutismen i Danmark: Det attende Hundredaars Indre Mission*. København: Karl Schønbergs Forlag, 1903.

Macpherson, C. B. *The Political Theory of Possessive Individualism: Hobbes to Locke*. Oxford: Clarendon Press, 1962.

Marin, Louis. *Portrait of the King*. Theory and History of Literature 57. Minneapolis: University of Minnesota Press, 1988.

Marquardt, Frank. "'Distinguishing Ourselves from the other Religions": Confessional Conflicts and their Influence on the Early Moravian Danish West Indies Mission'. *Journal of Moravian History* 19, no. 2 (2019): 133–55.

Marquardt, Frank. "'Konnexion durchs ganze Land". Die Herrnhuter Brüdergemeinde im kolonialen Sozialraum dänisch-Westindiens 1739-1765'. PhD. Diss., Carl von Ossietzky Universität, Oldenburg, 2022.

Marx, Karl. *Capital: A Critique of Political Economy, Vol. I*. In *Marx/Engels Collected Works*, vol. 35. Moscow: Progress Publishers, 1996.

Marx, Karl. 'Contribution to the Critique of Hegel's Philosophy of Law: Introduction'. In *Marx Engels Collected Works 3*, 175–87. Moscow: Progress Publishers, 1975.

Marx, Karl. *Das Kapital: Kritik der Politischen Ökonomie*. Marx Engels Werke, vol. 23. Berlin: Dietz Verlag, 1971.

Marx, Karl. 'On the Jewish Question'. In *Marx Engels Collected Works*, vol. 3, 146–74. Moscow: Progress Publishers, 1975.

Marx, Karl and Friedrich Engels. *The German Ideology*. Moscow: Progress Publishers, 1964.

Marx, Karl and Friedrich Engels. 'The Manifesto of the Communist Party'. In *Marx and Engels Collected Works*, vol. 6, 477–519. Moscow: Progress Publishers, 1976.

Marx, Wolf. *Die Saalkirche der deutschen Brüdergemeine im 18. Jahrhundert*. Leipzig: Dieterichsche Verlagsbuchhandlung, 1931.

Merten, Kai. *'Ich habe im Himmel keine Spur von dir gesehen.' Religionsbegegnungen in Grönland im 18. Jahrhundert*. Nordic Studies in Religion and Culture. Münster: LIT Verlag, 2020.

Mettele, Gisela. *Weltbürgertum oder Gottesreich: Die Herrnhuter Brüdergemeine als globale Gemeinschaft 1727–1857*. Bürgertum Neue Folge, Bd 4. Göttingen: Vandenhoeck & Ruprecht, 2009.

Meyer, Dietrich. *Zinzendorf und die Herrnhuter Brüdergemeine*. Göttingen: Vandenhoeck & Ruprecht, 2009.

Meyer, Gudrun, Peter Stein, Stephan Palmié and Horst Ulbricht. *Christian Georg Andreas Oldendorp: Historie der caraibische Inseln Sanct Thomas, Sanct Crux und Sanct Jean. Kommentarband*. Beiheft Unitas Fratrum. Herrnhut: Herrnhuter Verlag, 2010.

Mills, Charles W. *The Racial Contract*. Ithaca: Cornell University Press, 1997.

Mitropoulos, Angela. *Contract and Contagion: From Biopolitics to Oikonomia*. New York: Minor Compositions, 2012.

Müller, Karl. *200 Jahre Brüdermission I: Das erste Missionsjahrhundert*. Herrnhut: Verlag der Missionsbuchhandlung, 1931.

Müller, Karl. *Der Weg des Matthäus Stach. Ein Lebensbild des ersten Grönland-Missionars der Brüdergemeine. Aus alten Briefen und Tagebuchblättern zusammengestellt von Karl Müller*. Berlin: Furche-Verlag, 1926.

Noller, Matthias. *Kirchliche Historiographie zwischen Wissenschaft und religiöser Sinnstiftung: David Cranz (1723-1777) als Geschichtsschreiber der erneuerten Brüderunität*. Jabloniana, Band 6. Wiesbaden: Harrassowitz Verlag, 2016.

Ogilvie, Sheilagh. 'The Economics of Guilds'. *The Journal of Economic Perspectives* 28, no. 4 (2014): 169-92.

Ogilvie, Sheilagh. *The European Guilds: An Economic Analysis*. Princeton: Princeton University Press, 2019.

Oldendorp, C. G. A. *Geschichte der Mission der Evangelischen Brüder auf den caraibischen Inseln S. Thomas, S Croix und S. Jah. hrsg. durch J. J. Bossart*, 2 vols. n. p., 1777.

Oldendorp, C. G. A. *Historie der caribischen Inseln Sanct Thomas, Sanct Crux und Sanct Jan: Insbesondere der dasigen Neger und der Mission der Evangelischen Brüder unter denselben*, 2 vols. Abhandlungen und Berichte des Staatlichen Museums für Völkerkunde Dresden, Bd 51. Berlin: Verlag für Wissenschaft und Bildung, 2000.

Olsthoorn, Thea. 'Cranz's Greenland as a Stepping Stone to Labrador: Tracing the Profile of the Inuit'. In *Legacies of David Cranz's 'Historie von Grönland' (1765)*, edited by Felicity Jensz and Christina Petterson, 239-59. Christianities in the Trans-Atlantic World. London: Palgrave Macmillan, 2021.

Olsthoorn, Thea. 'Das Herz auf der Zunge: Der Streit der Herrnhuter mit Hans Egede wegen der Lehre'. *Unitas Fratrum* 79 (2020): 261-77.

Olsthoorn, Thea. '"Wir Haben keine Ohren." Kommunikationsprobleme und Missionsverständnisse bei der Verbreitung und Rezeption des Christentums in Grönland und Labrador im 18. Jahrhundert'. *Pietismus und Neuzeit* 39 (2013): 47-85.

Perelman, Michael. *The Invention of Capitalism: Classical Political Economy and the Secret History of Primitive Accumulation*. Durham: Duke University Press, 2000.

Pestana, Carla Gardina. *Protestant Empire: Religion and the Making of the British Atlantic World*. Philadelphia: University of Pennsylvania Press, 2009.

Petersen, Robert. 'Some Considerations Concerning the Greenlandic Longhouse'. *Folk* 16-17 (1974): 171-88.

Petterson, Christina. '"A Plague of the State and The Church": A Local Response to the Moravian Enterprise'. *Journal of Moravian History* 16, no. 1 (2016): 45-60.

Petterson, Christina. 'En Konge i sin Faders Sted – Bibel og Konge i den danske Enevælde'. In *Bibelske Genskrivninger*, edited by Jesper Høgenhaven and Mogens Müller, 413-34. Forum for Bibelsk Eksegese, 17. København: Museum Tusculanum, 2012.

Petterson, Christina. 'From Communal Economy to Economic Community: Changes in Moravian Entrepreneurial Activities in the Eighteenth Century'. *Journal for the History of Reformed Pietism* 3, no. 1 (2018): 25–48.

Petterson, Christina. 'Governing the Living Community of Jesus: Johann Friedrich Koeber's Letter on Leadership'. *Journal of Moravian History* 21, no. 2 (2021): 143–62.

Petterson, Christina. 'Moravians in Greenland: Barren Shores and Fruitful Missions'. In *Legacies of David Cranz's 1765 'Historie von Grönland,'* edited by Felicity Jensz and Christina Petterson, 29–46. London: Palgrave McMillan, 2021.

Petterson, Christina. 'Spangenberg and Zinzendorf on Slavery in the Danish West Indies'. *Journal of Moravian History* 21, no. 1 (2021): 34–59.

Petterson, Christina. 'The Community Archive in Christiansfeld between Local and Global'. In *Crossroads of Heritage and Religion: Legacy and Sustainability of World Heritage Site Moravian Christiansfeld*, 194–210. New York: Berghahn Books, 2022.

Petterson, Christina. *The Missionary, the Catechist and the Hunter: Foucault, Protestantism and Colonialism*. Studies in Critical Research on Religion 4. Leiden: Brill, 2014.

Petterson, Christina. *The Moravian Brethren in a Time of Transition: A Socio-Economic Analysis of a Religious Community in Eighteenth Century Saxony*. Historical Materialism 231. Leiden: Brill, 2021.

Petterson, Christina and Roland Boer. 'Bible at the Origins of Capitalist Theory'. In *Cascade Companion on Bible and Economics 5: Bible in an Age of Capital: Reading Scripture in Capitalist Contexts*, edited by Matthew Coomber. Forthcoming.

Petterson, Christina and Katherine M. Faull. 'Speaking about Marriage: Notes from the 1744 Married Choir Conferences'. *Journal of Moravian History* 17, no. 1 (2017): 58–103.

Peucker, Paul. 'A Family of Love: Another Look at Bethlehem's General Economy'. *Journal of Moravian History* 18, no. 2 (2018): 123–44.

Peucker, Paul. *A Time of Sifting: Mystical Marriage and the Crisis of Moravian Piety in the Eighteenth Century*. University Park: Penn State University Press, 2015.

Peucker, Paul. '"Gegen ein Regiment von Schwestern." Die Stellung der Frau in der Brüdergemeine nach Zinzendorfs Tod'. *Unitas Fratrum* 45/46 (1999): 61–72.

Peucker, Paul. *Herrnhut, 1722–1732: The Early Years of the Moravian Community*. Pietist, Moravian, and Anabaptist Studies. University Park: Penn State University Press, 2021.

Peucker, Paul. *Herrnhuter Wörterbuch. Kleines Lexikon von Brüderischen Begriffen*. Herrnhut: Herrnhut Unitätsarchiv, 2000.

Peucker, Paul. 'Aus allen Nationen: Nichteuropäer in den deutschen Brüdergemeinden des 18. Jahrhunderts'. *Unitas Fratrum* 59/60 (2007): 1–35.

Peucker, Paul. '"Inspired by Flames of Love": Homosexuality, Mysticism, and Moravian Brothers around 1750'. *Journal of the History of Sexuality* 15, no. 1 (2006): 30–64.

Peucker, Paul. 'Selection and Destruction in Moravian Archives between 1760 and 1810'. *Journal of Moravian History* 12, no. 2 (2012): 170–215.

Philipp, Guntram. 'Halle und Herrnhut. Ein Wirtschaftsgeschichtlicher Vergleich'. In *Reformation und Generalreformation. Luther und der Pietismus*, edited by Christian

Soboth and Thomas Müller-Bahlke, 125–205. Hallesche Forschungen 32. Halle: Verlag der Franckesche Stiftungen Halle, 2012.

Plett, Heinrich F. *Enargeia in Classical Antiquity and the Early Modern Age: The Aesthetics of Evidence*. Leiden: Brill, 2012.

Poulsen, Rasmus Rask. 'Living with World Heritage: Authority and Knowledge in Contemporary Moravian Christiansfeld'. In *Crossroads of Heritage and Religion: Legacy and Sustainability of World Heritage Site Moravian Christiansfeld*, edited by Tine Damsholt, Marie Riegels Melchior, Christina Petterson and Tine Reeh, 125–44. New York: Berghahn Books, 2022.

Raphael-Hernandez, Heike. 'Black Caribbean Empowerment and Early Eighteenth-Century Moravian Missions Documents'. *Slavery & Abolition* 36, no. 2 (2015): 319–34.

Raphael-Hernandez, Heike. 'The Right to Freedom: Eighteenth-Century Slave Resistance and Early Moravian Missions in the Danish West Indies and Dutch Suriname'. *Atlantic Studies* 14, no. 5 (2017): 457–75.

Reichel, Gerhard. 'Der "Senfkornorden Zinzendorfs." Ein Beitrag zur Kenntnis seiner Jugendentwicklung und seines Charakters'. In *Erster Sammelband über Zinzendorf: mit einem Vorwort von Erich Beyreuther und Gerhard Meyer*, edited by Gerhard Meyer and Erich Beyreuther, 141–372. Hildesheim: G. Olms, 1975.

Resløkken, Åmund Norum. 'The Soul of the Arctic: David Cranz's Account of the Religion or Superstitions of the Greenlanders and Its Impact on Nineteenth-Century Descriptions of Religion in Greenland'. In *Legacies of David Cranz's 'Historie von Grönland' (1765)*, edited by Felicity Jensz and Christina Petterson, 185–205. London: Palgrave Macmillan, 2021.

Richarz, Irmintraut. *Oikos, Haus und Haushalt*. Göttingen: Vandenhoeck & Ruprecht, 1991.

Risler, Jeremias. *Leben August Gottlieb Spangenbergs, Bischofs der Evangelischen Brüderkirche*. Barby and Leipzig: n.p., 1794.

Roper, Lyndal. *The Holy Household : Women and Morals, in Reformation Augsburg*. Oxford Studies in Social History. Oxford: Clarendon, 1989.

Rosenthal, Caitlin. *Accounting for Slavery: Masters and Management*. Cambridge, MA: Harvard University Press, 2018.

Rud, Søren. *Colonialism in Greenland: Tradition, Governance and Legacy*. Cambridge Imperial and Postcolonial Studies. Cambridge: Palgrave Macmillan, 2017.

Rud, Søren. 'Policing and Governance in Greenland: Rationalities of Police and Colonial Rule 1860–1953'. In *Policing Empires: Social Control, Political Transition, Postcolonial Legacies*, edited by Emmanuel Blanchard, Marieke Bloembergen and Amadine Lauro, 177–96. Bruxelles: Peter Lang, 2017.

Ruhland, Thomas. *Pietistische Konkurrenz und Naturgeschichte : Die Südasienmission der Herrnhuter Brüdergemeine und die Dänisch-Englisch-Hallesche Mission (1755–1802)*. Unitas Fratrum Beiheft 31. Herrnhut: Herrnhuter Verlag, 2018.

Ruhland, Thomas. 'The "United Brethren" and Johann Gerhard König: Cranz's History of Greenland as an Avenue to the Natural History of India'. In *Legacies of David*

Cranz's 'Historie von Grönland' (1765), edited by Felicity Jensz and Christina Petterson, 209–37. London: Palgrave Macmillan, 2021.

Ryan, John. 'Historical Note: Did Double-Entry Bookkeeping Contribute to Economic Development, Specifically the Introduction of Capitalism?' *Australasian Accounting, Business and Finance Journal* 8, no. 3 (2014): 85–97.

Sahle, Esther. *Quakers in the British Atlantic World, c.1660-1800*, People, Markets, Goods: Economies and Societies in History, vol. 18. Woodbridge: Boydell Press, 2021.

Schantz, Douglas H. *An Introduction to German Pietism: Protestant Renewal at the Dawn of Modern Europe*. Baltimore: The Johns Hopkins University Press, 2013.

Schermaier, Martin. 'Res Communes Omnium: The History of an Idea from Greek Philosophy to Grotian Jurisprudence'. *Grotiana* 30 (2009): 20–48.

Schilling, Heinz. *Konfessionalisierung und Staatsinteressen: Internationale Beziehungen 1559-1660*. Handbuch der Geschichte der internationalen Beziehungen, Bd 2. Paderborn: Ferdinand Schöningh, 2007.

Schilling, Heinz. *Martin Luther: Rebel in an Age of Upheaval*. Translated by Rona Johnston Gordon. Oxford: Oxford University Press, 2017.

Schilling, Heinz. *Religion, Political Culture, and the Emergence of Early Modern Society : Essays in German and Dutch History*. Studies in Medieval and Reformation Thought 50. Leiden: Brill, 1992.

Schmidt, Gottfried. 'Die Banden oder Gesellschaften im alten Herrnhut'. *Zeitschrift für Brüdergeschichte* III (1909): 145–207.

Schneider, Hans. 'Die "zürnenden Mutterkinder". Der Konflikt zwischen Halle und Herrnhut'. *Pietismus und Neuzeit* 29 (2004): 37–66.

Schneider, Hans. '"Philadelphische Brüder mit einem lutherischen Maul und mährischen Rock." Zu Zinzendorfs Kirchenverständnis'. In *Neue Aspekte der Zinzendorf-Forschung*, edited by Martin Brecht and Paul Peucker, 11–36. Göttingen: Vandenhoeck & Ruprecht, 2006.

Sebro, Louise. *Mellem afrikaner og kreol: Etnisk identitet og social navigation i Dansk Vestindien 1730-1770*. Historiska institutionen: Lunds Universitet, 2010.

Sebro, Louise. 'Mellem mange verdner: Netværk, vækkelse og transnationale forbindelser i det atlantiske rum i begyndelsen af 1700 tallet'. *Temp - Tidsskrift for Historie* 10, no. 20 (2020): 139–59.

Sensbach, Jon F. *A Separate Canaan : The Making of an Afro-Moravian World in North Carolina, 1763-1840*. Chapel Hill: Published for the Omohundro Institute of Early American History and Culture, Williamsburg, Virginia, by the University of North Carolina Press, 1998.

Sensbach, Jon F. 'Race and the Early Moravian Church: A Comparative Perspective'. *Transactions of the Moravian Historical Society* 31 (2000): 1–10.

Sensbach, Jon F. *Rebecca's Revival: Creating Black Christianity in the Atlantic World*. Cambridge, MA: Harvard University Press, 2005.

Sider, Gerald M. *Lumbee Indian Histories: Race, Ethnicity, and Indian Identity in the Southern United States*. Cambridge: Cambridge University Press, 1994.

Smaby, Beverly. "'No One Should Lust for Power... Women Least of All:" Dismantling Female Leadership among Eighteenth Century Moravians'. In *Pious Pursuits: German Moravians in the Atlantic World*, edited by Michele Gillespie and Robert Beachy, 159–75. European Expansion and Global Interaction 7. New York: Berghahn Books, 2007.

Smaby, Beverly P. *The Transformation of Moravian Bethlehem: From Communal Mission to Family Economy*. University Park: University of Pennsylvania Press, 1988.

Smith, Adam. *An Inquiry into the Nature and Causes of the Wealth of Nations*, 2 vols. London: Printed for W. Strahan; and T. Cadell, in the Strand, 1776.

Søgaard, Helge. *Christians Kirke. Den tyske Frederiks Kirke*. Edited by Elna Møller. Danmarks Kirker 21–22. København: Gads, 1975.

Sombart, Werner. 'Der Kapitalistische Unternehmer'. In *Werner Sombart: Die Modernität des Kapitalismus herausgegeben von Klaus Lichtblau*, 2nd edn, 241–300. Klassiker Der Sozialwissenschaften. Wiesbaden: Springer VS, 2019.

Sombart, Werner. *Der Bourgeois: Zur geistesgeschichte des modernen Wirtschaftsmenschen*. Berlin: Duncker und Humblot, (1913) 1987.

Sombart, Werner. *Der moderne Kapitalismus II: Das europäische Wirtschaftsleben im Zeitalter des Frühkapitalismus*, 5th edn. München & Leipzig: Duncker und Humblot, 1922.

Sombart, Werner. 'Economic Theory and Economic History'. *The Economic History Review* 2, no. 1 (1929): 1–19.

Sommer, Elisabeth. 'Gambling with God: The Use of the Lot by the Moravian Brethren in the Eighteenth Century'. *Journal of the History of Ideas* 59, no. 2 (1998): 267–86.

Sonenscher, Michael. *Capitalism: The Story Behind the Word*. Princeton: Princeton University Press, 2022.

Sonenscher, Michael. *Jean-Jacques Rousseau: The Division of Labour, the Politics of the Imagination and the Concept of Federal Government*. Leiden: Brill, 2020.

Sonenscher, Michael. *Work and Wages: Natural Law, Politics and the Eighteenth-Century French Trades*. Cambridge: Cambridge University Press, 2012.

Spangenberg, A. G. *Von der Arbeit der Evangelischen Brüder unter den Heiden*. Barby: Christian Friedrich Laur, 1782.

Stead, Geoffrey. *The Moravian Settlement at Fulneck 1742-1790*. Leeds: The Thoresby Society, 1999.

Stoler, Ann Laura. *Race and the Education of Desire: Foucault's History of Sexuality and the Colonial Order of Things*. Durham: Duke University Press, 1995.

Strom, Jonathan, Hartmut Lehmann and James Van Horn Melton. *Pietism in Germany and North America 1680–1820*. Burlington: Ashgate, 2009.

Teigeler, Otto. *Zinzendorf als Schüler in Halle 1710–1716. Persönliches Ergehen und Präformation eines Axioms*. Hallesche Forschungen 45. Wiesbaden: Harrassowitz Verlag, 2017.

The Moravian Archives. Bethlehem, Pennsylvania. *The Bethlehem Diary Volume I: 1742–1744*. Translated by Kenneth G. Hamilton. Bethlehem: Moravian Archives Bethlehem, 2001.

Thompson, E. P. *The Making of the English Working Class*. New York: Vintage Books, 1966.

Thomsen, Hanne. 'Ægte grønlændere og nye grønlændere — om forskellige opfattelser af grønlandskhed'. *Den Jyske Historiker* 81 (1998): 21–56.

Uttendörfer, Otto. *Alt-Herrnhut. Wirtschaftsgeschichte und religionssoziologie Herrnhuts während seiner ersten Zwanzig Jahre (1722–1742)*. Herrnhut: Verlag Missionsbuchhandlung, 1925.

Uttendörfer, Otto. *Die wichtigsten Missionsinstruktionen Zinzendorfs*. Herrnhut: Verlag der Missionsbuchhandlung, 1913.

Uttendörfer, Otto. *Wirtschaftsgeist und Wirtschaftsorganisation Herrnhuts und der Brüdergemeine von 1743 bis zum Ende des Jahrhunderts*. Herrnhut: Verlag der Missionsbuchhandlung Herrnhut, 1926.

Viemose, Jørgen. *Dansk kolonipolitik i Grønland*. København: Demos, 1977.

Voelz, James W. 'A Self-Conscious Reader-Response Interpretation of Romans 13:1–7'. In *The Personal Voice in Biblical Interpretation*, edited by Ingrid Rosa Kitzberger. London: Routledge, 1998.

Vogt, Peter. 'Christologie und Gender bei Zinzendorf'. In *Gender Im Pietismus: Netzwerke und Geschlechterkonstruktionen*, edited by Pia Schmid, 63–92. Halle: Verlag der Frankeschen Stiftung/Harrowitz Verlag, 2015.

Vogt, Peter. '"Honor to the Side": The Adoration of the Side Wound of Jesus in Eighteenth-Century Moravian Piety'. *Journal of Moravian History* 7 (2009): 83–106.

Vogt, Peter. 'Let our Commerce be Holy unto Thee! Economic Practice in the Eighteenth Century Moravian Church'. In *Pietismus und Ökonomie (1650–1750)*, edited by Wolfgang Breul, Benjamin Marschke and Alexander Schunka, 269–300. Arbeiten Zur Geschichte Des Pietismus 65. Göttingen: Vandenhoeck & Ruprecht, 2021.

Vogt, Peter. 'Zinzendorf's "Seventeen Points of Matrimony": A Fundamental Document on the Moravian Understanding of Marriage and Sexuality'. *Journal of Moravian History* 10 (2011): 39–67.

Vosa, Aira. 'Von der Tugend der Ehelosigkeit. Johann Georg Gichtels Einfluss auf August Gottlieb Spangenberg'. *Unitas Fratrum* 61/62 (2009): 9–21.

Wallerstein, Immanuel. *The Modern World-System 1–4*. Berkeley: University of California Press, 2011.

Wallerstein, Immanuel. *The Modern World-System 4. Centrist Liberalism Triumphant, 1789–1914*. Berkeley: University of California Press, 2011.

Ward, W. R. 'Zinzendorf and Money'. In *Church and Wealth*, edited by W. J. Shiels and Diana Wood, 283–305. Oxford: Blackwell, 1987.

Weber, Max. *Die protestantische Ethik und der Geist des Kapitalismus*. Tübingen: Mohr Siebeck, 1934.

Weber, Max. *The Protestant Ethic and the Spirit of Capitalism*. London: Routledge, 2001.

Wellenreuther, Hermann and Carola Wessel. *The Moravian Mission Diaries of David Zeisberger, 1772–1781*. University Park: Penn State University Press, 2005.

Wessel, Carola. '"Es ist also des Heilands sein Predigtstuhl so weit und groß als die ganze Welt." Zinzendorfs Überlegungen zur Mission'. In *Neue Aspekte der*

Zinzendorf-Forschung, edited by Martin Brecht and Paul Peucker, 163–73. Göttingen: Vandenhoeck & Ruprecht, 2006.

Wheeler, Rachel M. *To Live upon Hope: Mohicans and Missionaries in the Eighteenth-Century Northeast*. Ithaca: Cornell University Press, 2008.

White, Hayden. 'Interpretation in History'. In *Tropics of Discourse : Essays in Cultural Criticism*, 51–80. Baltimore: John Hopkins University Press, 1978.

White, Hayden. *Metahistory: The Historical Imagination in Nineteenth-Century Europe*. Baltimore: The Johns Hopkins University Press, 1983.

White, Hayden. *The Content of the Form: Narrative Discourse and Historical Representation*. Baltimore: The Johns Hopkins University Press, 1987.

White, Hayden. *The Fiction of Narrative: Essays on History, Literature, and Theory 1957–2007*. Baltimore: Johns Hopkins University Press, 2010.

White, Hayden. *Tropics of Discourse: Essays in Cultural Criticism*. Baltimore: John Hopkins University Press, 1978.

Wilhjelm, Henrik. 'Brødremissionens Overgivelse: Udviklingen i og omkring Brødremissionen i Grønland 1850–1900'. *Tidsskriftet Grønland* 6 (2000): 203–44.

Wilhjelm, Henrik. 'How a Man Accused of Being Wizard and Murderer Determined the Development of the Moravian Mission in Greenland'. In *Edice Moravian 13 (The Moravians in Polar Areas – Conference Proceedings from the VI. Moravian Conference)* 13 (2015): 35–41.

Wilhjelm, Henrik. 'Menneske (inuk) først og kristen så?: en vinkel på missionshistorien i Vestgrønland'. *Dansk Teologisk Tidsskrift* 68 (2005): 1–20.

Wollstadt, Hanns-Joachim. *Geordnetes Dienen in der Christlichen Gemeinde*. Arbeiten zur Pastoraltheologie 4. Göttingen: Vandenhoeck & Ruprecht, 1966.

Yamey, B. S. *Essays on the History of Accounting*. New York: Arno Press, 1978.

Index

America 46, 63, 68
Americas 37, 68, 70, 98
Antigua 76–7, 93–4, 124, 164
Arbo, Johann 53–5, 64

Baptism 22, 28, 30, 33, 114, 166
Barby 34, 100, 118, 120, 126
Berbice 77, 87, 93, 164
Bethel Plantation 106, 110–11, 126
   sale of 121–2, 127
   separate economy 118–20
Bethlehem, Pennsylvania 10, 14, 18, 42, 86–7, 107, 116, 180
   as centre of American mission 45, 75–7, 92–3, 98, 111, 113–24
   conflict with St Thomas 19, 42–4, 105–6, 125
   Debt recovery fund 48–9, 72, 75–6
   Dissolution of General economy 3, 12, 50–7, 170, 176, 179
   General Economy/communal household 9, 45–50, 125
   as part of centralization process 62–73, 84–5
bookkeeper 88, 117
bookkeeping 12, 73, 126, 178–80
British West Indies 75, 77, 84, 87, 100, 118
Bürgergeist 11–12, 73, 176–80
Business, Moravian 41, 49–50, 53, 120
   early capitalism and 11–12, 172, 177–80
   independent/private business 74, 124
   in the mission 86–7, 90, 95

Cammerhof, Friedrich 106, 111
   letter to St Thomas 42–5, 47, 55, 109, 128
Capitalism 1, 3, 128, 171, 182
   capital 7, 65–6, 70
   capitalist system 6–8, 101, 109

Danish West Indies 98, 128
   early 27, 42, 171, 176–7, 180
   Protestantism and 2, 10–11, 20, 171–6
Carté, Katherine (Engel) 9, 45, 47, 50, 99
   Decision to end General economy 63–4, 66
   mission 74–7
Central Council (*Ratskonferenz*) 45, 51, 58, 86
   and missions 84–5, 87
   replacing Zinzendorf 45, 61–2
centralization after 1760 10, 55–6, 58, 62, 91, 97
   effects of 99, 170, 180, 182
change (social) 4, 8, 10, 14, 23, 180
   Sombart on 11, 176–8
   Wallerstein on 36–7
choir houses 27, 28
   in Bethlehem 53–6, 65–6, 68, 74
   in Greenland 147, 155–8
choirs 27–8, 51, 92, 168–9
   in Greenland 151, 154–8, 166
   leadership 42, 45, 55, 162, 166–7, 180
   as Moravian way of life and ideology 10, 19, 25, 107, 165
   Single Brothers, Bethlehem 50, 56, 64
   Single Sisters, Bethlehem 50, 56
colonial administration 19, 48
colonial authorities/government 20, 64, 114, 124–5, 131, 133–5
colonial context 1, 29, 37, 128, 164
colonialism 151
colonial powers 3, 19, 82, 84, 88, 144, 147
colonial settlement 15, 22, 132, 133, 137, 143
communal household 3, 8, 9. *See also* General economy; Oeconomie
   Bethlehem as 44, 46
   break up of 49–50, 64, 68, 73–5
   in missions 51, 56–7, 124–5, 181

communication   33, 64, 119, 164
communion   16, 28, 30–1, 33, 160–3, 166, 169
Cranz, David   100 n.6, 167
credit   7, 86, 143, 149

Dalager, Lars   138
Damnitz, Hans Hermann von   49, 60
Danish West Indies   29, 33, 83, 84, 90, 100, 117
  archival resources   14–16
  colony   5, 98–9, 136, 150
  discussion at synod   92, 94, 96
  helpers   31–2
  inner and outer   41–2
  mission   3, 22, 75–7, 101, 127, 128, 164, 170
  organization   86, 97, 124–5
  relations with Bethlehem   42–4, 112–14
  restructure of economy   52, 77, 118–20, 179
  terminology   16–17
David, Christian   83, 109, 131, 151
debt recovery fund   48–9, 55, 67, 69, 72, 75
debts   48, 52, 64, 70, 72–3, 84
  Debts, St. Thomas   113, 115, 117
Deknatel, (Posaunenberg)   103, 107, 108, 112–14. *See also* New-Herrnhut, St Thomas
Directorial Board   55, 60, 62, 83–5
  Decision on General Economy (1761)   71–3, 76
  Establishment of Mission Deputation   87–8
  Report on Bethlehem (1761)   66–7, 75
Dober, Leonhard   22, 82, 88, 101–2
Dutch merchants   133, 137–8

economy   11–12, 18–19, 24, 57, 96, 112. *See also* General Economy
  balance between economy and mission   38, 43, 109, 125
  capitalist   177–8
  communal economy   46, 51–3, 56, 68–9, 72, 85
  exchange/market economy   2, 9, 44

  external economy   127, 128, 170
  frontier economy   19, 102
  global economy   1, 4–5, 6–8, 17, 38 (*see also* capitalism)
  household and   8, 10, 21, 112
  planned economy   179–80
  plantation economy   10, 81, 101
  religion and   171–6
  subsistence   10, 86, 156
Egede, Hans   131, 133, 135–6
Enge conferenz. *See* Inner Council
Engel, Katherine Carté. *See* Carté, Katherine
enslaved Moravians   26, 32–3, 127, 181
  as distinct from slaves   18, 108, 128, 182
enterprise   8, 11–12, 74, 95, 174, 177–9
  as outer matters   41–2, 132
  plantation   83, 117, 128
  separation from mission   119–20
Epiphany   90, 164, 168
Erbe, Hellmuth   12, 47, 64, 67
  and Bürgergeist   12, 73, 176, 179
establishments (business)   72, 86, 90–1, 96
Europe   2, 14, 37, 55, 147, 151–2
  centre of Moravian leadership   3, 15, 38, 76, 93, 147, 160
  comparisons with   105, 110, 127, 156, 166
  economic development Europe/colonies   1, 55, 98, 181
  gifts from   151–2
  and its colonies   4–5, 19
  Moravian practice in   26–9, 49, 50
  Moravian settlements in   72, 154
  provisions, resources from   10, 76, 86, 116, 144–5, 151, 170
  travel to and from   45–6, 64, 69, 104, 116, 155
European   153, 164, 170
Europeans   57, 151. *See also* non-European
  communities   19, 87, 167
  context   1, 42, 76
  household   158–9
  model   52–3, 65, 68, 73, 87, 158
  in Greenland   16, 29, 33, 146, 159, 160, 166–7

Index

non-Moravians   5, 29, 134
exchange   24, 104, 110, 147–9
exchange value   2, 7, 9

feudal
  feudalism   4, 10, 26, 42, 182
  feudal leader   23, 74
freedom   53, 55–6, 136, 146

Gemeinhaus   152. *See also* Saal
Gemeinnachrichten   15, 34, 159
Gemeintag   33, 163, 164, 168–9
General Economy
  decisions to end   58, 62–4
  dissolution   3, 14, 50–1, 75, 77
  and European model   52, 76
  and Koeber   12, 71
  organization of   9, 45, 55, 75, 85–6, 125
  Spangenberg   45–6, 56, 66, 71
Gnadenhütten   106–7
Godthaab (the colonial settlement)   131–4, 136–7, 149. *See also* Nuuk
  Merchant at   138, 142, 144
  mission   131, 133, 139 (*see also* Egede, Hans)
Grassmann, Andreas   135, 137, 161

Halle   5, 22, 59, 81, 93, 173
"Heathen Diacony" (*Heidendiakonie*)   94, 116, 145
Helfer-conferenz   119, 121
Helpers' conference   33, 119, 120, 127
Herrnhaag   28, 46, 60
Herrnhut   36, 49, 70
  Anton in   22, 82
  on Bethlehem   56, 66, 68, 71
  as centre   14–15, 52–3
  choirs in   27–8, 155, 165
  economic centralization in   10, 53, 55–6, 64, 114, 126
  economic problems   37, 48–9, 59
  founding of   5–6, 21, 167
  and Halle   5, 173
  Judith Issek in   165
  leadership in   59, 117, 125–7, 182
  mission deputation   119, 146, 159
  as proto-type   33, 65, 70, 87, 107, 164
  restructure in   18, 58, 63–4, 81

Historie der Caribischen Inseln. See Oldendorp, C. G. A.
history   12–13, 18, 178
  modern understandings of   34–5, 172–4
  Moravian history   21, 51, 152, 167, 168
  Moravian mission history   21, 160
  Moravian understanding of   18, 24, 35–6, 38, 171, 176, 180, 182
History of Greenland. *See* Cranz
House community (Hausgemeine)   9, 47, 86, 94
Household. *See also* Oeconomie
  Bethlehem as ideal   38, 42–4, 109
  communal   3, 8–9, 46, 48, 73, 181
  European household in
    Greenland   145, 158–60, 167, 170
  household management (St Thomas)   96, 111, 112, 117, 124–6
  Kalaalit Moravian   158–9
  mission households   1, 18, 44, 51, 99, 103
  models   10, 86
  Moravian practice   7, 21, 42
  pre-modern   10, 27, 158
  restructure of Bethlehem   50, 52, 54–7, 64, 74
  settlement household as contrast to communal   49–50, 65–6, 74, 85
House-meeting   29–30, 116, 142, 160, 162
Hüsgen, Jan   83, 100, 107, 109, 111, 115, 120, 127

individual
  assessment/speakings   161–2, 166, 169
  believer/member   2, 28, 56, 69, 165, 180
  charismatic individual   61–2, 96, 173
  of modernity   4, 34–5, 73, 74, 175
  Moravian understanding of   18, 25–7, 171, 176, 180–2
individualism liberal   2, 4, 23–6
industrial society   9, 20, 59

industry
  Bethlehem   49–51, 55–6, 65–6, 71, 74
  capitalist   172, 174
  Moravian (wirtschaft)   16, 41, 43–4, 59, 95–6, 170
  St Thomas   110, 114, 127
Inner Council
  correspondence   145, 159, 166, 167
  establishment   61–2
  on missions   76, 87, 93
Instruction (*Instruks*) of 1782   134, 142–3, 147, 149
inventory
  Bethlehem   84
  general   90, 179
  St Thomas   110–11, 114, 115, 119, 121, 126
Israel, Heinz   15, 151

Jamaica   76, 77, 92, 94, 124, 164
Judith Issek   155

Kangeq   142, 162
KGH (Royal Greenlandic Trade)   133–4, 140, 143
King
  as highest authority   141
  King Christian VI of Denmark   22, 82, 135–7
  King Frederik V of Denmark   138, 141
Koeber, Johann Friedrich   93, 96, 141
  Bethlehem   64, 66–8, 71, 85
  Bürgergeist   73–4, 179
  Inner Council   61–2
Korn, Jens   83, 110, 114–15, 117

labour
  divisions of   9–10, 85–6
  Greenland   144, 157
  individual labour   3, 4, 24, 50, 74, 175
  St Thomas   101–2, 105, 117, 120, 125
  slave-labour   126, 182
Labrador   17, 83, 84, 92, 138, 162, 164
Lamb   28, 43–4, 97, 153, 159
leadership. *See also* Europe; management; synod (pre-1760); Unity Elders Conference (UAC)
  Barby   115, 118, 120, 123
  Bethlehem   63, 64, 70–2, 105

centralized   5, 99
change in   58, 81, 96
Christ   169
division in outer and inner   42, 113
Europe   38, 127, 140–1, 147, 151, 160, 166
female   161, 166
Greenland   162, 166
Herrnhut   18–19, 55, 61–2, 64, 91, 92, 159, 179
Indigenous   31, 166
St Thomas   119, 121
structures   165–6
visitations   111
Lichtenfels   77, 140, 163
liturgy   41, 54
  liturgical day, gatherings   154, 163
  liturgical fellowships (choirs)   28, 165
  liturgical forms   33, 164
  liturgical organization   154, 163, 166
  liturgical texts   164–5
Loretz, Johann   34, 118, 124
lot   16, 30, 46
  lot casting for St Thomas   116, 124, 180
  lot decision Bethlehem   47, 53, 63–4, 180
  lot decision Greenland   30, 157, 161–3, 166
  lot decision Nazereth   71, 73
  mission-management   76, 93
  office of Chief Elder   169

Mack, Martin   118, 125
management   3, 16, 64, 113, 121, 141
  household   42, 55, 57, 96, 113, 117, 128
  mission   28, 93, 115, 146, 151
  rationalized   11–12, 177–9, 181, 182
  techniques slavery   115
manager   55, 103, 134
Marienborn   22, 46
  synod 1764   81, 91–6, 107, 151
market   50, 73–4
marriage   30, 37, 46, 134
Marschall, Friedrich von   63–4, 66–8, 72, 85, 96
Martin, Friedrich   22, 86, 103

Marx, Karl 35, 173, 175–6
  Capital 7–8, 12–13, 98 n.2, 176
  Meisterknecht (master servant) 102, 119, 120
member 27, 59, 141, 151, 169, 180
  aristocracy 6, 7, 59–60
  Bethlehem 53, 65–6, 71, 74
  choirs and racialised difference in members 165–7
  common humanity of 24, 180
  community of 34, 35
  enslaved members 104, 108, 123, 181
  European in Greenland 144, 159
  European settlements 27–8, 33, 88, 90, 165, 167
  Kalaallit 33, 153, 154, 162, 164
  Native American 92
  non-European 16, 23, 33, 94
  senior 15, 23, 160
membership 33, 62
Mettele, Gisela 23, 33, 91, 164, 182
mill 48, 95, 110, 115
mill construction 105, 115, 118
missionary practice 19, 21, 29, 38, 171
missionary work 1, 45, 47, 73, 75, 82, 96, 99, 105, 113
Mission Deputation 14, 19, 57, 58, 62, 87
  establishment 81, 85, 87–91
  Greenland 143, 145, 159
  management of missions 76–7
  reconstitution 1764 94–6
  report to the Marienborn synod 91–2
  St Thomas 118, 120, 121, 126
Mission Diakonie 60, 118 n.66, 179
mission organization 3, 18, 177
  early 19, 26, 30, 81–4
Missions (moravian) 21, 23, 38, 72, 182
  archival documentation 2–3, 14–16
  connection to community 23, 26, 96, 164–5, 168
  economy and 43–4, 90–1, 127–8, 170
  purpose 30–3, 38, 43, 88–9
Missions departement 14, 87, 121
money 5, 10, 44, 85, 109, 181
  capitalism and 3, 7, 57, 175–6
  exchange 74, 149
  pre-modern money 8–9
  sources of 60, 90, 179
  travel money 88

Monopoly 135, 138, 143, 145
Moravian (mährisch) 96, 131
Moravian Archives Bethlehem 14

National Helpers 30, 33, 169
Native American
  converts 26, 94
  missions 9, 30, 45, 47, 75–6, 82, 85, 92, 118
Nazareth 48, 51, 66, 68, 70–1, 73, 84
Netherlands 2, 49, 51, 82, 84, 152. *See also* Dutch
network 82, 102, 134
New-Herrnhut, Greenland 3, 16, 29, 32, 77, 131, 182
  choir-houses 155–7
  colonial restrictions 143, 149
  community life 164–7
  ideal settlement 92, 107
  mission station layout 151–3
  organization 162–3
New-Herrnhut, St. Thomas 3, 16, 44
  independent settlement 110, 118–19
  management 116, 120
  organization 106–7, 126
  purchase 103
  slaves assigned to 122–3
Niesky (Crumbay) 107–8, 112, 118, 122, 127
Nitschmann, Anna 58, 77
Nitschmann, David (bishop) 22, 82, 101–2
Nitschmann, David (Syndicus) 101 n.9, 135–7
Nitschmann, Rosina 161–4
non-European 33, 167
North America 5, 22, 46, 48, 92, 93, 101, 110
North Carolina 51, 68, 75, 82, 99
Nuuk 133–4

Oberlausitz 21, 59, 131
Oeconomie. *See also* household
  common household
    in Bethlehem 47, 54–7, 63, 65–8, 70–1, 73
    in the missions 83, 85, 86, 112, 123, 124, 146, 159
    outer 9, 54–5, 112, 150, 170

distinction between household and
outer Oeconomie 112,
114–15, 117
as household 8–9, 159
St Thomas Oeconomie 115–17
separation of household and outer
Oeconomie 118–21
Oldendorp, Christian Georg 17 n.47, 33,
41, 100 n.6, 105, 106, 109
Ortsgemeine 49, 51–2, 63–4, 68, 106–7.
See also settlement

Peucker, Paul 9, 51–2, 62 n.16
Philadelphianism 32
Pietism 2, 5–6, 11, 25, 172–5
Pilgergemeine
Bethlehem 9, 46–7, 85
Zinzendorf 53 n.55
Pilgrim (missionary) 43–5, 51, 65,
70 n.41, 71, 73
pilgrim-community 9, 46–8, 75
Plantation (sugar). *See also* Bethel
Plantation; New-Herrnhut, St.
Thomas
mission work on 15, 32, 104, 127,
154, 181
Moravian property 3, 86, 115–16,
170, 179, 182
Bethel 110–11, 117 n.59, 118–23,
126
New-Herrnhut 44, 84 n.8, 90,
103–7, 112
Moravian work on 101, 103, 109,
137 n.21
plantation industry 10, 44, 52, 83, 96,
101, 102, 113–14, 117, 128, 171
"Plantation Disposition" 43–4, 98–128
Plessen, Carl Adolph von 82–3, 103,
109, 137 n.21
production 5, 9–10, 48
blubber 134, 139, 156
forces of production 50, 52, 98
mode of 8, 98, 175, 180
sugar 19, 44, 86, 101, 105, 110,
112 n.49, 115, 116, 121, 125,
127–8
profit 2, 3, 12, 95, 138, 174, 179
in Bethlehem 50, 53, 74
Cammerhof 43–4

Max Weber and 174–6
in the missions 10, 86, 91, 96, 105,
120, 170, 182
profitable 110 n.41, 118, 127, 133, 179
Protestant, Protestantism 1, 2, 36, 100,
142 n.39, 176
Protestant Ethic and the Spirit of
Capitalism 11, 20, 172–5
provisions
from Europe 10, 84, 86, 90, 138,
144–5, 148
in Europe 59, 76 n.63, 94
management of 16, 116–17, 120,
156, 159

race 99
racial categories 17
racial difference 167
racialized 16, 166
Ratskonferenz. *See* Central Council
Rauch, Christian Heinrich. *See* vistitation
Rebhun 110, 118, 123. *See also* Bethel
Plantation

Saal 152, 168. *See also* Gemeinhaus
St Croix 76, 108, 117, 124, 164
interrelations between three
islands 112, 115
mission work 77, 92, 94
plantation management on 109,
137 n.21
smithy 127
visitation 112, 113, 118, 122
St John 76, 94, 108, 113, 124, 164
St Thomas 18–19, 61, 75
beginnings of mission 22, 82, 101,
102
bookkeeper, manager 95, 180
conflict with Bethlehem 42, 44, 105
congregation 104
Danish colony 1, 98, 136
Danish West Indies 3, 77, 164
economic status 92, 99, 101, 113,
118, 179
enslaved brothers and sisters 18, 33,
101, 181
household organization 10, 124–7
managed by Bethlehem 76, 111,
113–14

Index

mission 26, 81, 99, 110, 164
organization of mission 9, 16, 86, 94, 154, 181
restructure 50, 121
slaves 101, 121–3, 125–7, 181–2
sugar-plantation 90, 103–5, 107, 110, 113–14, 182
visitation 34, 105, 106, 111–23, 160
Seidel, Nathanael
  committee for restructuring Bethlehem 66–8, 72, 76
  departure for Bethlehem 63, 65, 72
  visitations St Thomas 83, 111, 114–16
settlement. *See also* Ortsgemeine
  Bethlehem as 49–50, 65, 68, 73, 74
  contrast to diaspora 28, 76
  in Europe 9, 51, 72, 91, 106–7, 154
  Georgia 46, 51
  Herrnhut 21, 70
  mission 15, 83, 94, 139, 147, 179
  Nazareth 70–1, 73
  difference between mission and settlement 85–6, 107
  choirs 19, 27–8, 155, 158
  colonial settlement 5, 98, 133–4, 137–8, 144
  Godthaab (Nuuk) 15, 22, 131, 132, 138, 142–3, 149
  Greenland mission 151, 153, 163, 165, 170
  as independent economic entity 120
  Kalalliit 154–6
Severin, Jakob 135–8
Single Brothers' Choir 28
  in Bethlehem 50, 54, 56, 64
  in Greenland 153, 157
Single Brothers' House 28
  in Bethlehem 53, 55, 68
  in Greenland 157
  in St Thomas 115
Single Sisters' Choir 28, 155, 168
  in Bethlehem 50, 56
  in Greenland 153, 155
  In Herrnhut 165
Single Sisters' House 28
  in Greenland 155, 157, 163
Slave, slaves 26, 37, 101, 102, 104, 109, 110
  access to 32, 103

Anton 22, 82
baptized 107–8
labour 126–7, 170
management 115, 117, 119–21
members 33, 108, 127, 128, 182
mission to 22, 26, 32, 75, 82, 125, 181
rebellion in Berbice 93
sale of 121–3
slave-holding 19, 26, 81, 107, 127
terminology slave and enslaved 17–18
slave-congregations 101, 154
Slave-owner, ownership 100, 101, 107, 114, 128, 182
inventory 111, 115, 126
Moravian owned 101, 104–9, 115, 126–8, 182
problem 105, 113
slavery 3, 99–101, 170, 171, 181
social conditions 101, 150
social contract 4, 25
social disruptions 8, 175
social life 13, 181
social organization 4, 10, 23, 27, 73, 155
social relations 71, 73, 74, 134, 175
social structures 4, 151, 153
Sombart, Werner 11–12, 175–9
Spangenberg, August Gottlieb
  in Bethlehem 45–8, 56, 66, 84
  letter to Greenland 168
  networks 45, 82
  radical pietist 46
  suggestions for restructure 70–5
  summons to Herrnhut 63, 64
  on the West Indies 102, 112–14, 160
speakings 16, 157, 161, 166, 169
spirit 73, 74, 182
  bourgeois spirit (*see* Bürgergeist)
  of capitalism 11, 172–5, 177
  of temptation 158
spiritual matters 18, 41–2, 87, 91, 109, 165, 167
Stach, Matthäus 22, 131, 136
state 4, 19, 37, 174
  Danish state 133, 135, 140–2
  German states 84, 180
subsistence 10, 12, 24, 86, 179
  Greenland 136, 156, 157, 170

sugar industry 10, 19, 44, 101, 116, 125, 127
  expansion 110-11
  profits 86, 96, 126
sugar plantation 3, 96, 112, 113, 126, 171, 182
sugar works (mills etc.) 104-5, 115
Suriname 57, 83
"the Suriname form" 126
Suriname letters 164
Suriname mission 22, 77, 82, 84, 87, 93
Suriname missionary 104
surplus 10, 45, 48, 50, 55, 64, 77
  surplus from slavery 101, 120, 126-8
  surplus value 7
synod (pre-1760) 44, 59-60, 82
Synod in Marienborn, 1764 19, 81, 91-6, 107, 151
  synod (general) 14, 57, 61, 87, 124, 159, 181

theological
  direction 64
  doctrines 174
  drive 172, 173
  foundations 160
  ideas 174
  issues 97
  mainstreaming 52
  organization 111
  reasoning 172
theology 11, 28, 37, 153
tobacco 55, 142-3
  as payment 147-9, 157
trade (craft) 10, 22, 82, 86, 115, 124
  in Bethlehem 48, 50, 51, 54
  St Thomas 82, 102-3, 105, 113-14, 118-19
trade (exchange) 4, 19, 24, 83, 181
  Moravian view on 94-5
trading companies 133-5, 138, 141
  KGH 140, 143, 146, 149, 181
transportation 89, 135-8, 149

Unity 9, 10, 33-4, 63, 86, 88, 125, 127, 139-41, 164, 167, 179-81
  debt 48, 72
  economy/property 55, 60, 72, 77, 94-5

leadership 61-2, 97, 118, 120, 159
  missions 85, 88
  organization 60, 61
  restructure of 12, 42, 52, 58, 62, 74, 77, 97, 99
Unity Elders Conference (UAC) 15, 34, 87, 91, 118, 121, 156
  arrangement of visitations 124, 146-7
  Greenlandic choir houses 156-7

Verbeek, Johann Renatus 117 n.59, 121-2, 126
visitation 34 n.48, 105, 111, 160
  Greenland 16, 161
    1740: Grassmann, Andreas 135
    1745: Nitschmann, Rosina 161, 163
    1751: Watteville 144-5, 158, 161, 169
    1771: Martin Sternberg 159-63
    1859: Ernst Reichel 161
  St Thomas 111, 124
    1736: Spangenberg 22 n.4, 111 n.46, 160
    1749: Watteville 104-7
    1753: Seidel 105 n.23, 107 n.31, 111-13
    1755: Rauch 98 n.1, 110 n.40, 113-14
    1759: Seidel 83, 114-16
    1784: Loretz 34, 118-19
    1797: Verbeek 34 n.49, 122

Wallerstein, Immanuel 37, 177
Watteville, Friedrich von 59-60, 61 n.12
Watteville, Henrietta Benigna von 61 n.12, 169
Watteville, Johannes von 61-2, 87, 110, 169
  as missionary correspondent 51, 65-6, 84, 163, 164
  visitation Greenland 144, 145, 159, 161
  visitation St Thomas 104-7, 111, 114
Weber, Georg 43, 107 n.31, 112-13
Weber, Max 2, 11, 20, 171-6
Weiss, Jonas Paul 61 n.13, 66-8, 85, 88
West India and Guinea Company 82, 98 n.1, 103 n.15

West Indies (Danish and British)   93, 95, 100, 102, 104, 105, 124
Wilhjelm, Henrik   22 n.5, 136 n.18, 155 n.12
workshop
  Bethlehem   43 n.8, 45, 50, 51, 73 n.49
  choir-houses and   28, 45
  Greenland   153
  St Thomas   3, 112

Zinzendorf, Nicolaus Ludwig von
  and Bethlehem   45–7, 51–2, 65
  and the Danish West Indies   102, 103, 109, 112
  death of   3, 18–19, 23, 42, 84, 114, 159, 163, 168 n.62
  organizational change   14, 53, 58–9, 61–2, 74, 91, 96–7, 99–100, 117, 128, 176
  founding of Herrnhut   21
  and Greenland   161, 164
  ideas and ideals of   9, 29–30, 37, 41 n.2, 59–60, 166
  Max Weber and   173
  and mission   17 n.46, 22, 32 n.44, 81–2, 93
  Pietist upbringing   5, 81–2

Printed in the USA
CPSIA information can be obtained
at www.ICGtesting.com
LVHW012343280624
784232LV00003B/217